F

Science, Society,
and Values

Science, Society, and Values

Toward a Sociology of Objectivity

Sal Restivo

Bethlehem: Lehigh University Press
London and Toronto: Associated University Presses

Associated University Presses
440 Forsgate Drive
Cranbury, NJ 08512

Associated University Presses
25 Sicilian Avenue
London WC1A 2QH, England

Associated University Presses
P.O. Box 338, Port Credit
Mississauga, Ontario
Canada L5G 4L8

The paper used in this publication meets the requirements
of the American National Standard for Permanence of Paper
for Printed Library Materials Z39.48–1984.

Library of Congress Cataloging-in-Publication Data

Restivo, Sal P.
    Science, society and values : toward a sociology of objectivity /
Sal Restivo.
        p.   cm.
    Includes bibliographic references and index.
    ISBN 0–934223–21–1 (alk. paper)
    1. Science—Social aspects. 2. Objectivity. I. Title.
Q175 .5.R46 1994
306.4'5—dc20   92–85310
                                                                    CIP

For John and Ruth Hill Useem

Contents

Preface

My work in the sociology of science has been guided by three agendas: to develop a sociological theory of science and scientific knowledge; to use the sociology of science as a vehicle for developing a sociology of objectivity; and to explore the relationships between science, objectivity, and human values. These are not agendas that one starts and finishes in any straightforward way. This book is an invitation to others to follow me along the various roads I have traveled in my quest for ways to live and to inquire. I don't expect that those who make the journey will all agree with everything or anything I've done or concluded. But I do think they will all be provoked to think a little more deeply or a little differently about science. And perhaps by the end of this journey, some at least will understand why and how I have begun to focus my efforts on showing the connection between anarchy and inquiry.

One form of scientism or another has plagued the sociology of science from its emergence in the works of nineteenth and early twentieth century thinkers such as Marx and Weber, through the period between the late 1930s and 1970 dominated by Robert Merton and his students, and into the age of the "new" social studies of science movement that began in the late 1960s. It has contaminated radical and liberal as well as conservative sociologies of science. I do not want to minimize the difficulty of trying to understand science without accepting the culture of science uncritically. But this is precisely what I have tried to do, although only in the course of working through the various problems I have tackled in the sociology of science. As a result, my work has not fallen neatly into the conventional categories of discourse and worldviews in the field.

I have sought more or less independently of readily identifiable labels and schools to determine the conditions under which we can maximize disinterestedness and a cultural commitment to the primacy of the person (conceived as a product and steward of the community and the environment), and minimize or eliminate all forms of political, military, and religious authority and any tendencies to transform well-founded knowledge into universal Truth. I have tried to sustain a realistic and materialist worldview without becoming a true believer in science. And I have tried to distance myself from relativism in both its antirealism guise and its disinterested science disguise. These strategies, in combination with my insistence that we keep our focus on the human face of science and on struggles to emancipate and liberate human beings, have given my work a distinctive flavor. I have argued that all cultures, communities, and selves are "arenas of objectivity," and that "objectivity communities" compete and contend for success, survival, and growth through the development and use of bodies of knowledge. There are, however, certain social formations that are better than others when it comes to generating knowledge that is minimally contaminated by narrow self and everyday social interests. The project of developing a relevant theory that links social formations, modes of inquiry, and human values is complicated by the necessity of establishing normative limits to inquiry, and the danger of becoming complacent and overconfident about what we "really" know. It now seems evident to me that anarchistic social formations, in the sense intended by such thinkers as Willian Morris, Peter Kropotkin, and Michael Bakunin, are in principle the sources of the most objective and liberating knowledge. It will take the larger part of this book to introduce the various factors that lead to this conclusion. And then it will turn out not that I have built an edifice topped by a theory of anarchy and inquiry, but only that I have built the foundation for such a theory. My most modest expectation is that by the time they reach the end of this book, readers will at least have some appreciation for the nature of my quest.

It may be useful to point out the parallels between my overall agenda and Karl Marx's agenda for transforming modern "bourgeois" science into human science in the process of transforming modern class society into a communist society. Anarchism has tempered the influence of Marx's views on my work. At the same time I have come to see the extent to which Marx himself was an anarchist in spirit. I have tried to avoid the authoritarian excesses implicit and explicit in Marx's radicalism, and the scientism in his notion of a science of society. But anarchists too have been troubled by these demons, and I have had to proceed carefully into this realm.

I sketch the background against which I have worked toward a critical sociology of science in Chapter 1. This chapter provides an introduction to *some* of the most important perspectives in the sociology of science. Chapter 2 establishes a crucial fact about modern science—that it is a social institution. The scientific revolution, I argue, must be understood as an organizational and institutional revolution. Without this understanding of science, criticisms of science and ideas about alternatives to science are incomprehensible. Sociological studies and criticisms of science need to be understood as being about an institution, and not simply about scientific statements or scientists, if naive relativism is going to be avoided. Chapter 2 helps to establish the social fact of modern science, embedded in and embodying modern industrial-technological culture. This is the fundamental insight on which virtually all that follows rests.

The consequences of viewing modern science as a social institution are brought out immediately in Chapters 3 and 4. These two chapters bring modern science under the general critique of modern culture. In particular, I criticize the idea of scientific progress. Following C. Wright Mills, I discuss the idea that science is just another part of the machinery of the modern ruling class milieu and the military-industrial complex.

Chapter 5, on the anthropology of science, is a critical introduction to one of the key parts of the science studies landscape. The anthropology of science has probably been the most important development in the history of science studies. The reason is simple: a number of on-site investigators were able for the first time to provide detailed information about how the objects known as scientific facts are manufactured in a modern laboratory. These details stimulated the development of theories of scientific knowledge that challenged cherished distinctions between basic and applied research, facts and values, cognitive and social aspects, science and technology, and objectivity and subjectivity. Platonic conceptions of pure ideas and assumptions about the a priori were also shaken up by these investigations. If any single approach in science studies can be identified as responsible for encouraging sociological explorations of scientific, mathematical, and logical knowledge, it has to be the anthropology of science.

From its very beginning in the late 1960s, science studies has been linked with science policy issues and problems. In Chapter 6, I sketch the radical and conservative implications of science studies for science policy. Are we interested in making science studies, like science, a tool of ruling elites? Or are we interested in using science studies to uncover, criticize, challenge, and change the power relations of science? The latter position, which I advocate, implies the end of science as we now know and study it (and eventually an end to science studies, too). I also consider the issue of science and policy in terms of applied social science research. My concept of a sociology of objectivity is used here to address the problems and prospects of a sociology of scientific validity.

The seventh and concluding chapter is on the sociology of objectivity. This chapter includes a section on the sociology of mathematics, an area of research that has been central to the development of the sociology of objectivity and of the sociology of mind and thinking.

As a representation of my program in the sociology of science, this volume is a companion to my book, *Mathematics in Society and History* (Kluwer Academic Publishers, 1992). Together these volumes represent the culmination of a period of research on natural science and mathematics, and simultaneously the foundation for my current research project (in collaboration with Randall Collins) on the theoretical sociology of mind.

Acknowledgments

I wish to thank several scholars whose influence and efforts on my behalf over many years have significantly furthered my intellectual life: Bernard Barber, the late David Bohm, Daryl Chubin, Randall Collins, Burkhart Holzner, Karin Knorr-Cetina, Julia Loughlin, Kenneth Manning, Joseph Needham, Lewis Pyenson, John Schumacher, Nathan Sivin, Leigh Star, Dirk Struik, Sharon Traweek, and Michael Zenzen.

Science, Society,
and Values

1

Introduction: The Sociology of Science

My objective in this introduction is to provide a view of the sociology of science from my perspective as a working sociologist of science. In particular, my aim is to sketch the context within which I have worked and the intellectual background against which I have developed a critical sociology of science.

The Emergence and Development of the Sociology of Science

The seeds of the sociology of science were planted by the social theorists who created the social sciences between 1850 and 1920. Karl Marx was one of the first of these theorists to articulate the notion that science is a social fact. Scientific activity, even when it is carried out by a single person, is a social act because it is a human act. It is not only the materials of scientific work and the language of the thinker that are social products. The very existence of the person engaged in science is a social activity. During the same era, Emile Durkheim speculated on the status of logical concepts as collective representations and elaborations, and Max Weber drew attention to the relationship between capitalism, Protestantism, and modern science. And in his essay on "Science as a Vocation," Weber examined the changes in early twentieth century German academic life caused by the centralization and monopolization of laboratory equipment. Other important contributions to our understanding of the social nature of science were made by Friedrich Nietzsche, Peter Kropotkin, Michael Bakunin, and, in the early 1920s, Oswald Spengler.[1]

The history of sociology has sometimes been referred to as a dialogue between Marx and Weber. That dialogue also played an important role in stimulating the development of the sociology of science. But Weber's voice had more influence on the initial development of the sociology of science as a distinct field of inquiry. This is evident in the works of the theorist Robert K. Merton, who has been called "the father of the sociology of science." Merton began his studies in the 1930s, focusing on the relations between science and other social activities and institutions. The 1930s also witnessed the emergence of the sociology of knowledge, and significant contributions to the study of science and society by Marxist scholars, such as Boris Hessen and E. Colman. Radical scientists such as J. D. Bernal criticized the social inequities in science and society, and outlined programs for socializing science. These scientists set an agenda for a sociology of science that focuses on social policy and social change in science and society.

The sociology of science was born in a world of intense ideological conflicts, political and philosophical debates about the nature and social relations of science, and unprecedented levels of international violence. And like intellectual strategies in general, sociologies of science became tools and weapons in the struggles between defenders of competing visions of "the good society," and between rulers, generals, merchants, and landowners driven by motives of power and greed.

Between 1940 and 1970, mainstream sociology of science was dominated by the works of Merton and his students and colleagues. A left-of-center intellectual early in his career, Merton emerged from the social, political, and intellectual turmoil of the 1930s a relatively conservative theoretical sociologist. His sociology of science became part of a tool kit and arsenal designed to protect and promote Western science and culture. The relatively explicit concern with military and ideological threats and challenges of fascism and Marxism in pre–World War II studies of science and society became a relatively implicit ingredient of post–World War II functionalist sociology of science.

Functionalist sociology of science was defined in part by its opposition to Marxist sociology of science. But the opposition between these two major paradigms was complicated. Functionalists sometimes found Marxist arguments about economic influences on science compelling; and Marxists often defended bourgeois science, at least by adopting its methods and slogans. And Marxists were, in general, no more prepared than functionalists to challenge the purity of certified scientific knowledge.

It required the political and social upheavals of the 1960s to sufficiently tarnish the image of science and scientists and create an intellectual atmosphere in which the sanctity of scientific knowledge itself could be challenged. Critiques of science, society, and functionalist sociology of science during the late 1960s and 1970s set the stage for a "new sociology of science." It would turn out that in significant respects this new sociology of science was not so new after all. But by resurrecting Durkheim's studies of classification and social structure, Spengler's writings on numbers and culture, and Ludwig Wittgenstein's remarks on the philosophical anthropology of science and mathematics, new sociologists of science were emboldened to explore the social, cultural, and historical aspects of scientific knowledge. As a consequence of their empirical studies of scientific practice and the social construction of scientific knowledge, the spectre of relativism was raised anew.

Perennial issues in the sociology of science and knowledge such as realism versus relativism, the nature of objectivity, and the grounds of scientific progress are being discussed and debated today in a post-Mertonian atmosphere of laboratory studies, meta-science studies, actor-network theories, and constructivist theories of science and mathematics, knowledge, and technology. Contemporary sociology of science is part of and sometimes synonymous with a hybrid interdisciplinary field variously known as science (or technology) studies, social studies of science (and/or technology), and science and technology studies.

There is clearly a 1970s watershed that separates the new and the old sociology of science. But in general neither old nor new sociologists of science linger on issues of class, power, ideology, and alienation. Both affirm that science as it is, with all of its social trappings, "works." The basic goal of old and new sociologists of science is in general to describe how science works, and explain why it works and why it works *that* way. The goal is not to analyze, let alone criticize or challenge modern science as a value system, a worldview, and a way of living and working. Even some critical sociologists of science temper their criticisms with the assumption that "socialized science," science in a socialist (or communist, or anarchist) society, or some sort of unadulterated science could realize the promise of a science that would benefit humanity. This book sets forth a critical sociology that integrates a concern with the social and cultural conditions of objective inquiry and a commitment to emancipatory and liberating values and social changes. The details of this paradigm will emerge during the course of my exposition. In the rest of this chapter, I want to sketch the major competing paradigms that make up the sociology of science and that have, in different ways and to different degrees,

influenced the critical sociology of science I champion. I begin by introducing the two major paradigms developed in the old sociology of
science, the Mertonian and the Marxist paradigms. I then discuss
paradigms developed by the new sociologists of science.

The Mertonian Paradigm

From the 1930s to the 1970s, Robert Merton was the dominant figure
in the sociology of science. The heart of the Mertonian paradigm is,
in the words of Norman Storer, "the powerful juxtaposition of the
normative structure of science with its institutionally distinctive reward system." The research program reflected in and guided by this
paradigm focuses on evaluation processes inside the social system of
science.[2] Merton helped to articulate the general sorts of problems
any sociologist of science, Marxist or non-Marxist, conflict theorist
or functionalist, would be interested in. He examined the factors affecting the fragility or resiliency of the functional autonomy of science, the social factors involved in the emergence and subsequent development of modern science, the sociocultural contexts most
conducive to scientific activity, and the relationship between age and
age structure and the cognitive structure and development of science.

   One of the key assumptions in the Mertonian paradigm is to some
extent basic in any sociology of science: science is a social institution that influences and is influenced by other social institutions. A
second assumption serves as a signature for the old sociology of science: *social* forces and *immanent* forces determine the nature and development of science, but the latter "probably" account for "the
greater part of science." The phrase "greater part of science" refers
specifically to scientific *knowledge*. And "immanent forces" refers
primarily to the so-called "inner logic of development" that "explains" how and why scientific ideas emerge and evolve. The new sociology of science, by contrast, is grounded in the claim that *all* of the
forces that shape science are social.

   The key ideas and findings in the Mertonian paradigm include the
norms of science and a set of cleverly named hypotheses. Based on
his reading of primary and secondary sources in the history of science, Merton concluded that there are four fundamental values or
norms that make up the ethos of science: universalism, communism,
disinterestedness, and organized skepticism. Like other Mertonian
claims, the claims about norms have been criticized because they are

aspects of the ideology of science rather than conclusions based on empirical studies of scientific practice.

Mertonian hypotheses include the Eureka Syndrome (the joy of discovery and the quest for recognition are two sides of the same coin), the Matthew Effect (greater increments of recognition for given scientific contributions accrue to scientists with established reputations, and recognition is withheld from deserving scientists of lesser renown), the Ratchet Effect (once a scientist achieves a certain level of eminence, he/she tends to remain at that level, although a scientist may experience a *relative* decline in prestige in comparison with successful newcomers), and the Principle of Retroactive Recognition (scientists identified with co-authors, especially junior scientists, eventually get the recognition they deserve if their later research becomes notable). He also suggested that all scientific discoveries are, at least in principle, multiples (an idea found in the writings of many prior science watchers). And he formulated hypotheses and speculated about cryptomnesia, adumbrationism, and the potential hazards of the Matthew Effect and the reward system in science for scientific progress.

It is important to be alert to the ideological implications of Merton's hypotheses. The theme of multiple discovery, for example, was not merely intended as an argument for supra-individual patterns in scientific discovery. (Such patterns could as easily be attributed to immanent as to social factors). The point was that the apparently selfish and individualistic behavior expressed in, for example, priority disputes was in fact a disinterested collective (institutional) defense of the value of originality in science. And the Matthew Effect is associated with the claim that any inequities on the individual level are compensated for by the gains to science as a whole that result from keeping research well-organized around clearly defined goals. Merton's students have furthered this ideological program in studies that defend the reward and peer review systems in science, and that attribute gender inequalities in science to merit rather than discrimination.[3]

Mertonian sociology of science does not linger on the human face of science. It uncritically affirms modern science as the paradigm for objective inquiry. In consort with traditional history and philosophy of science, it functions as an ideology, even an apology, for modern science with all its social trappings.

While Merton and other structural functionalist sociologists were establishing their intellectual and professional dominance in academic sociology of science in the United States during the 1940s and 1950s, Marxist sociology of science was kept alive by a small group of intellectuals and scholars. Their paradigm is the topic of the next section.

The Marxist Paradigm

Marx is the author of one of the foundational statements on science as a social activity. With Engels, he argued that even the simplest sensuous certainties are products of social, industrial, and commercial activities. Marx looked forward to the negation of modern (bourgeois) science and its transformation into human science—wholistic, unitary (but not "unified"), global, and dealienated.[4] This makes Marx's commitment to the Grand Paradigm of modern science—the methods and theories of capitalism's science—a little shaky. But it is fair to say that in general Marxists accept that Grand Paradigm, even though this conflicts with their opposition to bourgeois science. This conflict arises from the notion, shared with the Mertonians, that there is a "science" independent of the science that is the institutionalization of capitalism's mode of inquiry. The contradictions that result from this orientation have not prevented (and may have facilitated) Marxist inquiries in areas of science that are taboo for more conservative sociologists of science.

Marxists have pioneered studies of the relationship between modes of production and the forms and degree of specialization in mathematical work, the relationship between mathematical activity and other social activities, mathematical objects as cultural products and social constructs, and the effects of the mode of production (first order causes) and of the social organization of mathematical work (second order causes) on mathematical ideas. From this perspective, mathematical knowledge is neither something "out there" in an eternal and universal realm that we can somehow reveal, nor a product of "pure" mental activity, nor of "geniuses" who create it virtually out of thin air. In any given social formation, mathematics grows out of practical activity and corresponds to the prevailing mode(s) of production. But it is not a simple "reflex" of the "economic base." It reflects mediations, conflicts, and tensions among the various activities and products within a social formation. The more complex these mediations, conflicts, and tensions, the more difficult it will be to correlate "mathematics and society" in any simple fashion.[5]

A strong advocate of historical materialism or Marxist sociology would hold that there is no "external reality" *an und für sich.* All knowledge is conditioned by mental-and-physical activities, culture, and history. The best representative of this position happens to be outside the Marxist camp. In his analysis of mathematics, Oswald Spengler argues that *"There is not, and cannot be, number as such. There are several number-worlds as there are several cultures;"* in brief: "There is no mathematic, only mathematics."[6]

The most ambitious attempt to construct a conventional Marxist theory of "pure" thought is Alfred Sohn-Rethel's study, *Intellectual and Manual Labor*. According to Sohn-Rethel, (a) the original source of abstraction is commodity exchange; (b) this original abstraction contains the formal elements of conceptual thought articulated by the Greeks; and (c) the Greeks derived ideal abstraction from the real abstraction operative in exchange. Sohn-Rethel's general strategy of inquiry is a model of Marxist analysis. But he exaggerates the uniqueness and "purity" of Greek abstract thought, and places the emergence of abstraction much too late in the history of human intellectual evolution. And, like so many Marxists haunted by the ghost of Hegel, he lets enough idealism slip into his analysis to spiritualize his materialism.[7]

A Period of Transition

The takeoff of the sociology of science in the 1960s was stimulated by two "outsiders," Derek Price and Thomas Kuhn. They are the major links between the old and the new sociologies of science.[8]

Price and Kuhn were trained as physical scientists, but they made their careers in the history of science. Price's book, *Science Since Babylon*, published in 1963, helped to initiate the quantitatively oriented "science of science" movement. His pioneering efforts in quantitative history led to his well-known exponential model of long-term scientific growth.

Price showed that there are different growth patterns in the literatures of science and technology, attributed publication structures to underlying social networks called (following Robert Boyle) "invisible colleges," and warned that "Big Science" might become "saturated." Price's analysis of citation patterns presaged the citation analysis industry. He showed that articles in different disciplines have different "half-lives." Some disciplines are tightly clustered around a rapidly moving research front; other disciplines focus on their classics. Citation analysis revealed clusters of interrelated researchers, and showed that the network patterns for the sciences are different from those in the technological fields. A more advanced technique, co-citation analysis, has been used to study competition and the succession of dominant schools in various disciplines.[9]

Citation methods have yet to produce results of the sort Price envisioned for the science of science. Perhaps if citation analysis were better integrated with other approaches, it might help sociologists of science advance their theoretical understanding of science.[10]

But theoretical sociology of science has not benefitted much from the association of citation analysis with the counting interests of a variety of managers and administrators. The citation industry has been an arena of attacks and counterattacks; but it has moved across the 1970s watershed and into the new science studies as part of the scientometrics paradigm.[11]

Price's work has provided sociologists of science with techniques for the empirical and quantitative analysis of trends and variations in science. His ideas about invisible colleges have also been utilized and adapted in studies of the social system of science.

Diana Crane, for example, identified invisible colleges in various scientific disciplines. Joseph Ben-David and Randall Collins used a related method—tracing master-pupil chains—to analyze the social conditions underlying the development of experimental psychology. And Nicholas Mullins studied the network structure behind the molecular biology revolution of the 1950s. Later, Mullins and his colleagues developed a structural model of the transformations in network structures that coincide with different stages of "scientific revolution."[12] The concept of scientific revolutions was introduced by the other "outsider" who contributed to the 1960s take-off, Thomas Kuhn.

Kuhn is the best known "external influence" on the new sociology of science. While he influenced some of the sociologists of science who initiated the 1960s take-off and made the transition to the science studies movement of the 1970s, he was most influential among the creators of that movement. The story of Kuhn is important for an understanding of how my agenda deviates from the agendas of my colleagues in the new sociology of science. Therefore, I will postpone further discussion of Kuhn until later in this chapter. I want first to chart some of the other crucial developments of the 1960s, before turning to the 1970s paradigms.

In addition to the works of Price and Kuhn, the contributions of Joseph Ben-David and Warren Hagstrom were important factors in the emergence of the sociology of science as a viable and autonomous specialty. Ben-David initiated the comparative historical study of science as a social institution within mainstream sociology of science. In the early 1950s, Joseph Needham began publishing what would become a monumental project on the comparative history of science in China and the West. The Marxist sociology that guided Needham's work, however, did not play an important role in bringing historical and comparative materials and perspectives to bear on the development of academic sociology.

Ben-David argued that the social bases of science are not located so much in the surrounding society as in the place where scientists work. Local roles and institutions influence the amount and types of scientific products. Ben-David showed, for example, how innovations such as Freud's psychoanalysis and Pasteur's bacteriology were the results of "role hybrids" that developed when career pressures pushed scientists from high-status research roles into low-status practical roles. Ben-David and Collins later demonstrated that patterns of vacancies in a stagnant academic field (philosophy) combined with a shortage of positions for scientists in the new, highly competitive field of psychology led to career migrations that resulted in the development of experimental psychology in the nineteenth-century German universities. Political and organizational vicissitudes affecting the number of university positions in various specialties have been crucial factors in determining the times and places when and where scientific production is going to occur. Ben-David went on to discuss the historical variations in scientific roles over the past two thousand years. His work entered the new sociology of science in part as a result of the work of Randall Collins, whose conflict theory of science is discussed below.[13]

Another important research tradition was established by Warren Hagstrom's *The Scientific Community* (1965). Hagstrom used a variety of methods, especially in-depth interviews, to produce a description and theory of the behavior of scientists in various fields. He showed that competition was an important correlate of originality, illustrated patterns of information exchange and recognition, and pointed out the pathologies of secretiveness and fragmented communication that can arise in science. In spite of some methodological and conceptual limitations Hagstrom's study led to the first *general* sociological theory of the scientific community; other works before and since generally concentrated on specific areas of science. Norman Storer's *The Social System of Science*, published in 1966, is a notable exception. Storer's work was a theoretical synthesis of analyses of science as a social system.

A number of later researchers were influenced to varying degrees by Hagstrom's work. One was Lowell Hargens, who did an analysis of organizational differences among scientific disciplines. Another was Jerry Gaston, who studied competition and recognition among theorists and experimentalists in the British high-energy physics community. There is some theoretical convergence between these works and the studies by Ben-David. They show the influence of the amount of competition and of patterns of recognition on the rates and types of scientific production in different fields. The theoretical limitations of these studies can be traced to uncritical views of science as the "best" mode of inquiry and a well-functioning social system.[14]

Hagstrom's theoretical framework was based in part on Marcel Mauss' analysis of gift-exchange networks in primitive societies. Mauss was associated with a classical tradition in sociology established by Emile Durkheim. Durkheim and Mauss initiated an independent research program in the sociology of knowledge by attempting to show that ideas in primitive societies arise from and reflect social structures. This line of inquiry remained isolated, for the most part, from the philosophical and political themes in German (Max Scheler and Karl Mannheim) and Marxist sociology of knowledge. For many decades, the Durkheimians confined their analyses to the ideas and classification systems of primitive societies. Claude Levi-Strauss, for example, elaborated a quasi-Durkheimian structuralist theory of primitive modes of thought. In the 1960s, the Durkheimian model was applied to modern cultures by Basil Bernstein and Mary Douglas. Their analyses, however, were confined to the different cultural codes of stratified social systems and were not applied to science. Georges Gurvitch modified the Durkheimian framework using ideas from Marxism, intuitionism, and phenomenology to produce a very general dialectical sociology of knowledge.[15]

It was not until the mid-1970s that a full-fledged Durkheimian sociology of science appeared, helping to initiate the new science studies movement. David Bloor argued that scientists, like religious persons, divide the world into sacred and secular. Along with science advocates, they treat science as a sacred object. One consequence of this is that they are resistant to sociological and other explanatory analyses of science.

Bloor argues that just as Durkheim's analysis of rituals enables us to understand religion as a social product, a Durkheimian analysis of the sacred status of science can help us explain science (including scientific and mathematical knowledge) as a social fact.[16] Durkheim himself formulated some general propositions regarding the sorts of ideas that are produced under different conditions of social density and ritual interaction. These propositions have been formally stated by Randall Collins in his work on conflict theory.[17]

The End of the Mertonian Hegemony

The 1970s began with the publication of two books summarizing in one case a decade and in the other four decades of research in the sociology of science. They were, respectively, Ben-David's 1971 volume, and the 1973 collection of Merton's papers. The limitations of the old sociology of science were highlighted with the appearance of these books just as the new sociology of science was emerging.

One of Ben-David's major theses is that decentralized authority systems are more favorable to variety in ideas and experiments than centralized systems. This is a viable thesis, but one that Ben-David, like many other orthodox sociologists of science, applies quite readily to the "external" setting for science and rarely to the "internal" organization of science. Ben-David's conception of science is biased toward an idealistic notion of rational intellectual activity. He never gives us a satisfactory sociological definition of science. And he says very little about conflicts in contemporary science and their potential effects on knowledge production, or the human consequences and value implications of the social organization of science.

The Merton collection appeared at a time when several important studies, including one by Merton's students Stephen and Jonathan Cole, were showcasing the Mertonian paradigm.[18] But alternative sociologies of science were also beginning to emerge at this time in works by such researchers as Stephen and Hilary Rose, Leslie Sklair, and Barry Barnes.[19] There were strains of neo-functionalism in some of the new literature, but this was less a reflection of Merton's omnipresence than of the pernicious influence of the idea that science is a privileged mode of inquiry. At first, the Mertonian "foes" were a shadowy presence. Their main weapons were criticisms and alternative programmatic statements. But they very quickly established viable research centers, programs and journals. The journal *Science Studies* debuted in 1971 under the joint editorship of David Edge of Edinburgh and Roy MacLeod of Sussex. A few years later, the name of the journal was changed to *Social Studies of Science*. Merton himself stayed close to these developments; indeed, he became the first president of the Society for Social Studies of Science, founded in 1975.

Increasingly, students of science were being drawn from a variety of interdisciplinary programs. Many of them came—and continue to come—to science studies with degrees, advanced preparation, and professional experience in the physical and natural sciences, mathematics, and engineering. This helps account for the most notable change in the sociology of science during the past two decades: the development of research on and theories of scientific and mathematical knowledge.

The Mertonian paradigm continues to guide a great deal of research and theory in contemporary sociology of science. The Marxist paradigm is more prominent than in the past. But they share the spotlight with new paradigms. And the field is now sustained by and at several key centers such as Edinburgh, Bath, Bielefeld, and Amsterdam in Europe, Wollongong in Australia, and Rensselaer, San Diego, Cornell, MIT, and Virginia Polytech in the United States. There is a decidedly non- or anti-Mertonian bias in much of the work being published in the field today. But, as I have already suggested, close inspection of this literature reveals lingering traces of the Mertonian legacy. Michael Mulkay's discussion of the "revision" of the "customary view" (that is, the Mertonian paradigm) illustrates these lingering traces, and the promises and shortcomings of the new sociology of science.[20]

Mulkay's outline of the new sociology of science and knowledge takes account of a "new" view of nature and science developed in the works of Kuhn, N. Hanson, and others: (1) the uniformity of nature is an artifact of scientific accounts; (2) facts are theory-dependent and variable in meaning; (3) observation is an active interpretive process; and (4) knowledge claims are negotiated. Mulkay concludes that physical reality constrains but does not uniquely determine the conclusions of scientists. Even though Mulkay argues that scientific knowledge is a product of cultural contingencies, he adopts several "customary" ideas: (1) science is an autonomous research community; (2) physical and social realities can be demarcated; and (3) there are internal and external aspects of and influences on science. The new sociology of science that Mulkay describes stresses negotiation and has no central place for alienation, elitism, exploitation, or conflict. His description of scientific culture as a pluralistic arena of shared interpretive positions based on flexible symbolic resources should remind sociologists of Talcott Parson's conservative social system model.

In more radical new sociologies of science, context and cognition are inseparable, contingencies are conceived to be constitutive of knowledge, the focus is on "local historicity" (to borrow Harold Garfinkel's term) and transscientific networks rather than the mythical scientific community, and struggles for power and privilege come into view as central features of the intellectual strategy known as "scientific research." While the post-Mertonians are clearly sympathetic to these ideas, the revisionism adopted by researchers such as Mulkay inhibits efforts to develop a radical alternative to the Mertonian paradigm. The difficulty may arise in part because constructing sociologies of science is, in general, the work of academics who are supported by institutions that sustain and are sustained by a scientific or quasi-scientific worldview. Thus, it is not merely the "necessary truths" of science that compel loyalty, but the fact that the social roles of sociologists of science are usually embedded in a network of power and privilege that overlaps or is one with the social apparatus of science. Under such circumstances, it is not surprising that sociologists of science tend to detach science from its social apparatus before studying "it," and that their studies so often seem to turn into functionalist accounts. It is not so mysterious, then, to find that some sociologists of science can imagine alternative interpretations of science as a well-functioning institution, but that few can imagine a critique of and alternative to science in its prevailing institutional form.

The 1960s was a period of harbingers of a new sociology of science. In the last few paragraphs, I have introduced some of the characteristics of that sociology of science. In the following pages, I outline these characteristics in more detail, as I introduce major paradigms in the new sociology of science.

The Scientometrics Paradigm

The new sociology of science, as I have pointed out, is heir to important Mertonian legacies. The Mertonian paradigm has historical and quantitative elements that Merton himself tended to fuse in his work. Over the years, however, the quantitative dimension of the Mertonian paradigm gained in prominence. That legacy, refashioned and strengthened through Merton's collaboration with Derek Price and Eugene Garfield (the entrepreneur who started the citation industry in the 1950s), is a critical ingredient in the scientometrics paradigm that claims the allegiance of some new sociologists of science.[21]

Scientometrics is a catchall of quantitative analyses that focus mainly on archival sources, and the products and outcomes of scientific practice. For some researchers, scientometrics, encompassing bibliometrics (citation and productivity studies), science manpower and career studies, and science indicators compilations, is the sociology of science.[22] For the scientometrician, the world exists "out there" and can be sampled, measured, counted, captured, and revealed by "objective inquiries." They "make estimates" and "test hypotheses" rather than (as advocates of paradigms further removed from the Mertonian legacy would put it) "make knowledge claims" and "construct realities."

Scientometrics focuses on the present and the immediate future. Making predictions based on trends, patterns, and relationships is, for scientometricians, what science is all about. The goals of controlling and evaluating science to aid policy-making, applications, and understanding are implicit if not explicit in the National Science Foundations' *Science Indicators* reports and the commentaries on those and related reports. The same is true, though to a lesser extent, in some of the more basic bibliometric analyses of how journals, authors, and disciplines "behave."[23]

Scientometricians share an interventionist presumption: to know something about a trend, pattern, or relationship raises the prospect of manipulating and changing it. This orientation to and optimism about mastering the future requires assertions of certainty—even in the absence of compelling data. This highlights what it is about scientometrics that makes it an anachronism in the new sociology of science. Whereas most new sociologists of science are more or less faithful to the symmetry principle that true and false beliefs must be explained in the same way, scientometricians must declare what they believe to be true and seek to explain only those truths. Naturally, the tone of such declarations and explanations must be as agnostic, objective, value-free, and disinterested as possible. This is the credo of the unreconstructed realist.

One programmatic curiosity in the scientometric paradigm is that while they may, in the new sociology of science spirit, admit "cultural context" as a variable they deny that it has any significant effect on the ultimate content of science or subordinate it to the collective wisdom of a sovereign "scientific community." The scientific community knows best when it comes to self-governance, accountability, and reform. Some chinks have, however, appeared in the armor of this scientometric presumption. Mertonians who have, until recently, offered unqualified endorsements of federal peer review systems, and justified inequities in the allocation of incentives and rewards as systemically (read *functionally*) necessary and efficient are now apologizing for flaws in the rationality of the scientific community.[24] Luck has finally been recognized as a component of peer-review decisions—but not elitism, particularism, and all those other "aberrations" in the normative framework of science.[25] Once, however, fraud, whimsy, and error are allowed to have infiltrated science, how long will it be before it is recognized that the stratification system of science, its rational decision-making authority, and its omniscient certainty about future outcomes may be aberrant, on the wane, and impaired.[26]

The European, and especially the eastern European, science of science movement is most closely tied to the new sociology of science through the scientometric connection. That connection was strengthened some years ago when the journal *Scientometrics* was founded. The stress on prediction and the statistical present in this paradigm reflects its function in the state's policy apparatus. Government bureaucrats, business leaders, and other elites require (or have been convinced by scientometrics entrepreneurs that they require) information on science for directing and defending science policy, stimulating scientific progress, and increasing scientific productivity—all in the interests of elite scientists and the ruling class. It is not so much the quantitative that is vulnerable to criticism here but rather the enchanting invocation of number, method, and truth in the corridors—and alleyways—of power.

The Conflict Paradigm

The "crude" efforts of Marxists to initiate an explanatory sociology of science are the starting point for Randall Collins' conflict sociology of science.[27] His approach is an alternative to the Marxist and the Mertonian paradigms, although he draws heavily on the Marxist legacy. His objective is to build a multidimensional organizational model that avoids the "reductionist errors" of the Marxists. Collins applies explanatory principles of stratification and organization to the analysis of the external roles of scientists, the internal structure of science, the internal politics of seventeenth-century physics, and the determinants of social structure, individual careers, and rates of mobility in science.

Three postulates are at the heart of the conflict paradigm. The first is that individuals seek to maximize their subjective status in terms of the resources they and their rivals have access to. The second is that there are frequent points at which individuals seeking to maximize their subjective status come into conflict. The recurring social patterns associated with a given social structure are determined in part by how resources are brought to bear on the generation and resolution of those conflicts. This also creates social factions that will come into conflict in the future and thereby generate social changes. The third postulate is that ideas are weapons created out of social interests, sustained through the efforts of those people and groups who have the resources to uphold and defend them, and used in struggles for intellectual and social dominance. These postulates and the larger paradigm they support are, according to Collins, compatible with the existence of autonomous intellectual communities, recalcitrant facts, and the logical unfolding of scientific ideas. But he cautions that this compatibility is not self-evident. Later in this book, I will show what needs to be done to "sociologize" these scientific ideas.

In general, Collins argues that paradigms (his own included, presumably), scientific revolutions, and periods of normal science (following the categories and terms made popular by Thomas Kuhn) reflect political processes at work in the careers of individual scientists. The social contingencies that affect these developments are what we call the determinants of the course of "knowledge." The ideas that social contingencies determine the course of knowledge, and that facts are socially formulated are hallmarks of the new sociology of science. At least some of the new sociologists of science treat these ideas more radically; some in fact deny that facts exist in any sense other than as socially constructed, negotiated entities. Collins is a representative of the new sociology of science because he is ready to think of knowledge and facts in terms of social construction and social contingencies. His emphasis on conflict, however, is not widely shared. The new sociologists of science tend to be innovative when it comes to revealing how science "really" works. But they are rather conservative when it comes to dealing with conflicts, and critically analyzing and evaluating science as a value system and worldview.

The Strong Program

The most prolific and perhaps coherent paradigm in science studies, the strong program is anchored in programmatic statements formulated by Barry Barnes and David Bloor in the early 1970s. The basic tenets of the paradigm, following Bloor's conception of "the strong program in the sociology of knowledge" are: (1) beliefs and states of knowledge are products of social causes; (2) truth and falsity, rationality and irrationality, success and failure are all studied impartially; (3) true and false beliefs are symmetrically explained in terms of the same types of causes; and (4) the explanatory patterns in the strong program apply reflexively to the program itself.[28]

The strong program aims to break down the barriers to sociological studies of scientific and mathematical knowledge. Bloor argues that the major obstacle to a sociology of mathematics is the assumption that mathematics has a life and meaning of its own. He is sympathetic to Spengler's naturalistic study of scientific and mathematical knowledge, but this part of his work is troubled by contradictions.[29] Bloor believes in an eternal, material world that is the source of "permanent truth," yet he argues that belief in a material world does not justify concluding that there is a final, privileged state of adaptation to that world that could count as absolute knowledge or truth.

Bloor's "methodological relativism" is unhinged by the scientistic basis of the strong program: the best way to study science is to follow the procedures of the successful sciences. Here Bloor parts company with Spengler, for the strong program relativizes everything but science. This biases the reflexivity provision of the program by making it resistant to criticisms of and radical changes in science.

Bloor's trust in science is based on the assumption that the scientific method is, in fact, a method, that it is a finished, universally valid method, that we understand its complexities, and that we can apply it in a straightforward manner. Bloor's argument that there are alternative mathematical systems suggests that there are alternative scientific systems. But Bloor does not relativize science this way, and this is one indication that the strong program remains haunted by the Mertonian legacy.

An interests model has been defended within the strong program by the Edinburgh school, led by Barry Barnes.[30] The argument that science is interest driven challenges the idea of pure science. But some critics of the strong program claim that interest theory explains everything and nothing, and does so retrospectively.[31] And interest theorists leave themselves open to the charge that they ignore the interests that drive *their* research, even while they claim "reflexivity" as a basic part of their code of conduct.

One branch of the strong program has sought to extend and contemporize the relativism operationalized by the Edinburgh school. The Bath school, led by Harry Collins and Trevor Pinch, has focused on modern episodes of discovery and replication in the physical sciences.

In an effort to show that controversy is normal in mainstream as well as in marginal sciences, the Bath strong programmers have investigated the debates about the reality of psi phenomena (parapsychology), solar neutrinos, and learning among planaria.[32] Here too, however, fascinating cases have failed to convince realists or satisfy other less radical relativists that the strong program has been true to its tenets.[33] Intriguing episodes often resist generalization. Some of these cases share the deficiencies of internalist history: rank-and-file scientists, non-scientists, and the "external" culture seldom command attention.

Epistemologically, the strong program tends to link sociological and scientific rationality. As a consequence, it links the standards of what constitutes "correct" sociological research with the standards of the physical sciences.[34] This is another way of stating Bloor's dictum that if sociologists rely on the "proven" methods of science to *study* science, "all will be well."

A moderate version of the strong program focuses on the social structural bases of scientific practice and progress. Donald Campbell's work on descriptive and evolutionary epistemology shares a demarcationist perspective (there is a clear distinction between science and non-science or pseudo-science), but is grounded in a more dynamic conception of scientific change.[35] Campbell, for example, refers to the "iterative oscillations of theoretical emphases," and a "continual dialectic that never achieves a stable synthesis" in his descriptions of science. But Campbell, like Merton, Bloor, and, as we will see, Kuhn, remains committed to the Grand Paradigm of modern science.

An ontological realist, Campbell is oriented to a reality all knowers can share, but which they can only know indirectly and presumptively. One of the fundamental queries of Campbell's program is: in what kind of world would what kind of procedures lead a knowing community to improve the validity of its model of the world? Campbell argues that in order to fit theories and the world described (just as in the case of fitting organisms and environments) we require blind (wasteful, nonprescient) variation and selective retention. Wild speculation, then, is recommended for inclusion in the guidebook of strategies for discovery, but not necessarily for the guidebook on logic.

Campbell contends that the idea of "facts in themselves" is literally untrue, and part of the ideology of science. But instead of moving from this position forward to a radical reconceptualization of science, Campbell steps backwards; we must preserve this ideology because it represents an important functional truth. Campbell thus seems to have one foot in the Mertonian camp and (in his defense of "wildness" or "unjustified" variation) another foot in Paul Feyerabend's camp of dadaist or anarchist inquiry. According to Campbell, Feyerabend loves variation so much that he totally neglects selection and regards retention as the enemy of variation. This is not entirely fair to Feyerabend, but it does indicate Campbell's cautious affection for Feyerabend's wildness.[36]

Paul Thaggard has criticized Campbell's evolutionary epistemology. He argues against borrowing a model for scientific growth from Lamarck, Hegel, or Darwin. A viable model of scientific growth would, he argues, have to take account of at least the following factors: (1) the intentional, abductive activity of scientists in initially arriving at new theories and concepts; (2) the selection of theories according to criteria that reflect general aims; (3) the achievement of progress by sustained application of criteria; and (4) the rapid transmission of selected theories in highly organized scientific communities.[37] Other criticisms are implied in the critical sociology of science I advocate, and some of these will be made explicit in other sections of this work. But there are interesting parallels between the development of Campbell's evolutionary epistemology into a sociology of scientific validity and my notion of a sociology of objectivity. I will have an opportunity to consider these parallels later on.

The centerpiece of the strong program is the constructivist paradigm. There is some rationale for treating this as a separate paradigm because of its distinctive ethnographic foundations. In any event, since I discuss this at length in Chapter 5, I will devote just a few sentences to it here to help fill in my sketch of the contemporary science studies landscape.

In large part through the efforts of ethnographers of science, the new sociologists of science have come to view scientific knowledge as a social construction rather than a product of pure cognition or description. On this view, the social settings and contingencies of scientific work are embodied in scientific knowledge. Scientific knowledge is a product of social *work*, a *discursive* accomplishment. Ethnographers of science have drawn attention to selection-processes in scientific work, the *decision-impregnated* nature of science at all levels, the *transformational* processes that lead to facts and knowledge, and the *practical, analogical, socially situated, literary, symbolic*, and *indexical* nature of scientific reasoning.

There is no question that the constructivists have helped to break down myths and ideologies generated by armchair historians and memoir writers, idealists, and ideologues. On the other hand, they have also raised the spectre of relativism, and provoked debates be-tween relativists and realists. More on this later.

Breaking the Ties That Bind

The competing paradigms and perspectives in contemporary sociol-ogy of science can be described in a variety of ways. We can conceive the situation in terms of a circus with three main rings—the strong program (which is based on the premise that the best way to study sci-ence is to adopt the proven methods of science and treat all forms of knowledge and belief symmetrically, that is, independently of their presumed truth or falsity), laboratory studies, and scientometrics. The first two rings are clearly under the constructionist umbrella. The third represents a quantitative "science of science" approach. Critical sociology of science (or "the weak program") is a fourth ring. Surviv-ing Mertonanism could be considered a fifth ring.[38]

We can also carve out the main arenas in terms of the strong, mod-erate, and weak programs. This set of categories focuses attention on the fact that studies of science are guided by different world views. The strong program as I have already noted, is scientistic and oriented to the values of established Western culture; the weak program treats all programs (including itself) as worldviews; it is a political program first, and a program in theory and research second. This program, which I have advocated with Michael Zenzen, Daryl Chubin, and Julia Loughlin stresses the study of process and product, contextualism, evolutionary epistemology, a future orientation that highlights con-cern open to potential human and environmental consequences of given courses of social and scientific action, and criticism and recon-struction of science and social policies. Values, policy, and a concern for the quality of individual and social life are the hallmarks of the weak program. The moderate program (as I have noted), is really a variation on the strong program.[39] It proposes a dynamic picture of science as a dialectical process, and tends to bring almost everything about science into question—except scientific method. The weak pro-gram treats science as a mode of inquiry subject to criticism and to fundamental changes coincident with fundamental changes in its so-ciocultural surroundings.

Another way to view science studies is in terms of the historical in-terplay of two basic themes: scientist as worker (Marx) and scientist as elite professional (Weber). The Weberian view is central to the

Mertonian paradigm, and is evident as one theme in the new sociology of science. The theme of scientist as worker is found in the new sociology of science, but moreso as an element of scientific *practice* than an element of class conflict. Radical and conflict theorists are bringing power and conflict center stage in their efforts to explain science and scientific knowledge. There is also growing evidence that the more mainstream sociologists of science are taking up this theme. If this continues, we can expect that the sociology of science—through its radical science, scientometrics, and science policy connections—will provide substantial intellectual resources for conservatives and radicals alike in *fin de siècle* politics. On the intellectual side, the confluence of the various developments I have sketched may transform sociologists of science, whether Marxians or Weberians, conflict theorists or neo-functionalists, or realists or relativists into comparative historical anthropologists.

In the meantime, the sociology of science remains a diverse arena of competing paradigms and worldviews. In the next section, I discuss the nature and implications of Thomas Kuhn's influence on the new sociology of science. This will provide a transition from the general setting of the sociology of science to the specific setting of my own work in this field.

The Myth of Kuhn

The widespread adoption of the rhetoric of normal science, revolutionary science, paradigms, and exemplars by sociologists of science and sociologists in general suggests the strong influence that Thomas S. Kuhn's *The Structure of Scientific Revolutions* (1962, 1970) has had on sociological inquiry. But claims that Kuhn's work is anti-Mertonian, nonnormative, relativistic, an alternative to positivism and logical empiricism, and even compatible with Marxism are all part of the myth of the Kuhnian revolution in the sociology of science.[40] The central dogma in the Kuhnian mythology is that Kuhn's paradigm is a significant, indeed a radical, alternative to Merton's. Some Mertonians have been more perceptive about the Kuhnian mythology than have critics of Mertonian sociology of science. Gaston suggests (correctly I think) that Kuhn's reception is accounted for by the simplicity and vividness of his discussion of science. But Gaston's remark that there is a consensus about the importance of Kuhn's work ignores the resistance of historians of science to Kuhn's views on science and sci-

entific change. The important point is that Gaston recognizes the
compatibility of Merton and Kuhn.[41]

Ben-David notes that Kuhn and Merton were not opposed for at
least a decade following the publication of Kuhn's work on scientific
revolutions. British sociologists of science were the chief creators of
the anti-Mertonian Kuhn.[42] Ben-David's assessment of the British
and American reactions as consequences of different (not to mention
competing) intellectual traditions may be accurate.[43] But even the
British tended to adopt Kuhn as the standard-bearer for an analysis of
science that has been generally far less radical than proclaimed in the
advertisements for British anti-Mertonian sociology of science.
Kuhn may very well be a man for all sociology of science seasons, but
he seems peculiarly suited for neo-Mertonian revisionism.[44]

The Kuhnian Paradigm

Merton has commented on the anomaly of acolytes who fail to distinguish the substance from the fate of Kuhn's work.[45] He has also
pointed out numerous convergences between his work and Kuhn's.
Merton criticizes Kuhn's restrictive sociology but insists that he and
Kuhn are at one regarding the significance of the institutions and
values of science as contexts for cognitive decisions. This is interesting because according to some interpreters Kuhn has helped shift
the focus of attention in the sociology of science to cognitive factors.
But Kuhn has done little more than what Merton has done: drawn
attention to the social context for cognitive decisions. This is far
from revolutionary.

One of the curious features of Kuhn's "sociology of science" is that
it does not treat sociological factors as problematic. Kuhn notes, for
example, that normal science is educationally narrow, rigid, and ill-
designed to foster creativity.[46] This characterization is not incompatible with scientific progress because rigidity accrues to individuals in
Kuhn's theory. But he ignores the fact that rigidity accrues to organizations and institutions too. Bureaucratization, professionalization,
and social controls imposed by political authorities all contribute to
rigidity in collectivities. This sort of sociological myopia is further
reflected in Kuhn's assumption that the supply of innovators—young
scientists and those who have entered new areas of research, according to Kuhn—is independent of social conditions within and outside
of science.[47]

The Kuhnian mythology probably stems from the fact that Kuhn discusses scientific change in terms of a political model, uses the term revolution to describe a certain type of innovative period in science, and underscores the persuasive aspects of scientific discourse. But Kuhn's model is based on the modern political revolution, a form of social change generally characterized by the circulation of elites.

Kuhn argues that political and scientific revolutions are both associated with the perception among members of a small element of the political or scientific community that institutions are malfunctioning. This sense of malfunction leads to a crisis and fosters revolution.[48] The aim of the revolutionaries is to change institutions; their claim is that the changes are incompatible with the mechanisms for change offered by the institutions themselves. This viewpoint, with its emphasis on sensing malfunctions, obscures the unintended consequences of social actions preceding the crisis and the dialectical sources of change inherent in social structural contradictions.

According to Kuhn, the period of crisis polarizes competing parties in both political revolutions and scientific revolutions. In both cases, defenders of the old order confront advocates of a new order. At this stage, differences between the contending groups can no longer be resolved by recourse to normal political strategies or, in the case of science, normal methods and logic. Institutional governance breaks down. The competing groups cannot agree on means for achieving and evaluating change within existing institutional contexts, and they reject suprainstitutional modes of conflict resolution. The result is recourse to mass persuasion and then force. In scientific revolutions, Kuhn argues, the process of paradigm choice is eventually accomplished on the basis of the highest standard: the assent of the scientific community. The extrainstitutional nature of revolutions in politics and in science, Kuhn contends, is a key aspect of the evolution of institutions.

Kuhn has responded to his critics by diluting the Pareto-like political content of his theory. Like the Mertonians, he expresses satisfaction with what science is as a human enterprise, supports elitism in science, and interprets the pursuit of individual and cliquish interests as compatible with scientific progress. Resistance to new ideas and discoveries is, for Kuhn as for Merton, not a violation of the commitment to the pursuit of knowledge but evidence for consensus maintenance, a necessary condition for "normal science." The Mertonian Kuhn believes that science-as-it-is is a well functioning institution; it is the paradigmatic mode of inquiry, discovery, prediction, and explanation. Kuhn joins Merton in giving a prescriptive account of science thinly disguised as objective history and sociology of science; he binds science to a Grand Paradigm of methods, logic, and rationality that remains unperturbed as science goes through its sinusoidal dance of normal and revolutionary periods. The final irony is that while the true believers in the sociology and history of science have been congratulating each other on the Kuhnian revolution, Kuhn himself has been busy doing internalist history of science unencumbered by notions of paradigms, exemplars, and scientific revolutions.[49]

A debate emerged between followers of Kuhn and Karl Popper over the extent to which Kuhn shows that the actual process of science is independent of empirical falsification. Lakatos, Feyerabend, and others have questioned the unity of the different dimensions of "paradigm" which Kuhn articulated and have argued that science is actually a battleground of competing paradigms.[50] Few sociologists have taken up Kuhn's ideas and subjected them to empirical tests.[51] My work with R. Collins suggested that the patterns of change in mathematics are substantially different from those identified by Kuhn and rooted in paradigm conservatism. Kuhn's own examples of scientific revolutions are open to alternative interpretations. The empirical flaws in Ptolemaic astronomy, for example, were well-known for centuries before Copernicus, and can hardly be said to have finally accumulated to an unbearable point. Collins' model of intellectual change, which allows room for only a limited number of major positions in a given intellectual arena, draws attention to the rearrangements in the institutional and political foundations of the European intellectual world in the early 1500s. New sources of external support provided opportunities for strengthening new, weak, or peripheral intellectual factions. The Aristotelian-Ptolemaic orthodoxy of the late medieval universities became vulnerable to displacement. It was in this setting of competing world pictures that the Copernican model was proposed and won acceptance.[52] On another front, the physicist David Bohm has countered Kuhn's account of science with an argument for science in permanent revolution.[53]

Conclusion

The crucial point I want to stress about the new science studies paradigms is that they affirm the Grand Paradigm of modern science. They do not challenge or criticize modern science as a value system, a worldview, and a way of living and working.

The characterization that sociologists of science generally do not doubt or question the worth of science holds on both sides of the 1970s watershed that separates the old and the new sociology of science.[54] There are, of course, some Marxists, conflict theorists, sociologists, anarchists, and radical science advocates who do carry out critical analyses of modern science.[55] Their analyses tend to be generated as part of a general criticism of the modern social order. But even their criticisms are often reined in by the belief that "socialized science," science in a socialist (or communist, or anarchist) society, or some sort of unadulterated science could realize the promise of a science that would benefit humanity. These works not withstanding, the idea that modern science is at least as much a factor in as a solution for our personal, social, and environmental ills is not defended by very many sociologists of science. C. Wright Mills' conception of modern science as a subordinate part of "the wasteful absurdities of capitalism," the military order, and the national state is not ascendant in the sociology of science.[56]

The constructivist and relativist agendas in the new sociology of science have alarmed the guardians of the scientific community.[57] They view them as threats to the integrity, legitimacy, and autonomy of science, the realist assumptions of scientific inquiry, and the quest for truth and objective knowledge. But the leading "constructivists" and "relativists" are not anti-realists, and many explicitly defend the methods and worldview of science. Bruno Latour and Steve Woolgar, for example, do not deny the existence of facts or of reality. They do not view themselves as naive relativists. Karin Knorr-Cetina is also explicit about accepting the existence of an independent reality and divorcing constructivism from an idealist ontology. Latour's "recantation" is even more dramatic: ". . . in spite of our critiques—and to be fair, in spite of a few of our early claims—," the new sociologists of science are no more 'relativist' than Einstein." Relativism and constructivism have in fact been ways of fighting against "absolute definitions of observations that do not specify the practical work and material networks that give them meaning . . ." Even the high priest of (empirical) relativism, Harry Collins, views his work as a defense of the authority of science ("the best institution for generating knowledge about the natural world that we have") and of the ultimate (however uncertain and fallible) expertise of scientists.[58]

David Bloor's closing remarks in *Knowledge and Social Imagery* make quite clear what is at stake here:

I am more than happy to see sociology resting on the same foundations and assumptions as other sciences. This applies whatever their status and origin. Really sociology has no choice but to rest on these foundations, nor any more appropriate model to adopt. *For that foundation is our culture. Science is our form of knowledge* [my emphasis]. That the sociology of knowledge stands or falls with the other sciences seems to me both eminently desirable as a fate, and highly probable as a prediction.

Bloor has made important contributions to our understanding of the interdependence of science, culture, and the sociology of science. The problem, for a critical perspective, is that he approves of the modern forms of these social inventions.[59]

It should be clear by now why so much of what goes by the name of sociology of science, science studies, or science criticism remains fundamentally conservative on the question of the value of science: many of the most influential authorities on the "sociological" nature of science are science advocates. The idea that science "works" and a "science fix" orientation have been amplified by runaway technological "progress." In the heady atmosphere of material plenty, people have been seduced by the icons, myths, and ideologies of modern science. And sociologists of science cannot afford to alienate the scientists they study by criticizing their ideas and actions, including how their social roles, organizations, and products fit into society. It is precisely this sort of criticism of "our" science, "our" culture, and "our" sociology of science that I want to pursue and encourage.

In this introductory section, I have sketched the sociology of science landscape, and given some initial indications of what critical sociology of science stands for.[60] In the following sections, I develop a portrait of modern science that reveals the rationale for a critical sociology of science. At the same time, I develop the idea of a sociology of objectivity. By taking the reader on a more or less chronological tour of my studies in the sociology of science, I hope to convey some sense of how I avoided the perils of relativism and the excesses of realism and came to argue for a sociology of objectivity. In the later chapters of the book, I will bring out the connections between the idea of a critical sociology of science and a sociology of objectivity. And I will show why the sociology of science needs to be viewed as a special case of the sociology of inquiry. The final chapter is a look into the future based on translating Karl Marx's vision of "human science" into a vision of "human inquiry" grounded in a sociological theory of objectivity.

2
Ecology, Social Organization, and the Scientific Revolution

Prologue

A great deal of confusion has been caused in science studies by the failure to clearly distinguish between science as a social institution, and science as a set of factual or knowledge statements, or as an abstract or ideal social system, or as the serial biography of heroic individual scientists. As soon as we make this distinction, of course, we modify the second set of concepts. For example, once we understand science as a social institution, science as an autonomous, independent set of facts or statements is immediately recognized to be a mirage. The ideas I defend in this book depend on understanding science as a social institution. Therefore, this chapter has a central role to play in grounding my arguments because it provides a portrait of the origins of modern science as a social institution. In offering an alternative to conventional ideas about the origin of modern science, I also draw attention to a sociological conception of the scientific revolution. Without this sociological understanding of modern science and the scientific revolution, my general approach to, conception of, and criticism of modern science will be misunderstood and lead to fruitless and irrevelant debates about, for example, relativism versus realism.

Introduction

The "scientific revolution" that occurred in Western Europe beginning in the sixteenth century is the source of a critical and persistent problem in the history of science: Why did modern science emerge in Western Europe and not elsewhere? The unique emergence of modern science has been the subject of much scholarly research and commentary. Weber noted that "only in the West does science exist at a stage of development which we recognize today as valid." Price writes that none of the other great civilizations followed a scientific path comparable to that followed by European civilization: "It becomes clearer from our fragmentary historical understanding of their case histories that none of them was even approaching it." With respect to periodization in the history of science, there is a general consensus on dating the beginnings of the scientific revolution. The stages suggested by A. R. Hall are exemplary. The years 1500–1800 were preparatory; those since 1800 represent a period of accomplishment. The history of the scientific revolution effectively concludes early in the nineteenth century. "Rational science," on this view, was created in the seventeenth and eighteenth centuries, and the tactics and forms of modern scientific evolution established by the early 1800s.[1]

The contributions of sociologists on this problem have generally followed the conceptual guidelines established by Max Weber for studying modern science. Weber did not consider capitalism a factor in the *origin* of modern science. But he argued that economic conditions were extremely favorable to the *technical* utilization of scientific knowledge during the emergence of capitalism in the West.[2] Robert Merton, following Weber's suggestions, explored the reciprocal relations between science and other social institutions. His general conclusion was that science became "accredited and organized" as a consequence of changes in cultural values favorable to scientific activity. Arguments for the utility of science arose in the major institutional sectors of European society, including religion, the economy, and the military. These arguments, according to Merton, were "mainly prelude" to the institutionalization of science.[3] Later, Joseph Ben-David elaborated the utilitarian hypothesis in conjunction with his analysis of the establishment of the scientific role. Ben-David explicitly recognizes that the institutionalization of science was a precondition for the scientific revolution.

The problem Ben-David addresses is: "What made certain men in seventeenth-century Europe and nowhere before, view themselves as scientists and see the scientific role as one with unique and special obligations and possibilities?" In his effort to identify the necessary conditions for the emergence of the scientific role, Ben-David relies on the utilitarian thesis formulated by Weber and Merton. He claims that either some striking practical scientific discoveries had to convince people that science was an economically valuable occupation; or there had to be people convinced that scientific work was intrinsically worthwhile and at the same time in social positions that would allow them to persuade others of their conviction independent of any evidence that science was economically valuable. The social structural conditions necessary for the emergence and development of the scientific role, were, according to Ben-David, two-fold. First, the authority of the established church was weak, making doctrine a matter of individual interpretation. Second, there was a "class of people" oriented to economic and technological change, utopian rather than practical in their "intellectual policies," and possessed of potential power and influence but not yet in an authoritative and responsible position.[4]

Joseph Needham has arrived at conclusions consonant with Ben-David's basic thesis by studying a negative case, China. China has been the crucial comparative case for students of the West's scientific revolution because, in Ben-David's words, modern science "should have been intellectually possible" there.[5] Needham began his work to determine why modern science developed in Europe but not elsewhere. Early on, a second question occurred to him: why was Chinese science and technology in advance of European science and technology between the −1st and +15th centuries? Needham argues that Chinese bureaucratic feudalism provides an answer to both queries. The opposition of the mandarinate to any and all social activities which might threaten their position prevented the autonomous development of science. The structural foundation of mandarinate opposition was centralized bureaucratic power. There was little opportunity for increasing the mobility, status, and autonomy of individuals or classes in imperial China. "Merchants" and "scientists" represent the two most striking cases.[6] According to Needham, the centralization of power was due to "the spatial range of public works (river control, irrigation, and the building of transport canals) transcending time after time the barriers between the territories of individual feudal or proto-feudal lords." It was this idea that led me to think about the influence of environmental conditions on scientific activity, and to the relevance of human ecology for studying the scientific revolution problem. The sociological conception of modern science leads to a sociological reformulation of Needham's Problem: Why did scientific activity become functionally differentiated and institutionalized in Western Europe and not in China or elsewhere? This reformulation implies that what are usually considered the defining characteristics of modern science—e.g., mathematization, the interaction of theory and experiment, and universalism and rationalism as basic normative orientations—were historically dependent on the continuity in communication and innovation made possible by functional differentiation and institutionalization. This idea paves the way for an eminently Durkheimian sociological explanation of a social fact. Needham's General Sociocultural Hypothesis, which encompasses environmental and ecological factors in its broadest formulation, can now be seen to be appropriate to the problem as I have reformulated it:

> It may be said that while ideological, philosophical and theological differences are never to be undervalued, what mattered most of all was facilitating pressures of the transition from feudalism to mercantile and then industrial capitalism, pressures which did not effectively operate in any culture other than that of Western, Frankish, Europe.[7]

I will have more to say later in this book about the cultural roots of the scientific revolution. Here, the focus will be on ecological factors in the emergence of modern science.

Ecology, Science, and Society

Human ecology focuses on population aggregates adjusting to their physical environments by means of technology and social organization.[8] The relevance of this approach is based on two ideas. First, structural and functional institutional autonomy is the crucial organizational factor that accounts for the scientific revolution. Second, institutional autonomy is related to ecological factors. By adopting a dangerously broad but heuristically enriching view of China and Western Europe as "ecological units of analysis," it is possible to suggest an alternative to the explanations Weber, Merton, and Ben-David offered for the West's scientific revolution. Those explanations retain a saliency and power in contemporary scholarship that provides support for the notion of "pure science." So long as students of science accept, more or less uncritically, the utilitarian hypothesis and the Mertonian notion of reciprocal relations, the myth of pure science will retain a degree of viability in spite of increasingly intense challenges and criticisms.

In the following sections, I explore a human ecology of the scientific revolution. This leads to the claim that the emergence of Protestantism, modern capitalism, and modern science can be viewed as *parallel* institutional responses to a set of underlying ecological conditions. This idea is a contribution to the identification of the material foundations of objectivity communities and objective knowledge, a primary ingredient of the sociology of objectivity I articulate in the later sections of this book.

Autonomy in Science

As early as 1952, Bernard Barber was arguing against viewing science as "disembodied items of guaranteed knowledge and . . . a set of logical procedures for achieving such knowledge." Science, he argued, is a special kind of thought and behavior realized in different ways and to different degrees in different societies. For Barber, science is grounded in "the generic human attribute of empirical rationality."[9] It is easy to find more radical conceptions of science in earlier writings, notably in the works of Spengler and, for a less extreme example, Fleck.[10] But it is rare to find such a clear argument against the "European miracle" thesis in mainstream sociology, history, and philosophy of science. Scientific activity has occurred in all societies from prehistoric and ancient times to the present. What happened in Western Europe beginning about 1500 was not a "miracle" but an organizational revolution. It was in this period that the foundation for the emergence (one might say "precipitation") of science as a visible, differentiated part of Western European social life was established. In due course, science was organized as a social activity providing a livelihood for members of society who would come to be called "scientists."

The crucial missing link in traditional approaches to the scientific revolution problem is a sociological definition of modern science. Weber and Ben-David provide the elements for such a definition. My working definition of modern science, then, is the social activity of "a specific group of persons" occupying positions as "scientists" in specialized settings (such as scientific societies, research laboratories, and universities), all of whom "regard the scientific investigation of nature as a major source of truth about the world," all of whom submit the results of their activity to be "used and judged" by other scientists, and all of whom are rewarded (given sustenance) for their roles in "publicly recognized institutions enjoying far-reaching autonomy."[11] We will have reason to reconsider this definition in the light of developments in the new sociology of science. This will not, however, affect the significance of defining science in sociological terms: that is, that the development of what are usually considered the distinctive attributes of modern science (such as systematic and continuous interaction between theoretical explanation and experimentation, the mathematization of hypotheses, and universalism and rationalism as basic norms) was historically a consequence of the institutionalization of scientific activity. Only an institutionally autonomous social activity could have supported the combination of "continuity and rapid innovation" associated with the scientific revolution.[12]

Ben-David claims that several generations of "scientists" might have made a scientific revolution in Greece. The same may be said for China and for fourteenth century Arabic-Islamic science.[13] There is a sociological rationale for such claims, but it can only be sustained if we adopt a sociological definition of modern science. Institutional and role autonomy were necessary conditions for the scientific revolution; they are the organizational focus of my analysis.

Two important preconditions for the institutionalization of science in Western Europe were established by the medieval period: the independence of the towns, and the differentiation of the "intellectual" role in the universities. In medieval Europe, as in ancient China, India, and Egypt, students interested in "higher learning" were attracted to famous masters. But the European towns in which such masters lived were corporations independent of the King. Foreign students were not, therefore, under the King's protection.

The corporate organization of the universities was stimulated by the often violent confrontations between scholars and townspeople, and the failure of either the church or the state to regulate university affairs. Incorporation was not unique to the West, but it became much more important there than elsewhere. By the thirteenth century, the university was a relatively well-endowed, privileged, and autonomous intellectual community.[14] Furthermore, as Ben-David has shown, the presence of different intellectual specialities within one autonomous organization fostered greater and viable differentiation and helped establish the sciences in the universities. Differentiation and the establishment of the "intellectual" role preceded the emergence of the academies and the development of the scientific role.

The institutionalization of science can be said to begin with the shift of scientific activity from the medieval universities to the academies. (Science would grow and strengthen in these crucibles and eventually return to the universities). The earliest of these academies was the Academia Secretorum Naturae, founded in Naples in 1560.

The first Academia de Lincei (1603–1630) was founded in Rome, followed by the Academia del Cimento (Florence, 1657–1667), the Royal Society (London, 1662–), and the Académie des Sciences (Paris, 1666 –). The Societas Ereunetica (Rostock, 1622–ca.1642) was one of the earliest German academies. The Berlin Academy was founded in 1700 by Leibniz. The academies, books and journals sponsored by the academies, and journals such as the *Journal des Savants* (Paris 1665) and *Acta Eruditorum* (Leipzig, 1682) were the foundations of continuity in scientific activity. That activity now grew more or less in proportion to the general growth of population and wealth, and became increasingly autonomous. (I will have occasion from time to time to remind the reader that autonomy is an institutional or organizational concept, not a description of purity and complete independence from other social activities.) Increasing autonomy stimulated the development of the scientific identity and the institutionalization of the scientific role.[15]

There are, of course, earlier examples of scientific organizations. Scientific activity was unified and academies were founded under the Roman Empire. There were communities of "scientists" in Hellenistic Alexandria. And there was an Arabic-Islamic "scientific community" that stretched from Spain to Persia by the thirteenth century. But these and other even earlier examples in East and West must be considered "proto-scientific" in terms of my working definition of modern science. They do not exhibit the extensity of differentiation and autonomy, nor the levels of generational and intellectual continuity characteristic of scientific activity in Western Europe from 1500 on.[16]

China, for all of its triumphs in science and technology, did not undergo a "spontaneous autochthonous" (Needham's term) scientific revolution. This is illustrated, for example, by the failure of Chinese astronomers to develop a unified scientific system, the relatively "official" nature of Chinese science within the state bureaucracy, and the intellectually inhibiting atmosphere of the schools of mathematics.[17]

The status of the scholar was high in China. But in China, as elsewhere, scholars and intellectuals were usually political and religious figures (mandarin officials or priests, for example). (This should not be taken to mean that modern scholars, scientists, and intellectuals are involved in "pure" roles, only that role differentiation and specialization were not as well developed in the pre-modern period.) In some cases, scholars or intellectuals were honored and supported for their charismatic qualities; such individuals did not earn their living as members of established occupations. In Western Europe, by contrast, the seventeenth and eighteenth centuries witnessed the emergence of a recognized scientific role and identity, increasingly distinct from those of philosophers and theologians. The distinction was not lost when these occupational categories overlapped.[18] Given conditions unfavorable to the institutionalization of science in China, there was no opportunity for the Chinese to turn isolated examples and episodes of proto-typical scientific work into a scientific revolution.[19]

The decentralization of ecclesiastical and political authority in Western Europe helped pave the way for the emergence of modern science.[20] Once we have taken account of regional and temporal variations in decentralization and in the historical development of Western science, we are left with one crucial fact: a centralized bureaucratic state comparable to that of China (and other civilizations) did not take hold in Western Europe. Neither the church nor the state—nor any other institutional sphere—dominated the social terrain of Western Europe in the way that the agrarian bureaucracy dominated in China until modern times. The persistence of that bureaucratic form prevented or time and again aborted the emergence of relatively autonomous social groups, notably a merchant class, and of anything like the Protestant Reformation.[21] In Western Europe, it was just these social changes that enhanced the status of scientific activity and led to the establishment of the scientific role.[22]

To this point, my aim has been to establish the significance of social differentiation and institutional autonomy in the emergence of modern science, and the role of decentralized authority in fostering these social conditions. In the next part of this chapter, I examine authority patterns, social change, and scientific activity in China and Western Europe in terms of human ecology. The identification of Western Europe and China as "ecological units" simply acknowledges the interrelatedness of populations, social organizations, environments, and technologies in these civilizational areas. These units define two distinct culturally bounded histories generally acknowledged by students of Chinese and European history.[23] We can naturally anticipate more focused and detailed analyses of smaller units within these civilizational areas comparable to Ben-David's shifts in geographical focus as he outlines the stages in the development of the scientific role which finally emerges in the northern sector of Western Europe.[24] The key concept in the following analysis is "sustenance organization."

Sustenance Organization and Scientific Activity

The system of sustenance in Western Europe was organized around a farming economy that relied on rainfall. In China, sustenance organization was based on large-scale irrigation works and flood control. The control of sources of water over vast areas required an extensive division of and control over labor. Dams, reservoirs, aqueducts, and tunnels had to be built and maintained. These "preparatory" operations had to be complemented by equally large-scale "protective" operations such as the building of dikes and embankments to safeguard crops from periodic and excessive inundations. The division of labor was further complicated by the need to recruit for and staff the preparatory and protective functions. The complexity of the division of labor in China in contrast to the situation in Western Europe has been analyzed by Wittfogel.

Wittfogel notes that cooperation in hydraulic agriculture involves more than "digging, dredging, and damming," and the program of organizing these activities. Additional questions arise: how many persons are needed, and where can they be found; what quotas and selection criteria will be adopted; how will the labor pool be selected, notified, and mobilized. Even simple water control operations require high levels of integrative social action. The elaborate variations, such as those we find in China, require extensive and complex planning. Informal intercommunity cooperation in public projects is, according to an hypothesis formulated by Julian Steward, possible only in small-scale systems; an increase in scale—measured in terms of the size of dams and the number of miles of canals—is accompanied by an increase in the demand for labor and in "managerial density." Eventually, volunteers are replaced by corvée labor, and temporary supervisors give way to state-appointed bureaucrats.[25]

If irrigation farming depends, then, on the effective handling of a major supply of water, an extensive division of labor will be required to control the water. To the extent that large-scale irrigation agriculture requires an extensive division of labor, a high degree of coordination and social control will be needed to insure the effective operation of the agricultural system. Such large-scale systems tend to promote the centralization and concentration of authority.[26]

It may be that the managerial functions required for operating irrigation systems can be performed by community leaders rather than through a central authority.[27] Indeed, it seems that the construction and maintenance of irrigation systems in China was much more dependent on the initiation and action of local authorities than Wittfogel recognized.[28] But local authorities—landlords, or landlord families— were products of an Imperial system who held academic degrees, and possessed the official contacts academic degrees made possible. They exerted pressure on the central authority through their official contacts in order to insure the proper irrigation control necessary for growing quality crops. Provincial landlord cliques controlled provincial projects; more powerful cliques, possessing a "national vision," controlled larger state projects. None of this, however, alters the important fact that there was a central authority ultimately responsible for public works, maintaining social order, and collecting taxes.[29]

Lenski agrees that large-scale irrigation systems have probably been a factor in the growth of "autocracy." But he does not believe that they have been either a "dominant" or a "major" factor. He argues that the degree to which authority is centralized is influenced by such factors as the size of the territorial unit, the quality of transportation and communication facilities, the relative distribution of military skill and power in the population, and the nature of the laws of inheritance. But the influence of such factors is not independent of the tendency toward centralization of authority inherent in the practice of large-scale irrigation. Thus, to the extent that effective centralized authority involves accessibility to the subordinate population, the emergence of centralization in large-scale irrigation agriculture depends on the construction of extensive transportation and communication facilities. Such facilities, in turn, increase the potential for greater centralization in control and authority.[30]

The practice of large-scale irrigation in China fostered the growth of centrally controlled systems of navigation canals, roads, and postal systems. This intensified the central government's monopoly on control over transportation and communication facilities.[31] In contrast, the practice of rainfall agriculture in Western Europe was a factor in calling forth a decentralized system of authority in which local transportation and communication facilities were established long before governments with wider powers undertook the construction and control of such facilities.[32] This is evident in the basic features of European feudalism. It was never a uniform system, never, in James Westfall Thompson's words, "a meticulously differentiated society, a carefully graduated hierarchy rising to an apex in the King-supersuzerain, a neatly divided delegation of authority." Chinese bureaucratic feudalism was, *by contrast*, a more uniform system.

Local communities in China did not enjoy the corporate autonomy of their European counterparts. European feudalism was unique in this respect in relation not only to China but to all other feudalistic systems. Japanese feudalism, for example, was based to a greater degree on loyalty to superior authorities and a divine ruler. And in India the critical concept of "free contract" did not arise. Collective immunity from the power of rulers emerged *along with* the right to resist unjust authority. The conception of a contract as "a mutual engagement freely undertaken by free persons" took hold in Western Europe in a way and to a degree unknown in other civilizational areas.

The initial hypotheses that emerge from the discussion so far are: (1) the necessity for large-scale water works in China was a determinant of the Chinese form of feudalism with its associated pattern of centralized authority; (2) rainfall agriculture in the West stimulated the decentralization of authority and the Western form of feudalism. While these hypotheses are basic to the human ecology approach, they require some refinement. Specifically, Wittfogel's "oriental despotism" hypothesis can be refined, following Barrington Moore, as follows: the tendency toward the centralization of authority and "bureaucratic feudalism" in preindustrial societies is related to environmental conditions that necessitate the construction, coordination, and control of large-scale public works.[33] The necessity of large-scale public works in China was specifically the necessity for large-scale irrigation.

The "democratic possibilities" Moore associates with Western feudalism—and the lack of such possibilities in China—are illustrated by the variations in economic activity in China and Europe. In turning to an examination of these variations, I want to draw attention to: (1) the parallel between the potential for institutional and role autonomy in economic and intellectual activity that existed in Western Europe but not, to the same degree, in China; and (2) the realization of this potential in capitalist and scientific activities in the West.

Sustenance Organization and Capitalist Activity

Ben-David claimed that the development of science in the European universities was stimulated by the emergence of a merchant or capitalist class whose interests were consistent with, and reinforced an empirical, rational worldview.[34] An alternative hypothesis is that the emergence of both "modern science" and "modern capitalism" occurred in part as a response to certain ecological conditions. China's ecology inhibited the development of a social formation that could permit the full development and institutionalization of scientific and capitalist activities. The ecological conditions necessitating large-scale water control, their general organizational consequences, and the correlated inhibition of scientific organizations in China were sketched above. Here, a broader ecological perspective is introduced as we compare economic activities in China and Western Europe, and ask why capitalism became institutionalized in the West but not in the East.

The primary factors in the emergence and development of capitalist activity are competition and exchange in a "free" diversified market. The competitive process begins with the emergence of an aggregate demand that exceeds the supply of resources. It is followed by an increasing homogeneity among the competitors. Then "congestion" begins to selectively eliminate the weakest competitors. This is followed by the development of some form of differentiation according to territory, or intraterritorial specialization which involves dependence on but a noncompetitive relationship with those who command supplies.[35] Thus, the differentiation and multiplication of functions in a society depends on competition for resources. In any such development, population size, environmental productivity, and level of technology play conditioning roles.

Population size constitutes a limitation upon the extent of functional differentiation, and limits the opportunities for and the extent of specialization. Population size is in turn a function of the productivity of the environment. A poor environment cannot sustain a large population, although the number of people who in fact inhabit an environment is in part a function of the type of social organization they develop. (This assumes an environment that allows for some organizational options.)

The productivity of an environment is in great part a function of the level of technology. Technology in turn determines the efficiency of transportation and communication facilities; and these facilities affect the extent to which spatially separated activities can be interrelated. To the extent that a population is isolated or independent of exchange relationships, its resources are limited to those of the local habitat. The development of technology, an economic surplus, and transportation and communication facilities permit and promote functional interdependence between and among communities. A progressively larger environment is made accessible by relations of interdependence and exchange.[36] These generalizations reveal important differences in the human ecology of China and the West.

The division of labor in China was extensive, but it was not functionally differentiated along an exchange-of-surplus base. Local surpluses were commanded by the state for the rulers. There was no localized, independent development of and control over differentiated surpluses *comparable* to that which developed in Western Europe.[37]

The decentralization of authority in feudal Europe was a function of, and stimulated, regional exchange. This, in conjunction with population increase and scarcity of land, was a factor in the emergence of a class of private capitalists. The free movement of the European merchants and their ability to share in the competition for power was dependent on the decentralization of authority, and on the associated conflicts between the landed nobility, the church, and the ruling classes.[38]

China was relatively isolated from intercultural exchange. Local and indigenous factors thus conditioned the structure of Chinese life to a greater extent than was the case in the Near and Middle East, and Europe. China's relative isolation as a historical civilizational area was a matter of geography—the Gobi Desert and Mongolian Plateau to the north, the Himalayas, Pamirs, and Tibetan Plateau to the southwest and the Yunnan Plateau to the southeast were major physical barriers. These help account for China's *relative* isolation from the "arc of urbanization" that linked the lower Nile, the Mesopotamian heartland, the Indus Valley, and the Gangetic plain.[39] The impact of these factors was reinforced by the lack of an internal "urban market."[40] Taken together, these conditions were the principal obstacles to capitalist activity in China. As we will see in the following discussion, China's capacity for generating a differentiated surplus was relatively limited, and an ecologically fundamental factor in explaining the Chinese course of history. I begin by examining in more detail the human ecological requirements for capitalist activity.

Competition leads to an elaborate division of labor functionally differentiated along an exchange-of-surplus base only to the extent that the production of surpluses has been institutionalized through an appropriate form of social organization. Students of the origin of urbanization usually start with the assumption that a precondition for the cumulative differentiation of social activities is a level of agricultural production high enough to release a substantial part of the population from primary resource activities, and to permit their involvement in secondary, tertiary, and higher level resource activities. An appropriate form of social organization capable of accumulating surpluses is thus a necessary ingredient of urbanization; this in turn creates the appropriate arena for capitalist activity.[41]

Capitalist activity is oriented to profit through exchange. This requires (1) an environment which will yield not simply a surplus but a *differentiated* surplus, (2) a social organization for accumulating and exchanging surpluses (for profit); this implies the functional differentiation of interdependent, more or less autonomous "free agents"—individuals or communities. Modern capitalism in particular was dependent on an ecological milieu conducive to the establishment of an autonomous role for merchants and capitalists, and the institutionalization of their activities.

If the area of land available for cultivation and the "environment" is held constant, the quantity of food available for any unit of population is a function of population size and the degree of farming knowledge and level of farming technology. Until the eighteenth century, agricultural production in Europe was limited chiefly by the difficulty of restoring the fertility of the soil after cropping. There were at least three methods available for restoring soil fertility, but their use was limited. The difficulty of restoring soil fertility, in conjunction with population increases, led to pressure on the food supply. Increasing numbers of people were in consequence detached from the land. They represented potential occupants of ancillary sustenance positions. Indeed, Pirenne identified these landless masses as the ancestors of the merchant class.[42]

The manorial regime that was established during the ninth and tenth centuries generated the economic surplus required to support ancillary positions one or more levels removed from primary resource extraction. Through various forms of manorial taxation and fiscal exaction the landed aristocracy secured the revenue with which to support an emergent merchant class.[43]

From 1000 to 1700, the magnitude of population increase in China and Western Europe is estimated to have been about the same. But while improved farming practices did not occur in Western Europe until the eighteenth century, improvements in China at a much earlier period resulted in increased yields to meet the needs of the growing population. The most significant development in land utilization and food production in China during the past millennium was brought about by the cultivation of early-ripening rice and its extensive diffusion early in the eleventh century. This revolution in land use and production was based on taking advantage of relatively well-watered hills.[44]

During the greater part of the past thousand years, the food situation seems to have been much better in China that it was in Europe. Whereas the Europeans had to struggle with the problem of restoring soil fertility after cropping, the most striking feature of rice grown under irrigation is its indifference to soil fertility.[45] This helps account for the capacity of wet rice agriculture to stimulate intensified cultivation in response to population pressures. And it illustrates the fact that the Chinese did not exploit a differentiated surplus. The stronger point is that a human ecology analysis suggests that given such factors as the nature and distribution of resources and the level of technology in China, the initial exploitation of a differentiated surplus appears to have been a uniquely Western prerogative, at least on an appreciably large and sustained scale.

Earlier, I alluded to urbanization as a context for capitalist growth. In ecological theory, general "cultural growth" is associated with "regional intercommunication and interstimulation."[46] Communication and stimulation here imply not simply linkages but *symbiotic* linkages within a "naturally" (that is, ecologically given) differentiated area. The prerequisite, then, for general cultural growth is the juxtaposition of diverse subenvironments or cultures symbiotically exploited in social interaction.[47] The process of urbanization is fed by population increases and the development of a surplus. Technology injects "form and focus" into the process.[48]

Urbanization is thus a function of the exploitation and exchange of differentiated surpluses. The resultant interdependence between communities and the increase in specializations are important for general cultural growth, economic growth, and scientific growth.[49]

Between the second and fifteenth centuries, China's general cultural growth can, according to Needham, be "represented by a relatively slowly rising curve, noticeably running at a higher level, sometimes a much higher level, than European parallels."[50] The explanation for the exponential growth of European technology from the seventeenth century on, for the scientific revolution, and for modern capitalism, cannot therefore be based on absolutist claims about the differences between China and the West. China's growth pattern, however, was episodic. And the preconditions for an economic, technological, and scientific "take-off" could not take root in an environment unfavorable to an exchange-of-surplus form of sustenance organization. The "take-off" in Europe, and in particular Western Europe, was possible because of prior and concurrent developments in urban interdependence, and the proliferation of transportation, communication, and exchange linkages in an environment that was not merely relatively hospitable, but hospitable to an exchange-of-surplus form of sustenance organization.

The facilitative factors I have pointed to in accounting for the West's scientific revolution did, of course, also depend on cultural diffusion. The diffusion of technology, especially from China, appears to have played an especially critical role in the West's breakthroughs.[51]

The structural consequence of the ecological constraints operating in China was that merchants and craftspersons were low in status, discriminated against, and relatively immobile within the rigid stratification system that dominated imperial China. In contrast to the merchant class that emerged in Western Europe beginning as early as the ninth century, the Chinese merchants were dependent on and subordinate to the scholar-officials, and subject to state supervision and regulation. And Weber argued that the most distinctive characteristic of the European merchants was that they came to possess effective military power.[52]

In summary, ecological conditions in pre-modern Europe were more favorable than elsewhere for the eventual emergence of a functionally differentiated and *sustainable* exchange-of-surplus mode of production, distribution, and consumption; and this was a precondition for *sustained* capitalist and scientific activity and the eventual institutionalization of modern capitalism and modern science. Ecological conditions in China inhibited these developments, although in China and elsewhere episodes of capitalist and scientific activity occurred. Human ecology helps account for why these episodes could not be sustained in China and why the appropriate set of factors could and did eventually come together in the West and lead to the capitalist and scientific revolutions.

Protestantism, Capitalism, and Science

The essentially concurrent emergence of modern science, modern capitalism, and Protestantism made the search for mutual influences a natural research task. In *The Protestant Ethic and the Spirit of Capitalism*, Max Weber claimed there was a relationship between ascetic Protestantism and modern capitalism. He also noted the strong influence of the natural sciences on the development of modern capitalism. The development of the natural sciences was in turn stimulated by the interest of capitalists in applying scientific knowledge to practical problems. In Weber's terms, the defining characteristic of modern capitalism, organized rationality, was dependent on the calculability of certain technical factors made possible by developments in mathematics and experimental method.

Given the basis provided by Weber for viewing ascetic Protestantism as instrumental in the emergence of modern capitalism, Merton was able to argue that ascetic Protestantism was instrumental in the emergence of modern science. Specifically, Merton claimed that the Puritan ethic, an "ideal-typical expression of the value attitudes basic to ascetic Protestantism generally, so canalized the interests of seventeenth-century Englishmen as to constitute one important *element* in the enhanced cultivation of science." The glorification of God in His works, the welfare of society, rationality as a curb on the passions, and the demands of systematic, methodic, and diligent work were, according to Merton, expressed through the pursuit of science.[53]

In order to verify the general hypothesis that "the cultural attitudes induced by the Protestant ethic were favorable to science," Merton deduced and tested the specific hypothesis that "if the Protestant ethic involved an attitudinal set favorable to science and technology in so many ways, then we should find amongst Protestants a greater propensity for these fields of endeavor than one would expect simply on the basis of their representation in the total population." Merton's data indicated a "pronounced" association between Protestantism and scientific and technological interests, "even when extra-religious influences are as far as possible eliminated."[54]

The application of the Weber-Merton theses in the comparative study of science in China and Western Europe allowed Talcott Parsons to conclude that Protestantism, a doctrine of "rational mastery *over* the world," stimulated science whereas Confucianism (China's functional equivalent to Protestantism in this comparative exercise), a doctrine of "rational adaptation *to* the world" inhibited organized scientific activity.[55]

Parsons noted Weber's judgment that at the crucial time in China, India, and Western Europe the combination of non-religious factors was equally favorable to capitalistic development. Thus, Weber concluded that it was probably the religious element in the respective economic ethics that inhibited capitalism in the first two instances, and facilitated it in the third. A parallel judgment about science underlies efforts to attribute the differences in the histories of Chinese and Western science to differences in the religious ethics of China and the West. Weber argued that the Confucian ethical system fostered traditionalism in China. It provided the moral force for accepting the existing social order, especially the traditional religio-magical aspects of that order (state cult, ancestor worship, and popular magic). The Confucian gentleman was oriented to a traditional status ideal, based on the assimilation of the classics, the fixed body of traditional literary culture. The Protestant ethic was distinctly revolutionary by comparison. It is from this Weberian perspective that Merton sees the instrumental influence of Protestantism on Western science. From this same perspective, Balazs argues for the widely accepted claim that Confucian orthodoxy was unfavorable to any form of trial, experiment, innovation, or "free play of the mind," and in this respect was certainly a factor that inhibited the development of Chinese science.[56]

The so-called Puritan ethic thesis has been debated and challenged for decades, and has shown remarkable tenacity. The reason for this will become apparent shortly. But first, it must be recognized that the history of Protestant interference with the pursuit of science on the one hand, and the innovative contributions of the Chinese in science and technology documented by Needham on the other are enough to establish some doubts about the general Weberian perspective.[57] There is, however, a stronger argument for reconsidering the thesis.

Confucianism was an integral part of the Chinese imperial political framework.[58] The fact that Confucianism developed and changed in relation to the development of the state bureaucracy, and came to function as the legitimizing ethic of the empire, makes it reasonable to conceive Confucianism as a normative construction grounded in and reflective of the prevailing form of sustenance organization.[59] One might be tempted at this point to argue that Protestantism (as an ethical system) was a normative response to changes in the form of sustenance organization in Western Europe. Actually it seems more reasonable to identify rationalism-universalism as the relevant normative response and thus the appropriate functional equivalent to Confucianism. Protestantism then becomes a variegated but nonetheless systematic response within prevailing religious institutions to the rationalistic-universalistic ethic that permeated to greater and lesser degrees all sectors of Western European culture beginning with the Renaissance.

As an integral part of the imperial Chinese bureaucracy, Confucianism might in fact be considered epiphenomenal in terms of its inhibitory impact on autonomous scientific activity. Even this interpretation may exaggerate the influence of Confucianism. In the midst of Confucian traditionalism and Taoist threnodies about a lost Golden Age, other convictions flourished. Some Chinese believed that "true knowledge" had grown and could grow yet more if people would "look outward to things," and build upon what others had discovered in looking outward.

These are Needham's observations; and he notes further that one can quote from the manuscripts of any century conceptions of science as a "cumulative disinterested co-operative enterprise."[60] The failure of that idea to crystallize in China and its successful crystallization in Western Europe is, I have argued, best explained by taking account of ecological and organizational conditions inhibiting or conducive to autonomous social activities.

Conclusion

In 1938, Merton concluded that "the formal organization of values constituted by Puritanism led to the largely unwitting furtherance of modern science." In reflecting on this conclusion in 1970, he wrote that "before it became widely accepted as a value in its own right, science was required to justify itself to men in terms of values other than that of knowledge itself." Neither statement, given the material reviewed in this chapter, conveys an appropriate conception of the relationship between science, capitalism, and religion in the West. The problem is not, as Merton suggested in 1970, "to estimate the proportion of cases which can be ascribed to the Puritanism-science sequence and to the science-Puritanism sequence."[61] Nor is it to carry out the same estimation with respect to Puritanism and capitalism, and capitalism and science. The human ecology approach recommends against this simple "reciprocal influence" assumption.

The human ecology of the scientific revolution raises related questions about the "utilitarian hypothesis," and the emphasis on values and the roles of individual "men" in the "evolution" of science. Ben-David's attachment to the utilitarian hypothesis is reflected in his emphasis on "needs," "demand," "social value," and "social interests." This strains his institutional approach (as it does Merton's) and leads him to focus on questions such as whether this or that person did or did not regard him or herself a "scientist."[62] He argues that the development of science depended on the determination of the minority of science advocates to openly fight for its general recognition, "to express and develop its interest in science in public discussion and purposeful association." The more fundamental sociological questions, however, are: (1) what structural conditions were the crucibles of that determination (and what interests were in fact represented by that minority); and (2) what ecological and structural conditions made the institutionalization of science possible? This is not meant to detract from Ben-David's important contribution to our understanding of the function of decentralization in the emergence of modern science.

My aim in this chapter has been to explore the explanatory potential of human ecology in addressing the scientific revolution problem. The route through population, social organization, environment, and technology in China and Western Europe illustrated the importance of considering how ecological conditions condition social organization and culture. And it led to a conception of Protestantism, modern capitalism, and modern science as parallel responses in different institutional spheres to ecological conditions that fostered an exchange-based economy, political decentralization, and a rational-universal ethos. This helps explain why in spite of historical and geographical variations and differences in the religious, economic, and social life of modern European nations, the Puritan ethic thesis has resisted every effort to undermine it.

This chapter also introduces an important starting point for the sociology of objectivity by establishing a naturalistic linkage between ecology/environment and the sustenance activities of human beings. I will have opportunity later on to exploit this idea in defense of a materialist, realistic sociology of objectivity.

I have tried, within the limits of this analysis and independently of any errors of commission or omission to establish the importance of defining modern science in sociological terms. This is the basis for concluding that the institutionalization of science is the precondition for, and not itself, the scientific revolution; and that the scientific revolution was an organizational revolution and not a revolution in values, methods, or other matters of technique and orientation.

The parallel responses thesis suggests a more intimate relationship between science and capitalism than most students of the scientific revolution have recognized. I will consider this relationship again in a slightly different context when I discuss "The Science Machine" in Chapter 4.

3
Science, Society, and Progress

The idea that science is at the root of our social and environmental ills can only be convincing if we recognize that the referent for "modern science" or "Western science" *is a social institution.* This is important because "science" can have other referents, including idealistic ones. Because of this multiplicity of referents, many of the critics of modern science experience a dilemma similar to that expressed by Michael Bakunin:

> What I preach then is, to a certain extent, the *revolt of life against science,* or rather against the *government of science,* not to destroy science—that would be high treason to humanity—but to remand it to its place so that it can never leave again.[1]

The dilemma is that on the one hand, it seems intuitively clear or otherwise obvious that "science" in some sense has contributed to whatever social progress has been achieved on this planet. On the other hand, we entertain no such illusions about *modern science as a social institution.* The dilemma arises in another, related way to the extent that we associate science with *rationality.* Again, objections to rationality, and the claim that rationality has obstructed rather than facilitated social progress, appear to many of us to be unwarranted and perverse, and harbingers of the twin demons of *relativism* and *irrationalism.* Indeed, rationality (reason), science, and progress are often viewed as parts of an ideological triad. But just as in the case of science, we find upon closer examination that rationality too is if not a demon at least Janus-faced.

The Problem of Rationality

In the fourteenth century, the word *rational* meant *having the faculty of reasoning*, or *endowed with reason*; and *exercising (or being able to exercise) one's reason in a proper manner*. In other words, to be rational is to have *sound judgment*, to be *sensible*, to be *sane*. *Rational* was also opposed to *empirical*. These two words were applied to two classes of ancient physicians who, respectively: (1) deduced their treatment of cases from general principles; and (2) based their methods of practice on the results of observation and experiment rather than "scientific theory." Among the *empirical* physicians, a practice was adopted if it worked, even if the reasons for its efficacy were unknown. The term *empirical* was later applied to *unscientific physicians* or *quacks*.[2]

By the seventeenth century, the word *rationality* was being used to refer to *the quality of possessing reason*, and *the power of being able to exercise one's reason: the fact of being based on, or agreeable to reason* (or, a *rational or reasonable view, practice,* etc.); and *the tendency to regard everything from a purely rational point of view*.

Today, the lexicographical meaning of *rationality* is: the quality of being *rational*, which in turn is defined as *having reason or understanding*. The three basic etymological ingredients of *reason* are: *ratio*, or *proportion*; (re: to *count*); and *calculate*. These terms are associated with and in fact constitute the verb *to think*. *To reason* also has the sense *to fit*. This meaning is related to the Greek cognate, *arm*, which in turn is associated with *power* and *might*. *To arm* means: *to furnish with something that strengthens or protects*; *to fortify morally*; *to equip or ready for action or operation*; and *to equip or ready for struggle or resistance*. These are the etymological grounds for the standard definitions of *reason*: *a statement offered in explanation or justification; a rational ground or motive; a sufficient ground of explanation or logical defense; the thing that makes some fact intelligible* (in this sense, *reason* is a synonym for *cause*); *the power of comprehending, inferring or thinking, especially in orderly, rational ways* (here, *reason* is a synonym for *intelligence*); *the proper exercise of mind* (here, *reason* means *sanity*). *Rationality*, finally means *acceptability to reason, reasonableness*.

What stands out for the sociologist in the preceding lexicographical, etymological tour is the shadow of *community standards* that covers the terrain. Words such as *proper, sound, sensible, sane, acceptability*, and *orderly* imply (indeed are synonymous with) prevailing community standards. This is important because one notable aspect of the recurring arguments for and against *rationality* is that they are implicated in conflicts about community standards, and resistance to the authority of those who set, sustain, and protect community standards—and in the efforts by outsiders to wrestle that authority away from the insiders. There is, naturally, a labeling dimension in these conflicts. The label *rational* is applied to claims of superiority, the defense of a privileged status or position, and the justification of one's or a group's power to define what is proper, sound, sensible, and sane in a community. The *Rational* Christians, for example, claimed a superior rationality for their form of Christianity. In this sense, then, *rational* is not a synonym for *science* (from the point of view of modern scientists and scientific thinkers). From this perspective, every community establishes standards for what is reasonable and labels them *rational*. This helps account for the adjectification of rationality that gives us scientific rationality, legal rationality, theological rationality, and so on. There may, of course, be overlaps and mutual influences between and among different forms of rationality. But the idea of community-specific rationalities is often used as a way of demarcating science from other modes of thought and knowing. Science is viewed by demarcationists as the only *truly* rational mode of thought or knowing.

There are two basic forms of opposition to the demarcationist strategy based on the rationality criterion. One is the claim that there are *no* criteria that allow us to distinguish better and worse rationalities across the variety of human cultures, classes, and professions. This claim is often grounded in a misreading of the logic of the Azande made famous by E. Evans-Pritchard's descriptions of their witchcraft and oracular beliefs. The second is the claim that there is a basic set of reasoning principles, or rationalities, that are part of the repertoire of human cultures. Thus, the Azande, plumbers, garage mechanics, the ancient Greek philosophers, paranoids, and physicists all use the same basic principles of reasoning. For example, some anthropologists of science claim that the forms of "laboratory reasoning" are nothing more or less than applications of the unspecific properties of common sense rationalities identified by Harold Garfinkel: these include:[3]

1. a concern for making things comparable;
2. a concern for establishing a "good fit" between observation and interpretation;
3. a concern for timing, predictability, and correct procedures;
4. a search for previously successful means;

5. a conscious analysis of the alternatives and consequences of action;
6. an interest in the planning of strategies;
7. an awareness of choices and the grounds upon which these choices can be made.

There are, in other words, no rationalities peculiar to science. The formal features of reasoning show the scientist to be a *practical reasoner*. While there is some basis for the second claim, neither claim tells the whole story of rationality as a cultural resource. To begin to fill in the rest of the picture, let's consider the notion that rationality is a norm of science.

The sociologist of science Bernard Barber identifies *rationality* as a norm of science: it is "the critical approach to all the phenomena of human existence in the attempt to reduce them to ever more consistent, orderly, and generalized forms of understanding." Barber is one of the few sociologists of science who troubles to articulate and define rationality. Others take it for granted as a norm of science or inherent in science, or they ignore it. Robert Merton, for example, says virtually nothing about it in his essays.[4]

Philosophers of science have been more concerned with rationality than the sociologists. This is no surprise; the scientific community, like all other complex communities, has a division of labor—the philosophers of science are the moral entrepreneurs of that community. Twentieth century philosophers have defined rationality in several ways; I follow Laudan here:[5]

1. acting to maximize one's personal utilities;
2. believing in, and acting on, only those propositions which we have good grounds for believing to be true (or at least to be more likely than not);
3. a function of cost-benefit analysis;
4. putting forward statements which can be refuted.

Now it is easy enough to find cases in the history of science in which most if not all observers would agree "intuitively" that scientists in a given situation were being "rational" even though they failed to follow any standard "model" of rationality. Consider the following ploys of scientists identified by Laudan:[6]

1. invoke "non-refuting" anomalous problems as major objections to theories;

2. concentrate on clarifying concepts and the reduction of other sorts of conceptual problems;
3. pursue and investigate "promising" theories, even if those theories are less "adequate" than rival theories;
4. utilize metaphysical and methodological arguments against and in favor of theories and research traditions;
5. accept theories even though they are confronted by numerous anomalies;
6. accept theories which do *not* solve all of the empirical problems of their predecessors;
7. exhibit wild fluctuations regarding the importance of a problem, and even its status as a problem.

As we will see in a moment, Laudan does not use these examples as a basis for announcing the end of rationality. Let us first consider the arguments of some other critics of rationality in science.

Michael Mahoney has criticized the assumption that scientific *practice* is characterized by rationality.[7] He argues that illogical reasoning is often used in theory evaluation; the only viable means for identifying valid scientific theories available to us appears to be disconfirmation, but disconfirmation is limited in scope and does not actually fit what scientists do in practice; theories seem to be born refuted, since they are virtually always at odds with some data, even when they are first proposed; and (Duhem-Quine) there are no really critical or crucial tests for theories. In *The Retreat to Commitment*, W. W. Bartley applies the "tu quoque argument"—the "how do you know" argument—to rationalistic (reason-embracing) modes of knowing, and concludes that all such approaches are irrational.[8] They are irrational because: (1) they are supported by some sort of ultimate epistemological authority such as logic, revelation, or sense data; and (2) the authority of the ultimate authority is accepted on faith. Rationality is thus limited by the fact of the infinite regress of standards requiring justification. Since we are sooner or later going to have to make a dogmatic commitment, we can in principle make any commitment we want—therefore, Bartley argues, we are not in a position to be criticized for our commitment or to criticize the commitments of others.

Mahoney and Bartley both contend that the effort to justify traditional rationality is at the root of its irrationality. Laudan's critique of traditional rationality, by comparison, is that it involves accepting those statements about the world which we have good reason to believe are true. Progress, in turn, is usually viewed as a successive attainment of the truth by a process of approximations and self-corrections. He criticizes the argument that actual standards of rational appraisal have remained constant over time. Components of rational appraisal such as ideas about scientific testing, beliefs about inductive inference, and views about what is to count as an explanation have changed enormously. (Note that for Popper and Lakatos, scientific standards of rationality have *evolved*; but the issue is whether a particular theory was well-founded by *our* current standards of rationality.) Given the criticisms rationality is subject to, what should we do? Do we jettison or save rationality? Mahoney, Bartley, and Laudan *save* rationality using two different ploys. Mahoney and Bartley argue that rationality should be based on *criticism* rather than justification. Mahoney's *comprehensively critical rationalism* (CCR) does not rest on the claim that it is indubitably rational—it thereby avoids the "tu quoque." The CCR strategy is to reduce errors, not guarantee truths.

Laudan's ploy also jettisons justification, but replaces it with a practical approach. He makes rationality parasitic upon progress. Rational choices are progressive choices; they "increase the problem-solving effectiveness of the theories we accept." No assumptions are made about veracity or verisimilitude.[9]

Why should Mahoney, Bartley, Laudan and so many others *want* to save rationality? And what do their heroics cost them? Mahoney and Bartley end up arguing that logic is one of the basic methods for reducing error via criticism. They claim that logic is not immune to criticism. But certain *forms* of logic are *presupposed* in critical arguments. If we reject *modus ponens* and *modus tollens*, for example, we cannot argue in any meaningful sense. This may not be a justificationist strategy; but as we know from such things as the Lewis Principle (a contradiction entails *any* system) and DeMorgan's 4-valued logic, it is a *problematic* strategy.[10]

The costs for Laudan are perhaps more subtle. He basically engages in virtuoso philosophical acrobatics in order to save the label "rational" for science. He almost seems to go out of his way to avoid recognizing that he has a *sociological* problem on his hands, not a *philosophical* one.

What then is all the fuss about? What is at stake in these criticisms and defenses of rationality—and science? What threats are posed by the twin demons, relativism and irrationality? Barnes and Bloor have pointed out that the defense of relativism is in part a reaction to the Cult of Rationalism and the remarkable intensity of that cult's faith in Reason (and Science). Earlier, I alluded to the notion that what is at stake here is intellectual turf. Just so, Barnes and Bloor write:

A plausible hypothesis is that relativism is disliked because so many academics see it as a dampener on their moralizing. A dualist idiom, with its demarcations, contrasts, rankings and evaluations, is easily adapted to the tasks of political propaganda or self-congratulatory polemic. *This* is the enterprise that relativists threaten, not science . . . . If relativism has any appeal at all, it will be to those who wish to engage in that eccentric activity called "disinterested" research.[11]

Rationality is the mantle of those in power, those with authority. The exercise of power/authority inevitably causes wear and tear on the mantle—the result is the *routinization of rationality*, a process that weakens the adaptive potential of a rationality, and makes it susceptible to attack and defeat by a more flexible, unarticulated, unformed, diversified, alchemical system-in-becoming. Such a system in every age in which it emerges from the shadows is labeled relativism/irrationalism, the embryonic rationality of the successful attackers. The recurring rationality/irrationality-relativism (or science/anti-science) conflict is from this perspective a feature of the circulation of authority. Another way to look at this is: rationality formalizes an adaptive strategy; this inevitably means that the adaptive *potential* of the strategy becomes relatively fixed and ultimately declines (again, routinization of rationality). Still another way of looking at this is in Nietzsche's terms; if you are looking for peace and pleasure, then believe, if you are looking for truth, then inquire.

It is interesting to consider whether there has been a change in the way relativism is used within the science studies movement. In the early years of this movement, it seems that relativism was a tool used to criticize the behavioral relevance of the norms of science, including rationality. The relativists were outsiders then, underdogs. As their position has strengthened, as a consequence of the institutionalization of the science studies movement, it seems that relativism has slowly become transformed into a norm of science! Its complete transformation into the new *rationality norm* of a next generation of "scientists" may only be a matter of time (and may in fact already be evident in Latour's recantation.).

Science, rationality, and logic can all be capitalized, routinized, commodified, adopted as tools and symbols of established (especially state) interests, power, and authority, and ultimately used as barriers to free or open inquiry. This raises questions about the relationship between science and rationality on the one hand, and progress on the other. These questions are the focus of the following remarks.

Progress—and Social Progress

The Scientific Revolution made "science," "progress," and "rationality" synonymous. In what is generally recognized as the first modern, secular treatise on the theory of progress, *Digression on the Ancients and the Moderns* (1688), Fontenelle argued that scientific growth represented the clearest, most reliable mark of progress. This relationship between science and progress was expressed in the works of Comte and Spencer. Rousseau, by contrast, argued that "Our minds have been corrupted in proportion as the arts and sciences have improved." The twentieth century version of progress, Schwartz writes,

> . . . turns out to be a blindly hurtling technology that has carried man to the moon, split the atom, created a cornucopia of commodities for a privileged few of the earth, and holds out a promise to carry along with it the remainder of mankind.[12]

It is difficult to sustain the idea of progress in the face of the wide range of problems we are burdened with. The essence of the crisis is that the very forces of production we look to to mark progress are interlocked with the very problems that make us doubt whether there has been any progress. Camilleri for example, notes:

> The drug and the mental hospital have become the indispensable lubricating oil and reservicing factory needed to prevent the complete breakdown of the human engine.[13]

It is interesting to view the way in which the optimism rooted in the idea of progress and the idea of science is affected by the unavoidable realities of human experience. For example, about thirty years ago, a panel of distinguished scientists gathered to celebrate—of all things—the centennial of Joseph E. Seagram & Sons, Inc. They were asked to speculate on "The Next Hundred Years." The idea—or better, the ideology—of science and progress required that the scientists project a positive future. And they did. But what is interesting is the way many of them introduced their speculations.[14] The Nobel Laureate geneticist Herman J. Muller said that the future would be rosy,

> provided that the world does not fall prey to one of the four dangers of our times—war, dictatorship of any kind, overpopulation, or fanaticism— . . .

Harrison Brown prefaced his remarks with the words, ". . . If we survive the next century . . . ;" John Weir began, "If man survives . . ." The most bizarre opening sentence was Wernher von Braun's, "I believe the intercontinental ballistic missile is actually merely a humble beginning of much greater things to come."

The idea of *scientific* and *intellectual* progress was fueled by the seventeenth century advances in science and literature by such cultural giants as Galileo, Newton, Descartes, Molière, and Racine. The idea of *social* progress was added later. Early in the eighteenth century, the Abbé de Saint-Pierre advocated establishing political and ethical academies to promote social progress. Saint-Pierre and Turgot influenced the Encyclopedists. It was at this point that social progress became mated to the values of industrialization and incorporated in the ideology of the bourgeoisie.[15] Scientific, intellectual, and social progress were all aspects of the ideology of industrial civilization. But there have been attempts to identify a type of progress that is independent of material or technological progress. Veblen, for example, argued that the various sciences could be distinguished in terms of their proximity to the domain of technology. Thus, the physical sciences were closest to that domain, even integral with it, while such areas as political theory and economics were farther afield:

In the sciences which lie farther afield from the technological domain . . . the effect of the machine discipline may even yet be scarcely appreciable. In such lore as ethics, e.g., or political theory, or even economics, much of the norms of the regime of handicraft still stands over; and very much of the institutional preconceptions of natural rights, associated with the regime of handicrafts in point of genesis, growth and content, is not only still intact in this field of inquiry, but it can scarcely even be claimed that there is ground for serious apprehension of its prospective obsolescence. Indeed, something even more ancient than handicraft and natural rights may be found surviving in good vigor in this "moral" field of inquiry, where tests of authenticity and reality are still sought and found by those who cultivate these lines of inquiry that lie beyond the immediate sweep of the machine's discipline. Even the evolutionary process of cumulative causation as conceived by the adepts of these sciences is infused with a preternatural beneficent trend; so that "evolution" is conceived to mean amelioration or "improvement."[16]

Progress, then, can be viewed in terms of "amelioration" or "improvement" in a social or ethical sense. George Benello argues that

. . . if we use the term culture in its anthropological sense, there is good basis for saying that primitive South Sea Island cultures are considerably more advanced than our own machine-dominated society. What is implied is that there are certain psychological and ecological universals—laws which define the conditions under which human growth and self-realization can take place, no matter what the level of technology.

Although the material conditions of culture may change and evolve, the basic conditions under which the primacy of the person can be affirmed do not.[17]

I doubt that many anarchists, Marxists, and socialists who have embraced science and technology in their programs for social progress, human emancipation, and individual liberty would agree with the notion that progress based on primacy of the person could be independent of material or technological progress. The very development of the idea of the primacy of the person seems to be dependent on a certain level of social development grounded in scientific and technological advances.

Theodore Roszak, one of the foremost critics of modern science and of the very idea of scientific objectivity, distinguished two types of progress:

> . . . no one who is not lying himself blind to the obvious can help but despair of the well-being that a reductionist science and power-ridden technology can bring. Nothing humanly worthwhile can be achieved within the diminished reality of such a science and technics: nothing whatever. On that level, we "progress" only toward technocratic elitism, affluent alienation, environmental blight, nuclear suicide. Not an iota of the promise of industrialism will then be realized but it will be vastly outweighed by the "necessary evils" attending.
>
> But there is another progress that is not a cheat and a folly; the progress that has always been possible at every moment in time. It goes by many names. St. Bonaventura called it "the journey of the mind to God;" the Buddha called it the eightfold path; Lao Tzu called it finding "the Way." The way *back*. To the source from which the adventure of human culture takes its beginning. It is *this* progress which the good society exists to facilitate for all its members.[18]

This is another example, then, of the effort to conceive of progress in terms of ideas about dignity, liberty, integrity, creativity, community-mindedness, and ecological consciousness. My notion of social progress originates in such examples.

Social progress involves an increase in the capacity of human beings individually and collectively to identify, process, store, retrieve, and utilize information and knowledge; it is simultaneously measured by (a) the degree to which a community or society has established the sanctity of human life, the dignity of human beings, and, in Emma Goldman's words, "the right of every human being to liberty and well-being;" and (b) the degree of differentiation in a community or society. Herbert Read writes:

> If the individual is a unit in a corporate mass, his life will be limited, dull and mechanical. If the individual is a unit on his own, with space and potentiality for separate action, then he may be more subject to accident or chance, but at least he can expand and express himself. He can develop in the only real meaning of the word—develop in consciousness of strength, vitality, and joy.[19]

Social progress can move *vertically* to new levels and new ideas, and it can move *horizontally*, to spread new levels and new ideas across more and more of the social landscape. I have been at pains to illustrate why it is difficult to support the idea that "scientific progress" has facilitated or represented "social progress." Whatever positive impact science has had on social progress has been primarily on the horizontal level of ideas.

To the extent that social progress depends on new types and new levels of knowledge about the human condition, it has been facilitated by some aspects of scientific inquiry, even within the institutional boundaries of modern science. But in order to discard the cultural heritage embodied in the term "science," and to broaden the base of our methodological and theoretical resources, I prefer to work with the more general term "epistemic strategy." I use the term "human inquiry" for that epistemic strategy or strategies consistent with the idea of social progress. This term may be considered kin to Marx's conception of "human science," his projected mode of inquiry for a communistic society and an alternative to alienated science.[20]

Modern science is an epistemic strategy as well as a social institution. In general, epistemic strategies develop out of ignorance into configurations of conceptual schemas and theories based on cumulative experience, trial and error, "action in the world" (including various sorts of experimentation strategies). The result is the development of preferred epistemic strategies. Whatever our own preferred strategy, there is a heuristic advantage in critical, comparative studies of epistemic strategies. This provides a solid foundation on which to consider the possibility of a "best possible" epistemic strategy, or mode of inquiry. The "best possible" strategy might, for example, be the one that can incorporate and account for the full range of successes and failures in *all* epistemic strategies past and present. But this suggests a monolithic strategy. It would be better to encourage a range of "best possible" strategies, correlated with a range of dominant utilities such as understanding, technological reliability, intellectual coherence, truth and so on.[21]

It is conceivable that the range of epistemic strategies could be a manifestation of a covering strategy. In any case, best possible strategies characteristically play off tinkering, algorithmic procedures, and more or less formal procedures against one another. Overall, a general tinkering pattern predominates. Of course, experience provides broader and deeper foundations for supporting tinkering. Such foundations, however, should not be considered or treated as monolithic, static, and unchanging, and should not be viewed as logically, ontologically, or epistmologically prior to or independent of the theory and practice of inquiry. Foundations represent "what we know," but should not cast this "what we know" in stone. Foundations should be supportive but not rigid, directive but not dogmatic, well-founded but not ultimate. In tinkering, local resources and opportunities are selected and exploited in a "sculpting" of contingencies that lead to different types of social constructions, such as facts, theories, technologies, and myths.[22] The best possible epistemic strategy can never be a specific strategy such as Western science, Eastern mysticism, quantum physics, or Trobriand Island magic. Demarcationism as practiced by philosophers and others who want to clearly, unequivocally, and once and for all separate "science" from "non-science," "rationality" from "non-rationality," or "truth" from "falsity" is problematic for reasons rooted in the social nature of inquiry. But this realization does not entail either naive or radical relativism, or the impossibility of some sort of demarcation strategy. It is easy enough to understand why some sociologists, historians, and philosophers of science and knowledge have reached relativistic conclusions by superficially examining the famous Azande "poison oracle" case. But this is not a foundation for relativism. We *can* discriminate (demarcate, distinguish) among epistemic strategies based on the scale and scope of past successes, and the probability of future successes (on a larger scale and with increasing scope). There is, in fact, a general strategy found in all "successful" knowledge systems—certainly at the level of societies and cultures. To the degree that an epistemic strategy is in fact successful, to that degree the general strategy I allude to will prevail. This general strategy is distinguished by its *capacity* for criticism, reflexivity, and meta-inquiry. Variations in this capacity distinguish the Azande case from at least *some* cases of what people have indiscriminately labeled "science." The capacity for criticism, reflexivity, and meta-inquiry is directly proportional to the support for these aspects of inquiry—and the pervasiveness of such inquiry—in the society at large.

More specifically, the best possible epistemic strategy is demarcated from other strategies by the level and degree of development of the *critical* aspects of the various features and contexts of inquiry and everyday life—what Cliff Hooker refers to as the "schema of criticism."[23] Thus, we must be prepared to criticize facts, technological procedures, specific theories, the deepest and the most general levels of our conceptual frameworks, the very manner in which we rank these areas of criticism, and finally the established structures of research and criticism themselves. As we move up through these various levels of criticism, the time intervals for exploring and testing criticisms increases; ultimately, this approach can bring a millennia-long cultural and epistemic tradition into question. This critical enterprise is one that must be built into social structures at all levels—from the social structure of the self and mind to the social structure of a society, culture, or civilization. Democratic and anarchistic social structures embody this form of inquiry.

Let us look at this question of inquiry and social structure from another angle. On the one hand, research in the history and sociology of science clearly show that science is relative to social, political, and economic interests, values, culture, and history. On the other hand, we experience the recalcitrance of the world every day and everywhere in the causal or at least systematic relationship between actions and reactions, acts and consequences. The very fact that I am engaged in this enterprise means that I want to be a realist of some sort, but not the kind of realist who traps him/herself by seeking binding necessities and ultimate foundations that can prematurely stifle inquiry or close pathways to information and knowledge. This requires a capacity for not investing conjectures—no matter how self-evident, useful, or timeless they appear—with positive or absolute belief. The trick is to be able to grant the acceptability of *necessary* statements, and the weight of evidence, but to accept all such statements and evidence as no more than "well-founded." The anarchist who roots individual liberty in the denial of Authority in all forms is equally unwilling to participate in linguistic institutions such as the institution of proof.[24]

Anarchy, the Sociological Imagination, and Inquiry

The social institution of modern science has developed in association
with the development of modern industrial, capitalist society. By definition, the institutionalization of modern science involved tying
loosely organized pockets of scientific work together, and binding
them to state interests. Modern science is a tool of the state; and the
state represents and defends with all available means (including the
means of violence) the interests of a power elite driven by motives of
profit, territoriality, and material gain. This is not the whole story, of
course. For even while modern science—along with other modern
institutions such as education and religion—serves the state, or more
loosely, established interests, it is also—intentionally and uninten-
tionally—a major source of critical and creative energy that is aimed
at undermining unbridled state authority and promoting more reasoned ways of solving social, political, and economic problems than
now prevail. So too, there are cases of criticism, resistance, and rebellion within an otherwise conservative educational system designed primarily to feed the industrial and military systems with
"machined" humans, and to produce a relatively passive *citizenry* and
a relatively active *consumer-ry* willing (unknowingly, for the most
part) to trade active, intelligent participation in self-government for
the "freedom" to be poor, to go to the Shopping Mall, to drive the
freeways.

Those of us engaged in the dialogue this book is part of may dis-
agree about the extent to which modern science is a tool of state interests, and the extent to which it is a or the crucial source of criticism
and creativity in our society; or about the extent to which modern
science is elitist, competitive, and alienative on the one hand, or democratic, cooperative, and non-alienative on the other. But I think
we can agree that for modern science to play a facilitative role in social progress, it must be uncoupled from state interests, and from
anti-democratic social formations. And the ties between modern science and material or technological progress must be severed, since
science in the service of material or technological progress (as we
know it from the historical experience of the past three hundred
years) cannot serve social progress. I have already noted that these
proposals imply a radical transformation of science and society.

The emergence of modern science did not bring "scientific inquiry"
into being. However, it did help to focus attention on and articulate
ways of inquiry that did not follow party lines. This is reflected in the

idea that "disinterestedness" is a norm of science. The problem is that for an epistemic agent to achieve the goal of distinguishing material and non-material events, what is real and what is illusory, to discover how illusions, delusions, and hallucinations are grounded in material events, and to reveal in a constructive way the social foundations of his/her own thoughts, the agent must manage to work "objectively." It turns out that working objectively or being objective is not a simple matter of *deciding* to be objective, or relying on *intersubjective testing* in any conventional sense. Objectivity is a variable, and a complex social process. Basically, the most objective epistemic agents and communities are those that operate with the most general and diffuse interests. That is, the less one is committed to specific institutional or social interests—nationalism, Catholicism, Buddhism, the scientific bureaucracy, the nuclear power industry—the more objective one's knowledge is. This is the point so often missed when the norm of disinterestedness is discussed; disinterestedness is not rooted in social structures but instead conceived of as something floating about, spiritualized, without its feet on the ground. At the same time, one's distance from conventional and special interests makes one marginal, and creates a communication barrier between interest centers and peripheries. The objectivity generated on the periphery tends to be simultaneously of a higher quality than what is generated at the center, and alien to the needs and perspectives of the center.

C. Wright Mills drew attention to the "highly rational moral insensibility" of our era, raised to higher and more efficient levels by the "brisk generals and gentle scientists" who are planning the third world war:

> These actions are not necessarily sadistic; they are merely businesslike; they are not emotional at all; they are efficient, rational, technically clean cut. They are inhuman acts because they are impersonal.[25]

It may seem paradoxical to argue that modern science (allied with technology and progress) is a social problem because it is impersonal. After all, impersonal, machine-like truths and measures are supposed to guarantee that what we do is scientific and progressive. But it is precisely this notion of validation through proof-machines, logic-machines, language-machines, and number-machines that we must challenge in order to see the world of Science Machines and false progress described by Mills and others. The sociological imagination offers us a way out of this machine morass.

The core features of the sociological imagination as Mills conceived it are: (1) the distinction between personal *troubles* and public *issues*; (2) a focus on the intersection between biography and history in society; and (3) a concern with questions about social structure, the place of societies in history, and the varieties of men and women who have prevailed and are coming to prevail in society.[26] This perspective draws attention to new questions for the sociology of science: what do scientists produce, and how do they produce it; what resources do they use, and use up; what material byproducts and wastes do they produce; what good is what they produce, in what social contexts is it valued, and who values it; what costs, risks, and benefits does scientific work lead to for individuals, communities, classes, societies, and the ecological foundations of social life? Perhaps the most significant departure from traditional sociology of science Mill's perspective points to is a concern with questions about social relationships and quality of life. What is the relationship between scientists and various publics, clients, audiences, patrons; how do scientists relate to each other, their families and friends, their colleagues in other walks of life; what is their relationship as workers to the owners of the means of scientific production; what are their self-images, and how do they fit into the communities they live in; what are their goals, visions, and motives? The collective hagiography that portrays scientists as "ingenious," "creative," and "benefactors of humanity" does not tell us what sorts of people scientists are or what sorts of social worlds they are helping to build.

Normal sociologists of science in normal society have concluded that normal science is efficient, productive, and progressive. But normal science is a factor in the production and reproduction of a society burdened by widespread environmental, social, and personal stresses. Normal sociologies of science cannot help us see, let alone prevail in, a world of Science Machines and Cheerful Robots. Even the sort of Millsian perspective on science, society, and sociology of science that informs my views may prove too limited for the task of critique and renewal. Fundamental categories of experience must be examined, challenged, and changed to even begin to address the social problems of science and society. The dichotomy between "nature" and "culture," for example, has fostered a dominative, exploitative orientation to nature, women, workers, and the oppressed in general. A fascination with spectacular discoveries, inventions, and applications in the physical sciences, and with "genius," has blinded people to alienation in scientific work and in the lives of scientists. Inside and outside sociology proper, there has been (especially in the United States) resistance to unadulterated structural analysis. Individualistic and voluntaristic assumptions and perspectives have obstructed the development and diffusion of sociological conceptions of self, mind, cognition, and knowledge.

The full implications of sociology as a Copernican revolution that has moved the group, the collectivity, and social structure to the center of the social universe have yet to be realized in sociology.[27] This revolution has transformed the individual from a being of "soul" and "free will" to a set of social relations and a vehicle for thought collectives. This idea does not subordinate the individual to society. Rather, by giving us a better understanding of what an individual, a person, "really is," it helps us to recognize the liberating as well as oppressive nature of the variety of social formations human beings can be socialized in.

Sociologists have generally traced their origins to ideologues of modern industrial society, notably Saint-Simon and Auguste Comte. The Marxist origins of sociological thinking have not been ignored, but (again, especially in the United States) they have not received the attention they deserve. More importantly, the working class and anarchist origins of sociology have been ignored.[28] So have the origins of sociological thinking among women scholars and writers, and especially among feminists such as Harriet Martineau.[29] This "oversight" in particular has prevented the development of a sociology and a sociology of science infused with values, interests, and goals that would permit, indeed provoke, critical analyses of science and society. In particular, norms of skepticism and criticism have not been unleashed so that they could act on our deepest, our "unshakeable," beliefs and assumptions.

Recognizing the diverse origins of sociology depends on recognizing the distinction between the history of sociology as the history of a discipline and profession on the one hand, and of a way of looking at the world on the other. That distinction can help us to identify plural origins of science in general, and identify alternative, unrealized possibilities for the Scientific Revolution of the Galilean and Newtonian ages. That there is such an alternative in the history of science is illustrated by Carolyn Merchant in her study of women, ecology, and the Scientific Revolution.[30]

The ascendancy of a new sociological imagination would help transform and clarify some fundamental but still cloudy issues in the sociology of science. Thus, the sociological imagination is not neutral or relativist (in any naive or radical sense) on the question of truth. Mills argued that the social role of the intellectual involved a politics of truth, an absorption "in the attempt to know what is real and what is unreal."[31] He argued that social studies have consequences for norms of "truth and validity." These are not in any sense the statements of a naive realist. Mills consistently stressed the social structural roots of logic and even of mind. While he did not have the advantage of our current knowledge about the social processes of inquiry, he clearly appreciated the idea of a sociology of objectivity.

The sociological imagination is not, in Mills' hands, an abstract exercise. It is implicitly and explicitly a call to arms. It is not something to exercise in a political vacuum. It is true that Mills often spoke and wrote as a reformist rather than a revolutionary. But his proposals on social problems and social change challenged and continue to challenge prevailing social arrangements in fundamental ways. What sorts of rearrangements are necessary, for example, to transform intellectuals from hired hands to peers of the powerful, or to make intellectual work and politics coincident; what sorts of changes are necessary to develop "a free and knowledgeable public"? Mills addressed these problems and sought for solutions in conventional forms of democratic reform. In fact, such changes—like the changes feminist science critics seek—require much more far reaching social transformations than usually imagined. What sorts of social formations foster disinterestedness and objectivity? That is, under what conditions can inquiry proceed unburdened as much as possible from mundane interests and commitments, and within the most expansive network of information and knowledge possible? Based on the preceding conjectures, my answer is social formations in which the person has primacy, social formations that are diversified, cooperative, egalitarian, nonauthoritarian, participatory. The person has primacy in such social formations in an anarchist sense. That is, people are neither mere parts of social systems nor isolated individuals. Their potential for developing a multitude of mental, physical, and emotional dimensions of self is recognized and nourished; it is not surrendered to the authority of one or a few parts of the self, or to external real and imagined authorities. Social formations that allow for this sort of primacy offer the most fertile environments for inquiry because they do not, by definition, demand allegiances to specific institutional interests, or subordination to specific authorities. The values people rally around, for example, are very general. We are more likely to learn things that will promote individual liberty, enhance community life, and cultivate healthy environments in such social formations. There is no hope for evading the endemic conflicts, tensions, and contradictions of the human condition. The sociological imagination should not be viewed as a pathway to utopia. Rather, it should be seen as a guide to social change. And not only to social change on the grand scale, but also to marginal improvements in the conditions under which we live and inquire.

What is interesting about the relationship between anarchy (to stay with the term that represents the most advanced stages of democracy and communism) and objectivity is that it clearly and unequivocally makes objective inquiry a consequence of and a condition for social progress. To put it simply, objective inquiry is best pursued in anarchistic social formations, and is itself, at its best, anarchistic. Free Inquiry (to paraphrase a Feyerbend slogan) should always be subordinated to the Free Person in a Free Society, although in practice these form an interrelated mutually reinforcing web of freedoms. We should be practicing and promoting unfettered inquiry, inquiry unimpeded by Dogma, Authority, and narrowly defined Social Interests, inquiry driven by humane values and a well-developed and pervasive schema of criticism.

The anarchist tradition, then, stresses the need to separate inquiry from all forms of unbridled power and authority. Only this separation, and the elimination of the state altogether, can guarantee progressive inquiry and social progress. As Godwin argued with regard to the fundamental principle that government is incapable of affording any primary benefits to human beings:

> It is calculated to induce us to lament, not the apathy and indifference, but the inauspicious activity of government. It incites us to look for the moral improvement of the species, not in the multiplying of regulations, but in their repeal. It teaches us that truth and virtue, like commerce, will then flourish most, when least subjected to the mistaken guardianship of authority and laws. This maxim will rise upon us in its importance, in proportion as we connect it with the numerous departments of political justice to which it will be found to have relation. As fast as it shall be adopted into the practice of mankind, it may be expected to deliver us from a weight, intolerable to mind, and, in the highest degree, hostile to the progress of truth.[32]

My preference for democratic, and ultimately anarchistic, social formations is based on their capacity for de-capitalizing "Truth" and giving free rein to scepticism. Nietzsche's remarks on these two aspects of inquiry provide some of the basic ingredients for a philosophy of "nothing matters." The very idea of Truth is, he observes, "conclusive proof that not so much as a start has been made on that disciplining of the intellect and self-overcoming necessary for the discovery of any truth, even the very smallest." Truth in this sense is the province of the "man of conviction:"

> *Not* to see many things, not to be impartial in anything, to be a party through and through, to view all values from a strict and necessary perspective—this alone is the condition under which such a man exists at all. But he is thereby the antithesis, the *antagonist* of the truthful man—of truth . .
> 33

"Nothing matters" is, like Feyerabend's "Anything goes," a slogan of resistance to established Authority and not an invitation to value-less, undisciplined inquiry. The pervasiveness of scepticism and criticism which in part defines democratic and anarchistic social formations is anathema to Truths and Convictions. The formation of Social Interests is ideally and in principle impossible; for in communities and societies based on cooperation as opposed to those based on more or less deadly competition, social interests—reflections of *antagonist* interests—fuse with social *goals* and lose their potency as barriers to sceptical, critical inquiry.

In its negative aspect, the anarchist agenda is an offensive against all forms of authoritarianism, mysticism, and supernaturalism. In its positive aspect, it is a defense of and program for freedom and liberty in everyday life and in inquiry. Anarchy always has priority over inquiry—however much these two programs are intertwined. This is a forced choice, brought on by the course of historical and cultural development summarized in my "thug theory of history." Social and cultural change has been driven primarily by greed, profit motives, and the quest for power. As a result, we live in a world dominated by inhuman economics; terrorist, fascist, and authoritarian states; chemical disasters, ecological deterioration, and radiation accidents; the mechanization of selves and commodification of interpersonal relationships; and nuclear winter scenarios and the real possibility of nuclear annihilation. For the most part, this situation is a technologically intensified version of the "normal" human condition—at least in "civilized" societies.

The anarchists have been in the vanguard of those men, women, and children who have not stood idly by as we have been pushed and shoved by robber barons, pirates, profiteers, bureaucrats, and dictators toward *1984*, *Animal Farm*, and *Amerika*. The spirit of anarchy and its critique of modern science, technology, and society is present in all who stand with William Morris when he cries:

What! shall man go on generation after generation gaining fresh command over the powers of nature, gaining more and more luxurious appliances for the comfort of the body, yet generation after generation losing some portion of his natural senses: that is of his life and soul?[34]

These processes can be reversed—or at least slowed or attenuated—only to the extent that we recognize and act on the affinities that link anarchy and inquiry. Modern science cannot fit into this program—it cannot be a synonym for open inquiry because as a partner in structures of domination and authority over human beings and nature, it has wedded a "tyranny of abstractions" to the tyrannical "rule of men."[35]

Conclusion

In its current institutional incarnation, science is a threat to democracy and an obstacle to anarchy. It is politically and economically aligned with an elite class of military, banking, and corporate leaders who share a narrow view of what constitutes the "national interest" and whose "internationalism" and "global perspective" does not extend beyond considerations of territories and markets. Openness in science and society requires preparing citizens for participatory democracy through education rather than the narrow training that masquerades as education in our schools and universities (amply demonstrated by the standard treatments of religion, politics, economics, sex, and science). Open inquiry means that we can gather information and pursue knowledge without Church or State looking over our shoulders. Indeed, the very notion of objectivity depends on inquiry that is guided by broad and diffuse values and interests rather than by the values and interests of specific organizations, institutions, or social classes. The robustness of a mode of inquiry—a science, a rationality, a logic—is measured by the depth and scope of its schema of criticism. This implies that some modes of inquiry are better than others, and that they can be made better than their competitors in part by imbedding in them a fail-safe theorem: this mode of inquiry makes no justificatory claims about its own rationality, logic, or scientificity, and nothing in it or its products is to be construed as absolutely true, or absolute or certain in any sense; and in part by adding or enhancing a/the schema of criticism. The structual analogue for these factors in organizations, communities, and societies—and in persons—is necessarily a form of anarchy.

4

The Science Machine

The cultural meaning of modern science has always been in doubt. Every vision of a *mirabilis scientiae fundamenta* has been opposed by a conception of science as the product of an alienated human spirit. In some cases, this opposition is expressed as an attack on the very idea of science. In other cases, the conflict is between "true science" and science distorted by, for example, capitalists and technocrats. Sociologists of science are not, in general, concerned with doubts about and conflicts over the value of modern science. They are, implicitly or explicitly, science advocates. Their research tends to affirm, imitate, and justify modern science as a progressive, well-functioning social system, and the paradigmatic mode of inquiry. This is true, as I noted in the introductory chapters, on both sides of the 1970s watershed that separates the "old" and the "new" sociology of science.

The very existence of science studies as a profession is dependent on the goodwill of scientists as respondents and objects of observation and analysis, and the belief among scientists, intellectuals, scholars in general, and some members of the general public that science works and produces benefits for society. It is also clear that many of us assume that since "scientific methods" seem to be the only "reasonable" methods to adopt in inquiry, we must also adopt the competitiveness, elitism, alienation, machismo, and other social trappings of modern science (and society). This viewpoint is so deeply imbedded that even when we set out to *criticize* modern science, we adopt the "scientific approach" with all of its social baggage. And how many of us can afford—psychologically and professionally—to recognize (let alone act on the recognition) that the rationality of modern science is of a piece with the Alice in Wonderland rationality of power

politics, orthodox economics, and patterns of authority that has infiltrated every sphere of social life.

The new science studies has helped to uncover important social realities of science based on the seemingly trivial notion that scientists
are human and that science is a human activity. We have learned a
great deal about such things as the ways in which choosing particular
technical assumptions can, to use Brian Martin's phrase, "push an argument." We have deepened our understanding of the nature and significance of selecting, interpreting, and using evidence. We know that
in a specialized form of intellectual labor such as science, presupposi-
tions seem to be missing (one reason why science appears to be value-
free or unquestionably objective) only because they have become built
into scientific practice itself. And the more we inquire about why scientific research is carried out, who does it, who can use it, what it justifies, the more connections to "society" we uncover. And since society
in this case is highly stratified, we uncover the social ties between science and the power centers of society. This does not mean that all scientific knowledge is contaminated. But, as Brian Martin notes,

> . . . scientific knowledge is not solely the product of the quest for profit or
> the need to justify war. Rather, scientific knowledge—like the organization
> of the scientific community and the way scientific research is carried out—
> is selectively oriented towards these types of ends. In doing research, there
> are many areas which may be studied. Scientific knowledge is mainly de-
> veloped in those areas and in those ways which show promise of benefiting
> powerful groups in society. For example, in electronics, scientific knowl-
> edge is organized to help promote communication efficiency (usually one
> directional communication) and profit rather than ease of general access and
> local control.[1]

If we look at discussions of modern science that treat it as a well-
functioning and progressive enterprise, we will see that they entail a
certain worldview and in particular a theory of social relations. This
theory of social relations—which justifies elitism, competition, the
alienated activity of "normal science," and the separation of science
from ethics and values—is a barrier to social progress. Max Weber
describes the rationalization of worldviews as a universal, but above
all a European, historical process. Rationalization goes hand in hand
with the modernization of the state. In these processes, an other-
worldly authority, God, is transformed into a this-worldly authority,
Reason, as an immanent principle. This carries with it the potential
for the separation of rationality and science from ethics.

Researchers in science studies must stop thinking—publicly or privately—of "science" as "physics." The tendency to equate science and physics has obscured the significant discoveries of the social sciences, and made sciences such as ecology, biology, and chemistry second-class modes of inquiry. And the "science equals physics" equation along with a psychologistic, ahistorical, and asocial conception of consciousness and behavior has fueled misguided efforts to link scientific and mystical traditions. This has undermined the potential value of examining alternative cognitive strategies.

We need to pay more attention to the role of ideology in modern science. To say that there is an ideology of modern science means in part that there is a dogmatic support for modern science as a way of life, and a collective cultivation of false consciousness that *conceals* from scientists the psychological, social, and cultural grounds and consequences of their activities. False consciousness can also manifest itself as a *mistaken* interpretation of self and social role. The ideology of modern science sustains struggles for power and status, institutional survival, and the use of science (to the extent that it overemphasizes quantification, rigor, control, and prediction) as a resource for reducing personal anxieties and fears.

The pursuit of "science for its own sake" generally requires a commitment to work and professionalism (for example, the "publish or perish" imperative, and "grantsmanship"). This makes it difficult to find time for "outside" activities and intensifies the ideological hold of modern (professionalized, bureaucratized) science on scientists and on society. The convergence of the dysfunctions of professionalization and bureaucratization tends to increase specialization and over-specialization in a conflictful division of labor. Occupational and organizational closure (autonomy) increases under these conditions, and creative, critical intelligence, along with the more enlightened motives, are eroded. Ultimately, the ability of people socialized under such conditions to distinguish illusion and reality, hallucinations and external events (or at least to know about these distinctions) is threatened. The final price of run-away professionalization, in conjunction with bureaucratization, and the mechanization of the self, must be first the routinization of rationality, and then the loss of the critical faculties.

The tension between a commitment to science in the abstract and a recognition of the social problem of science is nowhere better illustrated than in feminist science studies. Feminist theorists such as Carolyn Merchant, Evelyn Fox Keller, Sandra Harding, and Elizabeth

Fee have added a new dimension to the critique of modern science by linking it to issues of gender and power.

Gender and Science

The Scientific Revolution, Carolyn Merchant argues, set nature, women, blacks, and wage laborers "toward a new status as 'natural' and human resources for the modern world system."[2] In fact, this reflected a general transformation of, in principle, all things, animals and people into commodities. The problem for the underclasses, underprivileged, and oppressed was that their commodified lives were dominated by more powerful human commodities. Among these more powerful commodities, the dominant roots of power were located in the social roles of men. They put a masculine stamp on the world, and thereby defined, constrained, and controlled nature, women, the disenfranchised generally, and modern science.[3]

The analysis of gender and science reveals the crucial flaw in the workmanship orientation to modern science: the failure to acknowledge the human meaning of methods, theories, and results. Merchant, for example, writes:

> Reproduction—hormones, menstruation, and pregnancy—is used to infer and justify the female economic dependence brought about in the seventeenth-century transition from subsistence to capitalist modes of production. For women, this aspect of the Scientific Revolution did not bring about the presumed intellectual enlightenment, objectivity, and liberation from ancient assumptions traditionally accorded it.[4]

In the scientific revolution, the interrogation of witches became a symbol for questioning nature. Merchant points out that the courtroom became the model for the inquisitorial process. And torture using mechanical devices to control disorder became a fundamental ingredient of the scientific method as power. As Keller reminds us,

> . . . if modern science evolved in, and helped to shape a particular social and political context, by the same token it evolved in conjunction with, and helped to shape, a particular ideology of gender.[5]

Arguments about science being gender-neutral or value-free are inevitably based on tearing individual scientific sentences or statements out of the social fabric in which they are conceived, produced, and used. Individual facts, or strings of facts, are then exhibited as science. But in order to understand feminist critiques of science, science must be seen as a social activity and a social institution.

An alternative science should not be conceived in terms of alternative scientific statements but rather in terms of alternative institutions and societies. This is clear even for equity issues that may at first appear to pose no threats to science-as-it-is. But the achievement of equal opportunity or comparable worth for women in science depends on such factors as reducing gender stereotyping, and gendered divisions of labor. It may even, as Sandra Harding argues, "require the complete elimination of sexism, classism, and racism in the societies that produce science." Harding also challenges the widely held view that "the feminist charge of masculine bias" leaves physics, chemistry, and the scientific worldview "untouched and untouchable." She points out the apparent contradiction between building a "successor science" and deconstructing science as we know it; her argument is that we need to pursue both goals:

> Each requires the success of the other, for an adequate successor science will have to be grounded on the resources provided by differences in women's social experience and emancipatory political projects; and an effective deconstruction of our culture's powerful science requires an equally powerful solidarity *against* regressive and mystifying modernist forces.[6]

I have reviewed some of the features of the feminist challenge that are consistent with the perspective on modern science being sketched in this chapter. There are certain limitations of the feminist challenge, however, limitations common to other arenas of science criticism. These limitations reflect the difficulty of loosening the grip of the icons of science and relinquishing the myth of pure science. Even feminist science studies and feminist science criticism that is pursued with the greatest degree of independence from traditional masculine biases relies, to varying but appreciable degrees, on the works of Thomas Kuhn and to a lesser extent, Bloor and the interest theorists in science studies—especially the Edinburgh group Bloor is associated with—as authoritative accounts of the sociology and history of science. I have already explained why neither Bloor nor Kuhn can be considered a critic of science in my sense. Bloor's approach requires adopting "the proven methods of science" and ignoring their social trappings. And Kuhn is first and foremost an internalist (in the traditional sense), a historian of science, and a firm believer in scientific progress.

Harding's misunderstanding of Kuhn is illustrated by the fact that she finds it ironic that his *The Structure of Scientific Revolutions*—which she reads as undermining "the notions of science central to the Vienna Circle"—was originally published as part of the International Encyclopedia of Unified Science project. But there is no irony in this association, as Kuhn himself has amply documented.[7]

Another example of the hold of traditional scientific ideology on feminist science studies is Harding's orientation to feminist scientists as "the new heirs of Archimedes as we interpret his legacy for our age."[8] Archimedes is lauded for "his inventiveness in creating a new kind of theorizing;" this is Archimedes as Icon, not Archimedes as military engineer.

While Harding is willing to consider (rhetorically at least) the idea of "a radically different science," Evelyn Fox Keller explicitly divorces herself from efforts to reject science or develop a "new" science. The reason she refuses to follow this line of feminist inquiry is, in her own words, the fact that "I am a scientist . . ." Her reasoning is compelling. Rejecting objectivity as a masculine ideal lends the feminists' collective voice to an "enemy chorus;" and it "dooms women to residing outside of the realpolitik modern culture." Keller rejects the call for a new science on the grounds that it destroys the positive features of modern science:

> The assumption that science *can* be replaced, de novo, reflects a view of science as pure social product, owing obedience to moral and political pressure from without. In this extreme relativism, science dissolves into ideology; any emancipatory function of modern science is negated, and the arbitration of truth recedes into the political domain.[9]

From the perspective I sketch in this book, Keller's aim—"the reclamation, from within science, of science, as a human instead of a masculine project, and the renunciation of the division of emotional and intellectual labor that maintains science as a male preserve"—is sociologically unrealistic. Harding seems to better appreciate the fact that renouncing "the division of emotional and intellectual labor that maintains science as a male preserve" means renouncing all that is associated with and implied by "science" and "scientist." At the very least, the sociology of science developed in this volume should alert Keller and other social critics who criticize science as "scientists" to the dangers of trying to import remnants of modern science into a new social order. As Elizabeth Fee has argued:

> At this point, while it is necessary to argue the case for the entrance of women into the scientific professions as presently constituted, it is also important to push the epistemological critique of science to the point where we can begin to construct a clear vision of alternate ways of creating knowledge.[10]

The fact is that the sociological perspective—in the strong structural sense I argue for—is not a prominent feature of feminist science studies and science criticism. This does not mean that their agenda does not draw attention to problems of social structure. But it does not do so in a way that radically sociologizes epistemology.

The Sociological Imagination

Sociologists of science, old and new, have had difficulty following Mills (1961: 8) in linking modern science to "the personal troubles of milieux" and "the public issues of social structure" for good reason.[11] What is missing from science criticism and from the sociology of science is the Millsian blend of structural analysis (sociology in the *strong* sense), social criticism, epistemological relevance, and an activist orientation to social change—in brief, the sociological imagination. I do not mean to imply that the Millsian program is completely free of all the science advocacy baggage. In Mills' work as in mine there is an unavoidable tension between: (1) new ways of seeing science that open up untraveled paths to critique and renewal in science, culture, and sociology; and (2) established methods of inquiry that short-circuit critique and renewal. My work as a whole is not an effort to transcend that tension but to exploit it.

Mills, Veblen, and other social critics of modern science have implicated it in problems of alienation, dehumanization, ecological deterioration, and nuclear escalation. They exhibit modern science not as a savior, panacea, cornucopia, or synonym for progress but rather as a social problem. Modern science, from this critical perspective, is a threat to democracy, the quality of human life, and even the very capacity of our planet to support life at all.[12] Moreover, because modern science is not simply *in* but *of* modern society, it is a social problem because modern society itself is a social problem. My aim in this chapter is to explore this conception of modern science, and reflect on its implications for critique and renewal in the sociology of science. I turn next, then, to a discussion of what I mean by the term, "social problem," and why I consider modern science *and* modern society social problems.

Modern Science as a Social Problem

In 1923, the biochemist J. B. S. Haldane published an essay titled *Daedalus, or Science and the Future*. Haldane painted a picture of an attractive future society created by applying science to the promotion of human happiness. Bertrand Russell replied to Haldane in an essay on *Icarus, or the Future of Science*. Russell wrote that much as he would like to agree with Haldane's forecast, his experience with statesmen and governments forced him to predict that science would be used "to promote the power of dominant groups rather than to make men happy." Daedalus taught his son Icarus to fly, but warned him not to stray too close to the sun. Icarus ignored the warning and plunged to his death. Russell warned that a similar fate would "overtake the populations whom modern men of science have taught to fly." Russell is more pessimistic than Haldane, but he is hesitant about holding Daedalus—and modern scientists—responsible for the fates of the individuals and societies they instruct.[13] Who *was* Daedalus, and *what* is modern science?

According to Greek mythology, Daedalus was the first mortal inventor. His career is marked by fantastic ingenuity coupled with jealousy, intrigue, and murder. He invents a machine that allows Minos' queen Pasiphae to copulate with a bull. The issue of this affair is hidden away in a labyrinth designed by Daedalus, and later killed by Theseus who uses a device invented by Daedalus to negotiate the labyrinth; Theseus also steals Pasiphae's daughter in the bargain. Daedalus eventually falls out of favor with the king and is imprisoned in a tower. Eventually, Daedalus fashions wings out of feathers and wax for himself and his son Icarus. Their escape from the tower is marred when Icarus ignores his father's admonitions, strays too close to the sun, and plunges to his death when the intense heat melts the wax on his wings. Daedalus survives, bitter and lamenting his own genius. Daedalus has a nephew, Talos, whose talent as an inventor he envies. Among Talos' inventions is the first saw. But Daedalus claims *he* invented the first saw. He resolves this earliest priority dispute (and the problem of having to contend with a rival) by pushing Talos off a tower. *This* Daedalus is, in fact, an appropriate symbol for modern science. Modern science, coupled with modern technology, has helped to fashion and sustain modern industrial, technological society. Sociologists of science have danced around this reality but not confronted it directly.

The idea that modern science is a viable, successful, and progres-

sive enterprise is not only common in the new sociology of science; it
is an idea that the most influential representatives of this field hold
dear. There is a parallel reluctance among students of social problems
to include modern science in their analyses, criticisms, and policy
studies. Social problems courses and textbooks do not, as a rule, devote space to modern science (although it may receive indirect attention in studies that deal with "technology").[14] One reason for this is
that modern science is not yet widely appreciated as a social phenomenon in the strong constructivist sense (that is, that scientific knowledge itself is a social construction). Another reason is the assumption that science (and especially something called "pure" science) and
technology are separate, relatively independent phenomena. Other
more general reasons were identified by C. Wright Mills in his 1943
paper on "The Professional Ideology of Social Pathologists." Mills
criticized the situational, case by case approach to social problems.[15]
This is a general problem in sociology, and is reflected in the tendency (illustrated in the organization of most introductory textbooks)
to describe and analyze society using a situational, institution by institution approach. The social structural approach Mills defended in
opposition to the "social pathologists" reveals the interdependencies
linking (in different ways and to different degrees) all the activities,
organizations, and institutions in a society; and it simultaneously establishes the need for theories which address these interdependencies.

My earlier assertion that "modern science is a social problem because modern society is a social problem" is a cryptic criticism of the
situational approach to social problems and a statement of allegiance
to Mills' concern for total social structures. By "social problem," I
want to convey nothing more complicated than the Millsian notion
that modern science is implicated in the personal troubles and public
issues of our time. The idea that modern *society* is, again in the Millsian sense, a "social problem" means that the object of the concerns
about personal troubles and public issues (and the focus of social
change agendas) is a total social structure rather than one or more
"dysfunctional" elements of that structure. This contrasts, for example, with a perspective that treats "the capitalist system and its ac-
companiments" as normal, and then looks to "its several parts, treating as problems those which do not function smoothly."[16]

The term "society," it should be stressed, poses a conceptual problem. In standard usage, it refers to an imaginary, undifferentiated
entity; and it tends to connote cooperation and "democracy." The
problem can be readily identified by considering what it means to use

the term "state" in place of "society." There are methodological and political implications of our concept of "society."

If one fragments society into "factors," into elemental bits, naturally one will then need quite a few of them to account for something, and one can never be sure they are all in. A formal emphasis upon "the whole" plus lack of total structural consideration plus a focus upon scattered situations does not make it easy to reform the status quo.[17]

The situational approach to the study of society and social problems has two important consequences for the study of science. First, it makes it possible to isolate science from other institutions, and classify it with the "healthy" as opposed to the "unhealthy" ones. Second, it means that even when science is examined critically, the total social structure is unlikely to become the focus of criticism and analysis. While I cannot describe all of the ramifications of a total social structural approach to the critical sociology of modern science here, I can at least provide some of the conceptual resources for such an approach.

Mills' critique of the ways in which "social problems" were conceived in his time is still relevant.[18] This is not only because some social problems research continues to be guided by the strategies Mills criticized. More importantly, contemporary strategies in social problems research and theory are subject to Mills' argument that they are not "of a sort usable in collective action which proceeds against, rather than well within, *more or less tolerated channels*" [my emphasis]. It is not at all clear, for example, that the fashionable "definitional" or "constructivist" (sometimes constructionist) approach avoids the pitfalls Mills identifies. I will return later in this chapter to the "realistic" and "activist" implications of the sociological imagination. It is important, however, to clarify a conceptual problem that cuts across the new sociology of science and contemporary social problems research and theory, and that is the relationship between constructivism and relativism.

It is important to understand modern science—including scientific knowledge—as a social construction in order to appreciate it as a social problem (in the Millsian sense). But there is some confusion—inside and outside of science studies—about what the constructivist interpretation of science means. The idea of social problems as social constructs is a key part of the framework of contemporary social problems research and theory.[19] In their critique of constructivism in social problems research, Woolgar and Pawluch assume that "con-

structivist" and "definitional" are synonymous, and that they entail
relativism as opposed to realism.[20] In any case, the genesis of constructivism in the new sociology of science is closely associated with
if not coincident with the sociological realism of ethnographic studies of scientific laboratories. In this context, constructivism is not
merely (or even) a matter of reality being constructed "by definition." It tends, rather, to be a fashionable way of talking about social
structures as the causal forces that generate thoughts and actions,
with a stress on the day-to-day, moment-to-moment activities of scientists as they go about producing and reproducing scientific culture.
There is thus no necessary connection between constructivism and
relativism. Given my earlier discussion of the fact that sociologists
of science such as Bloor and Knorr-Cetina are not relativists in any
anti-scientific sense, it should not be *assumed* that constructivism in
science studies and constructivism in social problems research mean
the same thing.

The foregoing should alert the reader to the fact that I proceed according to constructivist principles, but do not adopt any sort of
naive relativism. My approach is probably best described as "realistic" (rather than, for example, realist, let alone Realist!). The wed-
ding of constructivism and a realistic worldview does imply that
there are things that are true, and things that are false; and that
some sort of objective knowledge is possible. But constructivism
does not leave these ideas untouched; it transforms them into sociological concepts, and makes a sociology of objectivity necessary,
meaningful, and possible.

The argument that modern science is a social problem in the Millsian sense I have sketched depends on getting behind the facade of
ideology and icons in science to the "science machine," and exposing
the cultural roots of science. Mills observed that a variety of troubles
and issues are rooted and reflected in the relationships between modern science and other social institutions:

> . . . science seems to many less a creative ethos and a manner of orientation
> than a set of Science Machines, operated by technicians and controlled by
> economic and military men who neither embody nor understand science as
> ethos and orientation.[21]

There are in Mills' conception of the transformation of science into a
Science Machine by "military metaphysicians" echoes of Marx's notion of modern science as alienated, and Veblen's critique of modern
science as a machine-like product of our "matter-of-fact" industrial

and technological era. Thinkers with this turn of mind have described modern science as an "instrument of terror," a social activity driven by an assault on the natural world, profit motives, and the pursuit of war and violence.[22] In order to understand the grounds for such heresies, it is important that we distinguish clearly between isolated scientific biographies, methods, findings, experiments, and theories on the one hand, and, on the other, modern science as a social institution. By focusing on modern science as a social institution, we not only reveal the ways in which it is connected to and penetrated by other social institutions, we also transform biographies, methods, findings, experiments, and theories into social facts. This is the perspective I sketched in Chapter 3. It is a perspective that does not readily yield a conception of modern science as an autonomous (in the sense of independent) social system. Modern science *is* autonomous in a sociological sense to the extent that it is a structurally and functionally differentiated social activity. But the "parallel responses" thesis (Chapter 2) sets modern science into the very core of the modern state and its technological foundations. This idea requires some further discussion to clarify the distinction between structural autonomy and the autonomy of individuals.

Structural Autonomy

The concept of autonomy has played a key role in research on professions and bureaucracies. In general, students of autonomy in this context tend to focus on the autonomy of *individuals*, and in particular of professionals in bureaucracies.[23] In some cases, the focus may shift to the *social role*. But in neither case is the focus on autonomy as a *structural* variable, especially at the organizational and institutional levels of analysis.[24] Autonomy in this sense refers to the nature and degree of organizational or institutional demarcation and closure, and to the degree to which the boundaries of social activities and systems are distinct, permeable, open, or closed. The more, for example, a system can function independently of the resources of other systems, the more autonomous it is.

The structural sense of autonomy lends sociological meaning to the concepts "internal" and "external." The use of these concepts to refer to the two basic types of factors that can affect science, and to the distinction between contextual and non-contextual analysis has been properly criticized in the new sociology of science.[25] But these terms can be usefully applied in the context of analyzing the interaction of social systems that vary in terms of degree of closure, that is, degree of autonomy. Thus, an "internalist" approach would be an appropriate part of the research strategy for studying a relatively autonomous social activity or system. An internalist in the traditional sense of that term would generally consider factors such as scientific "ideas" independent of social forces. An internalist analysis in my sense would focus on the social structure of the system under study as a determinant of the knowledge produced in that system. The internal/external dichotomy is just one of a number of ideas that new sociologists of science have discarded or transformed conceptually. Another idea that has increasingly posed problems in science and technology studies is the "science," "technology," and "society" triad.

The Idea of Science, Technology and Society

The boundaries between these terms in traditional studies of science and technology have been more or less dissolved by some of the leading new sociologists of science. Harry Collins, for example, argues that his study of how scientific facts are established dissolves the boundaries that have traditionally separated science and technology and the rest of society in two ways:

First, it points to the continuity of the networks of social relationships within the scientific professions with networks in society as a whole. Second, it points to the analogy between cultural production in science and all other forms of social and conceptual innovation.[26] The important point that needs to be stressed about boundaries and networks in this context—and this is relevant to the discussions of structural autonomy—is that they are to varying degrees dynamic and protean.

The relative stability of boundaries and networks over a long period of time gives rise to systems we can determine degrees of autonomy for. But even when we are dealing with systems that have more or less well-defined institutional boundaries, we must be alert to changes, including periodic changes, in the character of those boundaries. They may be sufficiently fixed so that it makes sense to say they define an organization or an institution; but even within that framework, the boundaries may periodically break down. The system is thus more closed, more autonomous, at some times than at others.

Thus, Latour uses two expressions to refer to two aspects of the activities of scientists and engineers:

> . . . I will use the word *technoscience* from now on, to describe all the elements tied to the scientific contents no matter how dirty, unexpected or foreign they may seem, and the expression "science and technology," in quotation marks, to designate *what is kept of technoscience* once all the trials of responsibility have been settled.[27]

His conclusion is that "the name of the game will be to leave the boundaries open and to close them only when the people we follow close them."

My interpretation of Latour's conclusion is that whether it makes sense to talk about science, or technology, or technoscience, or wider cultural spheres depends on our perspective at any given time, and the degree of fluidity in the referents for our guiding concepts at the time we encounter them. In some cases, in fact, we may find we are studying a feature of "science" that is so widely diffused across and interdependent with other cultural spheres that we will need to use a new term to describe what we are studying.

Pinch and Bijker propose an interesting but less radical rationale for eliminating the distinction between "science" and "technology."[28] They argue that technology and science should be treated within the same social construction theory framework. Obviously, this sort of argument is a contribution to the more radical project Latour is engaged in. Establishing that technology is a social construct is to some extent less difficult than showing that scientific knowledge is a social construct; but it still contributes to the groundwork necessary for seeing, for example, technoscience where we have traditionally seen science and technology. In that sense, placing technology in its social context, and treating artifacts as "political," or more generally as social constructs, is relevant to the theory of the Science Machine.[29] But the relevance of this strategy tends to be limited because it can be carried out while implicitly or explicitly sustaining the traditional distinction between science and technology.[30]

Ruth Schwartz Cowan's work is a good example of how the contextualization of technology (in this case using the concept of "technological system") can be accomplished while implicitly treating science (by ignoring it) as a somehow separate and distinct phenomenon. And in the end, Cowan misses the linkages between the work process, technological systems, and social structure.[31] Her proposal for "neutralizing" the sexual connotation of household technology and the "senseless tyranny of spotless shirts and immaculate floors" is not a sociologically viable solution to the social problem of technology. The reason is that she fails to see the profound and far reaching structural changes necessary to achieve the goals she sets; and this failure reflects the fact that she does not see the sorts of connections embodied in a concept such as technoscience.

There is now a good reason on both empirical and conceptual grounds to argue that even in its more autonomous phases or sectors, modern science is of a piece with modern technology and the central values, interests, and structures of the more powerful classes in modern society. As I pursue my "social problem" thesis, I will continue to focus on "modern science," even though I have now provided a rationale for either dispensing with the term or using it more cautiously. But that rationale needs to be developed further, or developed in new directions (not only in this chapter but in science studies generally) before we can confidently adopt a new conception of the referent for "modern science."

The idea of the Science Machine and concepts such as technoscience help us to see the connections between and the fragility of the boundaries around science and technology and, simultaneously, the connections between science and other social activities. In the next section, I pursue these connections by sketching the emergence of modern science as one of the key ingredients of European expansionism.

The Cultural Roots of Modern Science

By 1500, on the eve of the scientific revolution, Europeans were taking command of the world's oceans and beginning to subjugate the highly developed cultures of the Americas. William McNeill identifies three "talismans of power" that enabled the Europeans to conquer oceans and cultures:

> . . . (1) a deep-rooted pugnacity and recklessness operating by means of (2) a complex military technology, most notably in naval matters; and (3) a population inured to a variety of diseases which had long been endemic throughout the Old World ecumene.[32]

European militarism had its roots in Bronze Age barbarian societies and the medieval military habits of the merchant classes and certain lesser aristocrats and landowners. It was in this most warlike of the major civilizations that modern science arose.

The maritime supremacy of the Europeans was the basis for the enlarged scope of their militarism beginning in the sixteenth century. Their superiority at sea was the result of deliberately blending science and practice, first in the Italian commercial cities and ultimately, under the guidance of Prince Henry the Navigator and his successors, in Portugal.[33] The scientific revolution institutionalized this inseparable blend of science and practice, science and technology.

Modern science has been primarily a tool of the ruling elites of modern societies from the time of its origin in sixteenth and seventeenth century Europe.[34] In its earliest stages of development modern science was part of the repertoire of "gentlemen" who were embracing capitalism and seeking to destroy the monopolies of the old landed aristocracy. But by as early as the 1690s in England, the tie between science (and in particular Newtonian science) the culture of the ruling Whig oligarchy, and the established church (in particular the latitudinarian hierarchy) was well-established:

> The scientific ideology of order and harmony preached from the pulpits complemented the political stability over which [the Whig] oligarchy presided.[35]

The scientific revolution organized the human and cultural capacity for inquiry in ways that stressed laws over necessities, the value of quantity over quality, and strategies of domination and exploitation over strategies based on an awareness of ecological interdependencies. As a product of the commercial, mercantile, and industrial revolutions that transformed Europe and the world between 1400 and 1900, modern science emerged and developed as an alienating and alienated mode of inquiry. It arose as the mental framework of capitalism, and the cognitive mode of industrialism.[36] Capital accumulation and industrial products and processes became prominent features of social life, and the primary factor in shaping our ways of thought, our science. We learned to think the way modern technological processes act.[37] Modern science (including scientists, and images and symbols of science) came into the world as a *commodity*, and has developed in close association with the discipline of the machine.[38] A number of researchers from Karl Marx to David Noble have recognized this, although many of them have implicitly or explicitly distinguished "science"—more or less "pure"—and a "modern science" adulterated by capitalism and technology.[39]

Given the stubbornness of the myth of pure science, it is important to continually stress that science in every form has always been as much a part of the economic, political and military fabric of society as modern science is. The "scientific community" did not, as Noble contends for example, have to overcome "Platonic prejudices." There is some legitimate confusion about the relationship between modern science in its formative stages and modern science in its fully institutionalized form. It might be argued or assumed that before science became a differentiated part of European social structure through institutionalization and the crystallization of the social role of the scientist that it was characterized by purity and Platonic prejudices. But even if this were the case in the earliest and most diffuse stages of the history of modern science, it is clear that once it became a major force in European culture it "took on an immensely practical posture that moved it from an intellectual pursuit to a source for industrialization."[40]

The idea of modern science in its earliest stages as a purely "intellectual pursuit," however, cannot sustain careful scrutiny. I have already noted that early modern science was a tool of "gentlemen capitalists," an elite on the road to ruling power. Moreover, seventeenth-century natural philosophers already expressed values of the "world politick" in their efforts to develop a mechanical description of the "world natural:"

> At every turn, that linkage ensured its integration into the larger culture and made its ideological formulation immediately and directly relevant to those who held, or sought to hold power in society and government.[41]

All of the foregoing needs to be kept in mind in order to fully appreciate Marx's comment that "modern industry . . . makes science a productive force distinct from labor and presses it into the service of capital;" this is the starting point for David Noble's study of science, technology, and the rise of corporate capitalism in *America by Design.*[42] The issue of "science" aside, it is fairly clear that *modern* science emerged as a means of capital accumulation, and thus an economic good and an article of commerce.

We can, as I hinted earlier, trace the roots of modern science to the knowledge producing activities of earlier cultures. Those activities are everywhere inseparable from military, political, and economic interests and power.[43] David Dickson, for example, writes:

> From its earliest origins in ancient Greece, Western science has enjoyed a close and productive relationship to military power. This relationship has

intensified in the forty years since the Second World War, a period in which, building on the experiences of that war, the rapid escalation of military force in both the East and West has been grounded increasingly on the application of advanced scientific knowledge to weapons of mass destruction. Science has done well out of its role, for the rise to positions of influence and favor of the scientific establishment in both hemispheres has been largely due to the contribution science has been able to make to new military technologies.[44]

The very foundations of modern science are permeated by a sense of the warmaking utility of scientific knowledge, expressed by the most brilliant as well as the most ordinary scientific practitioners. Most of the texts from the formative period of modern science that recommend science also point out its utility for improving the state's capacity for waging war more effectively and destroying life and property more efficiently:

> Early modern scientists identified with that small literate segment of the elite to whom power was presumed to be a natural prerogative.[45]

One way to illustrate this deep-rooted relationship between science and power is to reflect on the reality that lies behind the icons and myths of science.

Icons of Science

The social problems of modern science are masked by icons, myths and ideologies. Icons—Archimedes drawing pretty figures in the dust, Newton searching for shapely pebbles at the beach, and Einstein riding light beams in his mind—are objects of uncritical devotion. The myth of pure science is a cornerstone of modern science as a house of worship. And the ideologies of modern science have persuaded many of us to demarcate "science" and "technology," and to blame the latter for our social and environmental ills. No wonder, then, that it is difficult for us to see the alienative aspects of scientific work, and the connections between modern science and technology, ruling elites, state interests, and God as the symbol of moral order. What realities lie behind these icons, myths and ideologies? To begin to answer this question, we can turn first to some observations by an ambivalent sociologist of science, Robert Merton. For it was Robert Merton, the prime mover in fuctionalist sociology of science, who early in his career defended Boris Hessen's Marxist conjectures on the social and economic roots of Newton's *Principia* against G. N. Clark's effort to preserve at least some of the purity of Newtonian science.

Merton pointed out the importance of distinguishing "the personal attitudes of the individual men of science from the social role played by their research." A variety of motives, Merton argued, is compatible with "the demonstrable fact that the thematics of science in seventeenth century England were in large part determined by the social structure of the time." He also opposed Sombart's contention that science and technology were almost completely divorced in the seventeenth century. On the specific question of Newton's motives and the social relations of science in seventeenth century England, Merton writes:

> Newton's own motives do not alter the fact that astronomical observations, of which he made considerable use, were a product of Flamsteed's work in the Greenwich Observatory, which was constructed at the command of Charles II for the benefit of the Royal Navy. Nor do they negate the striking influence upon Newton's work of such practically-oriented scientists as Halley, Hooke, Wren, Huyghens and Boyle. Even in regard to motivation, Clark's thesis [regarding the primacy of disinterestedness among English scientists of this period] is debatable in view of the explicit awareness of many scientists in seventeenth century England concerning the practical implications of their research in pure science. It is neither an idle nor unguarded generalization that *every English scientist of this time* who was of sufficient distinction to merit mention in general histories of science at one point or another explicitly related at least some of his scientific research to immediate practical problems.[46]

In order to appreciate the significance of Merton's argument regarding the social relations of science and the motives of individual scientists it is useful to examine the idea of "pure science." An understanding of the sociology of pure science is a prerequisite for any critical study of the relationship between science and social progress. Let me begin by considering the two most important icons from before and after the period of the scientific revolution during which Newton lived and worked, and for which he is the preeminent iconographic representation. Newton's counterparts from the ancient and the contemporary world are Archimedes and Einstein.

Archimedes, like Newton, played down his role in practical affairs; at least that is the report we get from Plutarch. According to Plutarch, Archimedes "placed his whole ambition in those speculations in whose beauty and subtlety there is no admixture of the common needs of life." Plutarch of course, was writing nearly three hundred years after Archimedes' death. The distinguished historian of Greek mathematics T. C. Heath supports Plutarch's view by noting that Archimedes wrote only *one* "mechanical" treatise, the lost work *On Sphere-Making*. Heath equates "mechanical" with "construction," for the lost manuscript on sphere-making deals with the construction of a sphere representing motions of bodies in the heavenly system. Construction, however, is not the only sort of mechanical interest that can be opposed to "pure contemplation." In other works (some lost), Archimedes deals with such practical matters as the calendar, optics, centers of gravity, balances and levers. The fact that he was a great inventor, and that some of his inventions were designed for political and military purposes, cannot (Plutarch, Heath, and Archimedes himself not withstanding) be ignored as "incidental." It is unreasonable to suppose that Archimedes could completely detach his mechanical interests and talents from his interests and talents in so-called "pure mathematics." The coexistence of these talents and interests, amply documented, is sufficient grounds for arguing that Archimedes' mathematics was not a product of "pure contemplation."[47]

In his book on *Method*, discovered in 1906, Archimedes outlines the mechanical bases of his formal ("pure") geometric proofs. His tendency to suppress the "vulgar" roots of the results he presented in a logical format for public consumption is not an unusual strategy in the history of mathematics. His biography offers some clues regarding the roots of this strategy. Archimedes was the son of an astronomer (Pheidias), and an intimate (perhaps even a relative of) King Hieron. His *achieved* social position, at least, and the fact that he was in a position to generalize the generalizations of earlier mathematical workers, and then generalize his own generalizations (thus producing relatively high levels of abstraction) could easily have led him and admiring biographers (ulterior motives aside) to emphasize that his inquiries were not prompted by "vulgar" considerations. And whatever Archimedes' motives in any particular situation, they cannot alter the fact of his relationship to political and military authorities of his city, a relationship that tells us something about the ties between science and society.

The case of Albert Einstein, the most prominent icon in twentieth century science, is more complicated than the cases of Archimedes and Newton with respect to the relationship between individual motives and social roles. Einstein worked in an era of professionalized science. Twentieth century science is more highly professionalized and bureaucratized than earlier forms of science or inquiry. It is thus easier for individual scientists to work in apparent dissociation from the practical concerns of everyday life and vulgar political and economical interests because they are shielded by complex institutional relationships. It is therefore crucial to examine the "scientific community's" relationship to the wider society, and to the state, in order to understand the social role of an individual scientist.

Einstein's activities illustrate how the scientific community—through its own internal social structure and its ties to state interests—can protect and provide for its members, and even provide niches within which one can engage in the sort of private thinking sometimes labeled "pure contemplation." Einstein wrote:

> I believe with Schopenhauer that one of the strongest motives that leads men to art and science is escape from everyday life with its crudity and hopeless dreariness, from the fetters of one's own ever-shifting desires.[48]

But Einstein's social role—and more generally the relationship between science and society—is revealed in the public relations of Albert Einstein. There is no need to impugn Einstein's motives or his humanitarian spirit to recognize that there is something sinister in all of those photographs showing Einstein posing with kings, queens, prime ministers and presidents. The shadow of Adolf Hitler that darkens these photographs should not lead us to make the mistake of viewing the states represented in them as benevolent; it should not keep us from seeing that what is sinister about these photographs is not what they tell us about Einstein and King Albert or Einstein and President Harding, but rather what they tell us about science and the state. Let me pursue this further by turning to a brief exploration of the more general relationships between pure science and society.

The Myth of Purity

The iconography of science is rooted in the myth of pure science. The idea that pure science is a purely intellectual or cognitive creation untouched by social facts has been pretty much undermined if not yet demolished by sociologists and social theorists from Durkheim and Fleck to contemporary researchers in science studies. How, then, are we to understand what it is that pure science—so often personified in Archimedes, Newton, and Einstein—represents? Let us consider this question in terms of the purest of the pure sciences, pure mathematics.

Pyenson defines pure mathematics as mathematics "pursued for its intrinsic interest, not as a tool in the service of other interests." By introducing the notion of interests, Pyenson shifts our focus from the individual experience of mathematical thought to the politics of pure mathematics. In his *A Mathematician's Apology*, G. H. Hardy wrote:

> I have never done anything "useful." No discovery of mine has made, or is likely to make, directly or indirectly, for good or ill, the least difference to the amenity of the world.[49]

The noted chemist Soddy considered Hardy's views a scandal: "From such cloistered clowning, the world sickens." But J. R. Newman calls Hardy's statement "nonsense;" Hardy's Law is important in the study of Rh-blood groups and the treatment of haemolytic disease in newborns; and his work on Reimann's zeta function has been used in studying furnace temperatures. Hardy's radical defense of purity must be understood as an intellectual strategy. The fact is that Hardy hated war and the application of mathematics to problems in ballistics and aerodynamics. Thus, one aspect of the politics of pure mathematics is that it is an intellectual strategy for responding to social problems, issues, and conflicts.[50]

Within mathematics, the argument that there is a politics of pure mathematics is supported by the perennial rift between pure and applied mathematicians on university faculties. Peano's conflicts with Volterra and other members of the mathematics faculty at the University of Turin are one example of this rift from the early history of professionalized mathematics.[51] A number of mathematicians have told me that if I want to understand the social dynamics of contemporary mathematics, I should look at the conflicts between pure and applied mathematics and mathematicians. Such conflicts reflect disagreements about how mathematical knowledge should be used, and struggles for scarce resources within the university system and in the larger funding arena.

There is no need to deny "the search for knowledge" as an individual or even as a collective goal to recognize that the relevance of pure research to societal interests may be something else besides the production of knowledge for its own sake. Pure science may, for example, function as a *demonstration* of the *capacity* for research in a society. Such demonstrations can be the basis for intimidating enemies, projecting status claims, or establishing territorial functions. Today, putting the label "pure science" on the research being carried out in the various national camps and outposts of Antarctica is a way of maintaining informal territorial claims. Because of its generality, pure mathematics plays an important role in establishing the purity of scientific disciplines. One of the few political leaders to acknowledge the political function of pure mathematics was Napoleon I, who said that "The advancement and perfection of mathematics is intimately connected with the prosperity of the state."

Purism, then, is an intellectual strategy that has multiple roots and functions. As a *political* strategy, it can demarcate and defend the pursuit of knowledge from military, economic, and political interests one is opposed to; it can be *used* by ruling elites to establish territorial claims indirectly; and it can help political leaders keep tabs on and control over creative and innovative researchers.

It should be noted that a certain amount of trained incompetence is necessary if scientists are going to exhibit ignorance or be mistaken about their social roles. Sharon Traweek's anthropological studies of the high energy physics community illustrate some of the social mechanisms that bring about this trained incompetence. Physicists are trained, for example, to value certain emotional qualities (for example, meticulousness, patience, and persistence); and they are introduced to highly idealized portraits of great scientists—"geniuses"—as role models. To become physicists, they have to go through a process of intense professional socialization. The focus of this process is physics and the physics community.[52] The result is that the social contexts of their activities are obscured, and their conceptions of their social roles narrowed dramatically. Under such conditions, state ideologies and alienation can find their way into the "purest" of motives.

Labeling science "pure" is an intellectual strategy that can serve political, religious, economic, military and psychological functions. One of the most important social functions of the purity label is to mitigate resistance to and criticism of established interests. The state, for example, may grant scientists who adopt the purity label the freedom to pursue their individual research interests, so long as what they do keeps them from criticizing or resisting state actions, and especially so long as they do not interfere with the state's efforts to appropriate their discoveries and inventions in pursuit of military, economic or political goals. "Basic" or "pure" science can easily end up focusing on mechanisms instead of causes. As a result, problems can be abstracted from their social contexts, and solutions sought that do not threaten prevailing social arrangements. The focus on basic cellular biology in cancer research, for example, assumes a solution that interrupts the carcinogen process rather than one that rearranges the social order to remove carcinogens from the environment.[53]

To the extent that ideologies of purity stress "science for its own sake" they reinforce an individualistic (atomistic, separated, alienated) orientation to work and obstruct the development and pursuit of interests outside science, including the realization of the collective interests of scientists as workers. To the extent that they stress the independence of scientific knowledge from social interests, historical and social contexts, and individual subjective experiences they help to isolate and alienate not only that knowledge but the knowledge producers from the social processes of production and reproduction in science. To the extent that ideologies of purity reify the realm of purity, they function as justifications for authority (of ideas and heroic figures in the sciences, as well as of texts and teachers), and reinforce the principle of authority in everyday life.

Psychologically, purism can be used to satisfy an individual's need for and interest in purity in general as an emotional resource or defense mechanism. This form of purism can become severely pathological if the fear of earthly pleasures and conflicts of everyday life produce an extreme aversion to anything considered unclean or polluting. An intellectualized purism can develop among "floating intellectuals" who are not committed to or constrained by established social institutions, *but* have failed to develop strong independent ways of establishing for themselves what is true and what is false. This form of purism is associated with weakly formed social, political, philosophical or religious interests.

Religion and science are often mated in psychological purism and its variations. This is especially the case in mathematics and mathematized sciences. Consistency and completeness, hallmarks of pure mathematics, are central features of the Holy. Pure mathematics and religion were, for example, closely linked in the lives and works of George Boole and W. R. Hamilton. The religious imperative is widely recognized as a feature of early modern science, but its manifestation in contemporary mathematics is not so apparent. Gauss still held to an idea common to his peers and predecessors, that pure science exposes the immortal nucleus of the human soul. Already with Gauss, however, we find a transition from worship of God to worship of Nature as the object of human reason. Gauss still believed in an eternal, just, omniscient, omnipresent God. He was always trying to harmonize mathematical principles with his meditations on the future of the human soul. Cantor believed in the

Platonic reality of infinite sets because their reality had—he claimed—been revealed to him by God. And Bourbaki (the pseudonym for an influential group of early twentieth century mathematicians) claimed that mathematical problems evoke aesthetic and religious emotions.

The ideology of pure science—and especially of pure mathematics—grows in large part out of ideologies of God and Nature as ultimate authorities. In the end, authority comes to reside in the realm of Logic. Classical logic, for example (as the intuitionist mathematician L. E. J. Brouwer recognized), is an abstraction from, first, the mathematics of finite sets and then the mathematics of finite subsets. These mundane origins were forgotten when Logic was elevated to a position prior to and beyond all mathematics. The substitute God (the Durkheimian spirit cannot be missed here), Logic, was then applied to the mathematics of infinite sets without any justification. Reified realms serve as *moral* imperatives and constraints that in one way or another: (1) bind us to established professional and state interests; and (2) reinforce obedience at the expense of criticism and rebellion in our relationships within established institutions. This is the case even where we are left "alone" to pursue our "own" interests guided by our "own" curiosity to understand the way the world works, and in spite of any irreverent thoughts and actions that at best may make a few waves at the local organizational level. Finally, marginal scientists can give up or fail to develop their own ways of determining what is true and what is false, and instead rely on an intellectualized notion of pure standards. The problem, of course, is that they conceive these standards as transcendent rather than as social constructs, reflections of the work of a community or culture. This orientation to purity undermines the scientist's ability to recognize, criticize, and if necessary, take action against established interests embodied in specific individuals, roles and institutions.

In general, then, ideologies of purity, like religion, can drain away our individual and collective capacities for criticism and rebellion. Constructivism in science studies can help us to identify the social interests at work in generating and sustaining ideologies of purity. But it can only do this if it is extricated from its still intimate relationship with an authoritative Science. Only then can the idea of the social construction of science and knowledge become a force for social criticism and social change.

Finally, I want to reflect on the ways in which the lack of a strong sociological conception of science can inhibit the recognition of crucial features of the social relations of science. The context for these reflections was my response to analyses of secrecy in university-based research.[54] Some writers on this topic are rather optimistic about the ultimate effects of the growing ties between industry and universities on academic freedom; others are pessimistic. Some are more enthusiastic defenders of *laissez-rechercher* or *laissez-innover* than others. And some are readier than others to justify social controls on the flow on scientific information. But in general (and with some notable exceptions), the analyses I examined were guided by the elitist and professionalist values of the scientific, academic, legal, military, political, and business communities.

Reflections on Science, Secrecy, and Democracy

There are conflicts between and among these communities, but they tend to occur within a broader system of shared and compatible values and interests. A common factor is that, within the communities, contemporary problems in the social control of science are regarded as matters to work out through compromises and trade-offs, the traditional tools of the "political realists" whose views have so far dominated the science and secrecy debate. Some of these political realists admit that the contemporary social relations of science call for greater vigilance, but they neglect a vital point. Their perspective does not focus attention on what David Dickson refers to as the central feature of the relationship between science and society today: "The control of science has become a key element in the control of American society."[55]

The science and secrecy debate has been carried out in a social and political context that implicitly and explicitly places "the national interest," "national security," and the interests and values of elite professionals above the public interest and the values of participatory democracy. But Eric Holtzman has detected a "disheartening shift" and "chilly undertones" in the social relations of science—changes that Holtzman believes will threaten democratic institutions and values.[56] It is therefore important to stress the public interest in the social control of science, and to consider the science and secrecy issue from a participatory democracy perspective.

It is also important to challenge the notion that secrecy in science is a matter of "idiosyncratic and individualistic styles of behavior," or simply a manifestation of "human social behavior."[57] Secrecy in science (and in society) is a social phenomenon, but this basic social fact is often neglected. By focusing on the narrower question of "trade-offs," for example, the political realism that dominates the debate tends to be reinforced. The sustained sociological interpretation needed to uncover the social roots and consequences of secrecy and openness in science and society has not been forthcoming.[58]

Science, Social Structure, and Human Values

Ideas and practices regarding science and secrecy exist in organizational, cultural, and historical contexts. Scientific institutions, scientific knowledge, and scientists themselves are social constructions. Political and economic decisions by ruling elites affect everything from the place of science in the occupational structure to the social structure of the scientific community. Scientists (especially the "statesmen" of science), their ideologues, the public, the media, and other social agents and agencies are constantly creating and recreating both "the image of science and the scientist" and "the scientist's role in society." As the social organization of science, the relationships between science and the state, and the prevailing values in society change, so also do the theory and practice of openness and secrecy in science.[59] Certainly within any sufficiently complex social structure there is room for individuality and idiosyncrasy. But it is the ability to see past the individual and the idiosyncratic to actual, emerging, and potential social structures that leads to sociological understanding of social phenomena.

There are, of course, always constraints on science. Sometimes these constraints are imposed from the "outside" (by religious or political authorities, for example). Sometimes they are applied from the "inside" (when, for example, scientific authorities find it necessary, convenient, or prudent to carry out self-policing actions). The sources and forms of constraints on science depend on the extent to which scientific activity is institutionally autonomous. The culture of science and the wider culture are the sources of the values that reflect and guide scientists' behavior. Laws, socialization, and professionalization help determine whether scientists will or will not: (a) work in ways that damage the environment or compromise the integrity and welfare of people and animals; (b) engage in fraudulent activities; or (c) be secretive.

When the social structure of science changes, science and scientists change. And the three historically convergent social processes of institutionalization, professionalization, and bureaucratization have profoundly affected contemporary science. As these processes have unfolded, organized science has moved from the periphery to the center of the established social order and been enveloped by the interests and values of ruling elites. Such complex social realities make it difficult to capture and contain science with such static labels as "traditional science," "traditional goals of science," "basic science," "applied science," "norms of science," and even "science" and "scientist." Biologist Clifford Grobstein strongly implies that "shibboleths" of science or the academy (for example, "the right to teach, to debate, and to investigate—openly and without restriction . . .") are more important than scientific or academic practice.[60] Among other things, however, a shibboleth is a criterion for distinguishing one group from another. The uncritical use of shibboleths of science obscures their function as resources for and symbols of demarcation, elitism, and professionalism. It also obscures the existence of opposing interests and values in science, and of conflicts between science and other social institutions. Shibboleths are not guarantors of honesty, trust, and openness; nor do they insure that what scientists do will benefit humanity. Many scientists and science watchers have the mistaken but perhaps comforting idea that shibboleths (like norms and values) are important determinants of scientific behavior but are independent of social structures. Thus, emphasizing the "force of norms" in science is empty rhetoric unless there is an accompanying analysis of scientists' capacity to actualize norms and values, a capacity that depends on access to material and symbolic resources and social networks. If we want to understand and explain science and scientists, we have to study scientific practice. The fallacy of assuming that "science is (must be, should be) what science was" or that "science will always be what science is today" can be avoided only if we remain vigilant observers of what scientists are doing in their laboratories and offices.[61]

"The freedom of the academy" (in particular, as the home of "pure science") is a central shibboleth of university life and science. The precise meaning of the phrase may elude us, but it is clear that the academy's freedom to pursue its own interests and to criticize itself and its surroundings (including the state) is limited and fragile. It is limited by the interrelations between universities and government, business, the military, and the legal system, which create overlapping institutional values and interests. Academic freedom is fragile because academics, like court magicians, are ultimately servants of and at the mercy of the state—even when they are pursuing their "own" interests in the laboratory, or thinking "pure" thoughts in their armchairs. If the magician or academician becomes too independent, or if the interests of the state change, doing magic or science or carrying on any form of inquiry suddenly becomes a much more risky enterprise. An academy cannot be "free" in the sense that it can transcend environment, biology and culture. It can, however, be free (or freed) from the constraints of human authorities inside and outside of its social boundaries.

According to Rosemary Chalk, secret practices in science are "idiosyncratic and individualistic styles of behavior rather than the professional norm." But secrecy hardly makes sense outside of a social context. Even as an "aberration" it might signal a threat to open communication posed by emerging or potential changes in social structures and values. Secrecy is a natural ingredient of some social arrangements. A highly competitive science, for example, is a fertile ground for secrecy. Professionalism, and strong ties to business, government and the military all nourish secrecy in science. Too often, scientists and science watchers fail to see the structural forces that make secrecy (and fraud for that matter) likely or inevitable. They are apt to be defensive and claim in the absence of "hard evidence" that secrecy is an aberration, that it is no more prevalent today than it was in the past. Journalistic accounts of secrecy and fraud in science might prompt them to call for research to produce the necessary "hard evidence." Even in the absence of direct evidence, however, it is possible to judge whether secrecy is or is becoming a serious problem in science by exercising a little sociological imagination. Without denying the value of empirical data, sociological theory suggests that secrecy and fraud are increasingly likely in the wake of contemporary changes in the social organization and social relations of science which have prompted responses ranging from AAAS projects to David Dickson's study of " the new politics of science." Indications that secrecy is an increasingly prevalent feature of social life can also be used as evidence for secrecy in science; the relevance of this sort of evidence becomes apparent once we recognize that science is in and of society, not apart from it.[62]

Science in a Stratified Society

Social factors (e.g., competition, property, pure research, and differential access to information) that are problematic from a democratic perspective are simply characteristics of a society that is functioning well for many writers on this topic. Standards in science do not function independently of cultural values as a whole. Nor can science in a stratified society "benefit society as a whole." Holtzman recognizes this fact, but his perspective needs to be widened.[63] The Third World, the oppressed majority in South Africa, and the oppressed peoples of America are all entitled to access to the information they need to improve their life chances and life styles. One of the ways that ruling elites gain and hold power is by preventing citizens from having access to, or from achieving some understanding of, certain types of information. To achieve such power in contemporary society requires not just mechanisms of oppression, but also methods of material and ideological control over science, scientists, and science education. The myth that the United states is a pluralist society thus ignores facts of social stratification. It also obscures the fact that, ultimately, citizens have no legal or peaceful recourse when a government decides to use violence to protect its own interests—including its interests in the "best" scientists, the most advanced scientific methods, and the most up-to-date scientific information. Justifications for secrecy in science often fail to identify explicitly the antagonistic relationships that make secrecy necessary (except for the crude references to "enemies"). The antagonistic parties, their specific interests, and their relative political and economical power are rarely acknowledged, especially when the opposing parties are members of the same society. The justification of secrecy on the grounds of "national security" or "the national interest" ignores the opposition between elite interests and the interests of a wide range of publics.

Elites find the over-simplified conception of "society" useful because it helps them to establish an identity between their interests and "the public interest." In addition to the myth of pluralism (buttressed by a laissez-faire, nonregulatory, economic and political philosophy), elitists' interests are also served by the myth of value-free, value-neutral science, and the presentation of an optimistic public face.[64] One especially optimistic author, Robert Rosenweig, virtually articulates the classic "Robber Baron" philosophy that in an "imperfect world," the strategies required to keep society functioning smoothly will inevitably result in "some pain," "some embarrassment," and "some bad things."[65] He asks us (including those of us who are most likely to experience and suffer from the pain, the embarrassment, the bad things) to "have faith" in the "resiliency" of the system.

From an elitist perspective, competition is a valued aspect of scientific behavior. Competition is not, however, healthy for science as a public interest activity. The competitiveness inspired by priority concerns, for example, is at the root of the iron law of miseponymy—

eponymous rewards do not accrue to "innovators" and "discoverers" but to latecomers who have more power, prestige, visibility or charisma.[66] Iron laws are notoriously flexible; but there is sufficient truth in the miseponymy law to suggest, at least, the inherent dangers of competitiveness in science.

The concept of "intellectual property" fits well into elitist discourse on science and secrecy. The rhetoric of property and laissez-faire by itself is hardly enough to sustain the assertion that many of the participants are "capitalists of science." But given additional facts, such as the concept of "knowledge as real estate," I find it hard to resist the temptation to use the capitalist label.[67] For the sake of analysis, viewing information and knowledge as resources is useful. Such an approach places the analyst in a better position to appreciate the full social implications of viewing science as property. We can then seek to identify different types of intellectual property, the values associated with each type, and the relationships between propertied and underpropertied classes.

Because modern societies are stratified, it is unreasonable to claim that "society" supports universities as arenas of "pure research." The allegedly "pure" and "aesthetic" motives of academic science are the products of institutional autonomy, and the degree of institutional autonomy is dependent on the relations between science and the state. In practice, even the purest motives in science tend to be turned inward to satisfy alienated individual or professional interests. And, of course, there are various interest groups that have more or less invested in the universities and their "high tradition." To evaluate the nature and functions of the university system we need some measures of "quality education," measures that deal with human values. It is unrealistic to assume, for example, that aside from the problems raised by ties between universities and corporations, U.S. campuses are free of problems.

If we consider social stratification in an international context, then the role of intelligence communities in the flow of information takes on a significance rarely acknowledged in the science and secrecy debates. No matter what domestic controls a country places on science, there will always be (given prevailing social structures) pressures to keep information flowing within the intelligence communities, and therefore between and among ruling elites and their scientific advisors. Controls on science therefore tend to affect principally the flow of information between ruling elites and their publics.

If we stop to consider whether Rosenzweig's "bad things" can be avoided, then we have to take "tinkering" with science and society seriously. Elites are obviously cautious about this possibility. Their arguments against the need for tinkering generally take the form of rhetorical flourishes about how well science and society "work."[68] From a democratic perspective, however, there is a pressing need for social tinkering.

The democratic challenge in the controversy about science and secrecy is, as Marcel La Follette urges, to preserve and uphold "the highest traditions of scholarship and academic freedom . . . for the good of all."[69] To meet the challenge, we have to acknowledge what is rhetoric and what is substance in our defense of the ideals of inquiry; we have to recognize the intimate connections between inquiry and other social and cultural activities; and we have to acknowledge that the defense of open inquiry and participatory democracy involves political struggle as well as research, seminars, and scholarly articles. To insure openness in inquiry and society, we must reinforce democratic principles and institutions where they are thriving, rehabilitate them where they are being eroded or corroding, and establish them where they do not yet exist.

In the chapter that follows, I discuss the impact of studying "science in action" on our views about what science is and how it works. The idea that science and especially scientific knowledge, is a social construct could hardly have arisen—and certainly would not have had much persuasive power—without working with, watching and listening to scientists "at the bench."

5

The Anthropology of Science

Introduction

How are we to account for the myths and icons of pure science? In part, they reflect the fact that until recently, the nature of scientific work has been told at second and third hand in scholarly forums and media, and in journalistic and anecdotal essays, biographies and memoirs. Two of the basic ways in which sociologists and anthropologists have sought to enter into the everyday worlds of working scientists are through interviews and on-site observations. My own appreciation of science as a social fact really began when I interviewed visiting foreign scientists at a number of American universities in the late 1960s. It was not as if prior to this experience I did not have some first hand exposure to science in action. Four years of a secondary level engineering and science education, several semesters as an electrical engineering major in college, and an interest in electrical experiments had given me some sense of how science works. But what was missing in these experiences was a sociological perspective. As a result, even though I appreciated the fact that handbooks, textbooks, and classroom learning never seemed to overcome the need to tinker and improve (with equations as well as with actual components and circuits), I was not able to understand the fully social nature of what I was accomplishing as an "individual." I was still heavily under the influence of hundreds of biographies, manuals, textbooks, science teachers, and classroom experiments.

I begin this chapter by briefly reviewing the study I did of visiting foreign scientists. One of my aims is to show how the study allowed me to bring notions of ideology to bear on my conception of science. But the substantive conclusions I reached in this study are also still, I believe, interesting, and in fact relevant to the current experiences of visiting foreign scientists at American universities. It will also be apparent that many of the central themes in my later work came to the surface in this study, including a concern with the conditions of scientific work and an orientation to examining the role of science as a liberating or constraining force in human life.

In the second section of this chapter, I introduce a second approach to discovering "what is really going on in science."

The Third Culture of Science: What Are Scientists Saying?

Studies of and ideas about the global community defined the broad intellectual arena within which my study of visiting foreign scientists was conceived and carried out. The twentieth century has been marked by an extraordinary increase in the scale of world events. The historical process of sociocultural increases in scale is known as "ecumenization," the development of links between and across local primary communities, local or regional sociopolitical units, and civilizations. Ecumenization is rooted in the cross-societal or cross-cultural movement of persons engaged in the "prosaic activities" of trade, diplomacy, transportation, communication, missionary work, translation, tourism, science, scholarship, and journalism.[1] These activities have led to the emergence of social systems variously described as lateralizations, supercultures, and third cultures.[2] The "international scientific community" is considered a paradigm for such trans- or supra-societal systems, and the activities of scientists are considered critical forces for ecumenization.[3] Scientists have been defined as "strategic human capital" and "elites" whose normative orientations are a basis for global cooperation and the development of a world community.[4] Many of these ideas are incorporated in the idea of the third culture of science.

The Third Culture of Science

Following the general definition of "third culture" developed by John and Ruth Hill Useem, the third culture of science is defined as those cultural patterns created, shared, and learned by scientists of different societies who are engaged in relating their societies or sections thereof to each other. The Useems consider such patterns to be crucial forces for modernization.[5] Since the relationship between science and progress has generally been considered to be positive and unproblematic, it is not surprising that the dependence of national development and modernization, international cooperation, and global unification on the materials, knowledge, and values generated by science has been widely affirmed.[6] But the actual nature and consequences of third cultural activities for scientists, science, and societies have not been systematically studied. This was true at the time I carried out my study of the third culture of science, and remains basically true today. The introduction of the concepts of transcientific (or transepistemic) center and of technoscience in recent years has provided a conceptual basis for carrying out third culture research, but we have yet to see a sustained empirical program develop in this area.

Studies and speculations on international science and society have addressed four basic questions: (1) does involvement in the prosaic activities of the third culture of science stimulate an awareness of and constitute participation in, an emerging world encompassing ecumene; (2) do these activities facilitate the development of cooperative links between and among sovereign nations through the creation of strong, enduring interpersonal ties between scientists of different nations; (3) where scientists from "developing" countries are visitors in "developed" host countries, do their activities contribute to the "development" of their home countries; and (4) does activity in the scientific third culture integrate scientists into a supra-national scientific social system. The tendency has been for scholars and intellectuals to answer these questions affirmatively and optimistically but with little or no empirical evidence to support their positions. This seemed to me to be a matter of myths and ideologies about science, and my study of visiting foreign scientists was designed to provide some empirical bases for judging whether and how the third culture of science was linked to global awareness and ecumenization.

The visiting foreign scientist in America is a participant in a system of "international education" which has a well-defined ideological foundation. Whether they are thought of as members of the "international scientific community," creators of third cultural patterns, or participants in an experiment in international understanding, visiting foreign scientists in America work in settings which are assumed to stimulate an expansion of individual consciousness and to serve a complex set of national and international interests. Educational exchange, institution-building, technical and economic assistance, and the development of national scientific communities through third cultural networks are conceived as systems "designed to facilitate the process of modernization." This perspective is affirmed in the rationale for exchange programs and visiting scholar activities.

In a National Academy of Science study of postdoctoral education in the United States carried out during the same period I was working on my project, many university administrators argued that international education is "a responsibility of the world's richest country." And at a national conference on higher education and development in 1967, a United States State Department official noted that America faces the problem of "how education in America, for the foreign and American student alike, can help bring together the advanced and developing world."[7] I was uneasy about these points of view on the building of an international or world community around the activities of scientists and educators. These views seemed to be grounded in the myth of an "international scientific community." My study of visiting foreign scientists was thus initially conceived as a small contribution to bridging the gap between myth and reality in the international system of education and training. In the process of carrying out this study, I began to develop an appreciation for the ideological functions of the myth of an international scientific community and the myth of pure science. The tension between the myths and realities of science would eventually give rise to my notion of a sociology of objectivity.

In an anticipation of my later involvement in and support of ethnographic studies of science, this project focused on the conditions under which visiting foreign scientists at American universities work, and the types of ideas and activities these conditions stimulate and reinforce. The idea that conditions of work were major determinants of knowledge systems was not novel. The notion that this applied to *scientific* knowledge was. Here I associated myself with a still embryonic "new sociology of science." Within a few years, the idea that scientific knowledge was socially constructed would become a major theme and slogan of the science studies movement, stimulated in great part by the work of the ethnographers of science. In my study, the ideas and activities I focused on were related to the conception of international science as a modernization system, a system of "prosaic activities" in an emerging ecumene, and a critical supra-societal system many scholars and intellectuals considered to be a microcosm of an emerging world order.

Working Conditions and Ideas

Adam Smith, Karl Marx, and Thorstein Veblen are among the classical contributors to the conception of work as a significant determinant of worldviews, ideologies, and cognitive mappings. The most unequivocal expression of this idea, as formulated by Friedson, is that "what people do is *more* an outcome of the pressure of the situation they are in than of what they have earlier 'internalized'." More generally, Wilensky has noted that "occupational cultures (rooted in common tasks, work schedules, job training, and career patterns) are sometimes better predictors of behavior than both social class and pre-job experience."[8]

Scientific occupations are generally classified as "professions." Professions can be considered ideal-type occupational institutions characterized by a body of "systematic knowledge or doctrine acquired only through long prescribed training." Professionalization can thus be conceived as a process which tends to intensify and extend the impact of work on an individual's ideas and activities.[9]

It is reasonable, then, to assume that conditions of scientific work in the third-cultural milieu in which visitors work at American universities are primary determinants of their ideas and activities. My working hypothesis was that conditions of work in the third culture of science—specifically, in the milieux selected for study—are not conducive to the expansion of ecumenical consciousness, and that they do not stimulate the development of significant cooperative links between and among nations. This working hypothesis challenges the idea that the third culture of science is a microcosm of an emerging world community.

When I began this study, I did not share the optimism expressed by many scientists and students of science regarding the significance of international science as a world unifying force. Their optimism seemed to me to be based more on an idealized conception of science and scientists than on empirical evidence and theoretical analysis. In the course of my research, this ill-defined skepticism crystallized as I began to focus on the dysfunctional effects of professionalization and bureaucratization on scientific activities.

A Note on Method

A colleague, C. K. Vanderpool, and I conducted in-depth interviews with eighty-two visiting foreign scientists at three midwestern universities. Data were also gathered from visitors at four other midwestern universities using a mailed questionnaire. A stratified random sampling design proved impossible to implement because the only sampling lists available to us were inaccurate. This was not—and could not have been—discovered until we began our field interviews. Our response was to attempt to reach all those visitors who *were* available and who met our criteria for inclusion in the sample. We defined "visiting foreign scientists" as follows: all foreign citizens not considered students (e.g., visiting professors, lecturers, instructors, advanced research and teaching fellows and associates, visiting scholars, academic guests, specialists and all such foreign senior participants in educational programs) who are physical, biological, or social scientists; who were in residence at a university we selected as a research site; who were on campus for one month or longer during the academic year 1969–70 and summer session 1970, when the field work for this study was conducted; and who are permanent residents of a foreign country.[10]

Universities were selected as research sites if they had hosted 100 or more visiting foreign "scholars" (data for "scientists" were not available) each year for several preceding years, that is, universities which were *likely* to have 100 or more visiting foreign scholars during the 1969–1970 academic year.[11]

The limitations of using data on "scholars," and of restricting sampling to midwestern universities can be evaluated in part by noting that: (1) nearly three-quarters of the visiting foreign scholars in any given year between 1965 and 1972 were in the physical and life sciences, medical sciences, social sciences, and engineering; and (2) approximately one-third of these visiting scholars in any given year between 1965 and 1972 were in residence at midwestern universities and colleges. Three major universities with established graduate and professional schools were selected as interviews sites. These universities were characterized by: (1) some disparity in "quality rating" based on an index derived from the Carter report ratings; (2) some diversity in community setting; and (3) accessibility, determined by time and travel funds available for the study.[12]

Eighty-two of a projected 100 interviews were completed. A mailed questionnaire was then designed to broaden the data based on selected topics from the interview schedule. Additional information on the sampling procedures and on the characteristics of the sample are provided in the endnotes for this chapter.[13]

The cross-cultural experiences of the visitors can be summarized as follows: (1) most are citizens of the countries in which they were born; (2) nearly sixty percent had never visited a developed country for scientific study or research (excluding their present U.S. visit); more than eighty percent had never traveled to a developing country for study or research; (3) only 2.5 percent of the interviewees are children of a third-culture marriage, that is, the marriage of citizens of two different countries; (4) approximately ninety percent of the interviewees are married to persons whose country of birth is the same as their own.[14]

While these visitors had not been very mobile in physical terms, they had experienced some psychic mobility which stimulated their personal identification with the "international scientific community." Approximately seventy percent of the respondents experienced some form of interaction with foreign scientists in their home countries. However, the interaction was described as minimal and superficial. In many cases, such "interaction" consisted of attending one or a few lectures by a visiting American scientist.

More than seventy percent of the visitors in this sample are married; among interviewees, nearly eighty percent are married; and most of these visitors were accompanied to America by their families.

Conditions of Work

"Conditions of scientific work" include: subject matter (symbolic, physical, natural, social), mode (theoretical, experimental clinical, technological), orientation (basic, applied), work setting (laboratory, office, library), interaction set (works alone, with one or a few colleagues or assistants, in small or large groups), research costs and sources of funds. Visitors were predominantly physical and biological scientists working in theoretical and/or experimental modes. Their "basic science" orientation is reflected in the following data: (1) approximately ninety percent (base $n = 61$) of the interviewees characterized their work as "basic;"[15] (2) nearly sixty-five percent ($n = 50$) believe that their colleagues define them as basic researchers; and (3) more than half ($n = 74$) report that they would most like to be remembered for a "basic contribution to science." The pervasiveness of this orientation is further reflected in the importance of basic science as a factor determining questionnaire respondents' choices of research problems—nearly eighty percent ($n = 138$) consider it "very important;" only about four percent consider it "not at all important."

Most of the visitors—about two-thirds ($n = 123$)—report that they spend most of their working hours in a laboratory. Among interviewees, about one-quarter work alone, a few (six) work with one other person, and about twenty percent ($n = 80$) work in groups of eight or more scientists and supporting technicians.

Finally, almost half of the visitors ($n = 207$) report that their research depends to a great extent on large-scale funding, that is, funding by governments, large corporations, and major private foundations.

From these data, an idealized profile of the visiting foreign scientist can be sketched: a scientist working alone or in a small group with colleagues, pursuing what he/she and his/her colleagues define as basic research, with the objective of making a fundamental contribution to science; his/her interests center on theory and/or experimentation requiring consistent and continuous activity, with a good amount of time devoted to laboratory work.

These conditions of work tend to isolate the visitors from extra-scientific settings. The isolation is reinforced by several factors which are more or less directly related to conditions of work. The visitor is isolated from the teaching and administrative responsibilities and obligations associated with the full-time, permanent faculty role; he/she is isolated from the regular-faculty, career-tenure line. Scarcity of time (due, for example, to visa restrictions) and funds dictate a strict schedule of research and writing. "Supervisors" or "bosses" (two terms commonly used by interviewees when referring to their project directors), usually senior members of the tenured faculty, and/or department chairs actively intervene in situations that would require the visitor to take time out from his or her research or to be otherwise distracted; project directors and chairs help visitors with, for example, payroll problems, aquisition of research space and materials, and, to some extent, personal problems.

The visitor is further isolated by virtue of his/her non-citizen, transient status in the community. Many interviewees referred to this as an important asset of their role; it allows them more uninterrupted time for research than they would have in their home countries. The visitor has virtually none of the day-to-day responsibilities and obligations of the permanent members of a community or neighborhood.

The tight, rigorous work schedule makes it difficult for the visitor to become involved in the life of the community, and in the nonscientific "culture" of the United States. In some cases this isolation is reinforced by a spouse who, because he or she lacks professional ties in the community or university, and/or has language difficulties, does not encourage the visitor to "encounter the culture." The visitor is prevented or discouraged from eating out, sightseeing, or socializing regularly with people in the community. The objection raised by one spouse was that she did not want to be "embarrassed" in public. Her husband, a young Indian physical scientist, wanted to "get out more," to "eat hamburgers and drink Cokes," but would not do so because of his wife's feelings.

There are two interrelated consequences of working under such conditions: (1) isolation from non-work settings; and (2) role intensification—the role repertoire of the visitor is limited; science defines a major portion of all his/her activities.

Role intensification is stimulated by the continuity of conditions of scientific work between the United States and the visitor's home country. The degree of continuity is indicated by interviewees' responses to the question: "Was there anything unanticipated or surprising about your work experience in the United States?" Nearly sixty percent said "No." Conditions of work in the United States were experienced as essentially similar to work conditions in their home countries. The differences encountered were rarely differences in the conditions of work discussed above. A visitor from England, for example, commented on the relatively poor quality of laboratory equipment at his host university; the equipment there is purchased by the department or university, whereas he was used to constructing or supervising the construction of his own equipment in a campus workshop. Several scientists from developing countries commented on the greater accessibility of high quality equipment and materials in the United States, and the higher degree of "professionalism" among their American colleagues in contrast to the "poor scientific attitude" of their home country colleagues. But "conditions of work," while they may have been experienced as more nearly ideal for some visitors, were not significantly discontinuous with their home country experiences. Encountering a more nearly ideal environment for research work, in fact, appears to support the expectations of visitors who have learned what a "good" scientific environment should be like, but have not worked in one until coming to the United States. The differences, in any case, between conditions of work in the U.S. and those in the home country appear to be primarily differences which stimulate role intensification. The more ideal work environment may stimulate the visitor to invest himself fully into his/her work, thus furthering isolation and role intensification.

A more ideal "technology" (more easily accessible and of higher quality) may make work more satisfying and encourage the visitor to spend longer hours working than he/she is used to. The evidence for this in terms of a comparison of work involvement in the U.S. and in the home country is not, however, unequivocal. There is a difference in perceived patterns of authority here and in the home countries of respondents. Sixty percent of the respondents ($n = 79$) expressed an awareness of such a difference. They reported that their relationships with superiors in their host departments were more "democratic" than their relationships with superiors in their home country departments. Their American chairs and project directors encouraged and supported their research to a greater extent than was true of home country counterparts.

Tendencies to social isolation and role intensification are not conducive to stimulating and/or reinforcing cognitive and behavioral involvement with social change. Even where interviewees expressed a desire to learn more about the United States, they indicated how little time they had for actually doing so. Several interviewees noted, outside the context of the interview proper, their need to "get away on weekends to relax." Among this small sub-sample, activities selected for weekends tended to reinforce off-the-job social isolation: hiking alone, or in small groups, for example, was a favorite form of leisure for several of these respondents. Approximately fifty-six percent of questionnaire respondents ($n = 134$) felt that "every scientist and scholar should be directly involved in the decision making processes of his/her home country." Almost sixty-seven percent of respondents ($n = 215$), however, are distinguished by their lack of involvement in non-scientific organizations and activities at all socio-political levels—neighborhood, community, and national. Still another indication of their lack of socio-political involvement is the fact that only about eight percent of the questionnaire respondents ($n = 134$) are members of professional associations organized around the goal of promoting social responsibility in science. Most interviewees explained that they were "too involved in work" (here and in their home countries) to participate in extra-scientific activities.

Work, even in a third-cultural setting, can narrow rather than broaden an individual's experiences and perspectives. The disparity between the actual role of the visiting foreign scientists and the role imagined or wished for by many students of science and society is sufficient on the basis of what little evidence has been accumulated to warrant a closer examination of the consequences of international education, exchange programs, and related linkage systems than has hitherto been undertaken. The work role of the visitor, intimately linked to American "basic science," is rarely defined by the visitor or hosts specifically in terms of the visitor's potential contribution to his/her home country's development, or to world development.

What of the visitor's work role in relation to constructing links (scientific as well as more general "cultural" links) between America and his/her home country? Except for scientific (and other) elites, such links appear to be fragile. Once the visitor returns to his/her home country, his/her immediate situation takes priority over his/her host country experiences. To the extent that American scientists remain a part of his/her network, they do so in a predominantly if not exclusively professional way.[16] Visitors do not, in any case, appear peculiar in the extent to which they manifest a concern for or orientation to societal or global change. Their "international outlook" gives no evidence of being especially extensive or deeply internalized in comparison to what one might expect to find among other professionals.[17] This problem is discussed further below.

Social Organization and Ideology

In the process of professionalization, an occupation becomes "relatively colleague orientated."[18] The goals of professionalization are to limit the impact of subjective elements on performance and service, and to develop, maintain, and police standards of performance and service. Not incidentally, professional associations explicitly orient themselves to raising and maintaining the status of their members in the community and in society.

Carr-Saunders viewed professionalization as "one of the hopeful features of the time."[19] But the tendency toward occupational demarcation or "closure" in the professionalizing process creates an easily actualized potential for subordinating reason to dogma, and service to the community (or society, or humanity) to self-service. The "grim fight for status" and the general dictates of professionalism allow the scientists to exempt themselves from social responsibility. Indeed, Horowitz has argued that the price of professional training may ultimately be the loss of any capacity for objectivity.[20]

The significance of the dysfunctions of professionalization is increased with the recognition that they dovetail with the dysfunctions of bureaucratization. These two processes are linked, at least to the extent that they are concomitant, in the modern history of industrializing societies. Professionalization has been associated with "the increasingly specialized division of labor, the explosion of knowledge, and the rising demand for expertise in the management of a highly technical and highly bureaucratized society."[21] The convergence of the dysfunctions of professionalization and bureaucratization implies a tendency in occupations toward closure and dogma—an ethnocentrism of work, and a decrease in the capacity of organizations and individuals to respond to problems in creative, critical and socially responsible ways. The medical profession may well represent a standard for this model.[22] The visiting foreign scientist comes to work in an American science milieu which is highly bureaucratized and a source of international standards, symbols or images of professionalism in science. Under these conditions, "science for its own sake" is institutionalized as part of the ideology of professional scientists. By defining themselves as "basic scientists," interviewees effectively negated their own expressions of social responsibility. When asked whether they felt a sense of social responsibility for the possible social consequences of their research, nearly sixty percent of *all* respondents replied "definitely;" approximately thirty percent indicated "somewhat;" and about eleven percent responded "not at all" ($n = 214$). But when interviewees were probed on this question, they responded that since they were involved in "basic research," social responsibility was either: (1) inherent in what they were doing; or (2) irrelevant because there was no way to predict the consequences of their work. A thirty-three year old postdoctoral scientist said simply that he "believed in the efficacy of well-done research," and in the "goodness of basic research."

Among the minority of the scientists interviewed who noted direct links between their sense of social responsibility and their present research was a thirty-five year old biochemist who said he used to "synthesize compounds which no one else had, just for that reason." Now, however, he has a "better feeling" since he has recognized the relationship between enzyme reactions in tissues and the prevention and cure of illness. An interesting and unique response was offered by an advanced Ph.D. candidate in enzymology. He was certain his work, and work in the field generally, would have a "great influence" on society. But neither he, nor any other individual scientist is responsible for this influence—"Every scientist works on a particular problem which leads to one collective principle which is their influence." The important qualification he added was that the "*great* scientist *is* responsible," because "he" is more intimately and directly acquainted with and responsible for the "collective principle."

Only 6 percent of questionnaire respondents ($n = 140$) felt their research might have an adverse effect on humanity; 45 percent indicated "no foreseeable effect." This finding is consistent with interviewee conceptions of the basic scientist as, by definition, socially responsible. The pervasive faith in the "goodness" of basic science characteristic of respondents is further indicated by responses among interviewees to two questions: more than three-quarters of these scientists ($n = 79$) believe that scientists are important for achieving the ideal future they foresee for their home countries; and 70 percent feel that the ideal future they foresee will be achieved ($n = 70$). Their optimism about short-term developments in their home countries, as well as in the world, is consistent with their optimism about science and its function in society—basic research is good in and of itself, and contributes to the development of humanity.

To define one's research as "basic" can function as an explanation and justification for what amounts to an obligation to eschew responsibility for the present and future social consequences of one's scientific work. This interpretation is based on the idea that science is a social process involving human beings whose activities can be facilitated or obstructed by the way they organize, the resources they have available, and their relationships to other sectors of society. Nature and "reality" are not arbitrary; but science is not an autonomous, self-correcting, "pure" process which develops or progresses according to its own internal laws, shaped only by what is scientifically "real." At the very least, proponents of pure science, of the inherent "goodness" of basic research, should be willing to subject their ideas to the same forms of scientific inquiry scientists are expected to exhibit in their own research.

Since the late 1960s there has been a growing unwillingness among scientists to accept uncritically statements such as the following by a zoologist interviewee: "My role as a scientist, insofar as society is concerned, is negligible; what I produce is negligible in its consequences." Physicist Charles Schwartz, for example, issued a reminder to his colleagues that ". . . in order to decide whether some given organization is in fact free, pure, and disconnected from the troubles of the world is a matter for objective evaluation, not wish fulfillment." Barry Commoner, an advocate of social responsibility in science has noted that: "Scientists can no longer evade the social, political, economic, and moral consequences of what they do in the laboratory."[23]

Haberer was, at the time of this study, among the few students of science and society who had explicitly discussed the articulation of an ideology of science which focuses on the "intrinsic value of knowledge." He suggested that contrary to the views of the "theologians of science," modern science has manifested an "instrumentalism, characterized by an inversion of priorities whereby knowledge as a power incarnate became its primary impetus and the disinterested search for knowledge became of secondary importance."[24]

Implicated in what Gouldner calls "prestigious and 'high science' methodologies" and, working in an environment which stimulates social isolation and role intensification, the visiting foreign scientist may be more likely to fully internalize and express (or to do so to a greater degree) the ideology of science than his/her American colleague.[25] The younger visitors, and especially those who come to the United States from the periphery of the "international scientific community," may be, like some religious converts, uncritical promulgators of a strictly defined, sometimes caricatured conception of science and the scientific role.

Coser has argued that the "fairly unambiguous belief in progress" in science and society characteristic of the scientific community prior to the development of the atomic bomb is no longer adhered to. While this is certainly true for a certain segment of the scientific community, it is far from true of respondents in this study. In general, their view is consistent with the "conventional Western view of science;" science is conceived "as a source of cultural liberation and human welfare that is marred only occasionally, marginally, accidentally."[26]

Looking Backward: In Defense of Pure Tolerance

The concluding question on the interview schedule (slightly revised for the mailed questionnaire) was: "Looking over all your experiences here, in other countries, and back home, what effect have they had on the way you view the world?" Respondents invariably answered this question with some reference to "increased tolerance." This pattern can be interpreted in at least two ways: one, it can be viewed as a manifestation of an emerging post-modern global perspective. In that case, tolerance, following James Martin, would be conceived as the opposite of ethnocentrism; two, it can be interpreted as manifesting an unwavering commitment to the modern world, the world-as-it-is.[27] I am persuaded on the basis of my interviews that the latter is the more viable of the two interpretations.

Responses in the interview situation on this question were difficult to elicit. They were always formulated with reference to an international system, as opposed to a world system. Responses were consistently vague, even under probing. They were also vague among questionnaire respondents, many of whom failed to respond to the question at all. Many interviewees indicated that they had not given this type of question much thought; for most interviewees it was clear from the way they responded that they had not thought much about the impact of their third-cultural experiences. There was, in most cases, a visible "searching" (expressed in facial and other physical gestures) as the visitor sought to articulate changes that had taken place but were still poorly understood, or for changes he or she felt should have been experienced. Even with probing, responses were generally brief; they were broad, abstract, often far removed from day-to-day experience. Seventeen (20.8%) of the interviewees reported their experiences had "no impact" on them; 65 (79.2%) expressed an awareness of changes.

Nearly 60 percent of the interviewees reported developing a broader perspective on humanity. Most of their responses reflect in some degree an increased awareness of the unity of humanity. But they do not manifest an active commitment to and involvement with an increase in the interdependence among the peoples of the world. They take for granted the existence of a competitive system of sovereign nation-states. They do not manifest a self-conscious striving to confront and incorporate some form of post-modern ecumenical perspective. The consequences of their experiences appear, in general, pedestrian when contrasted with images created by prophets of a science-based, science-generated world community.

Final Observations on Visiting Foreign Scientists

The "prosaic activities" of visiting foreign scientists are related, from their perspective, to learning and improving research skills: this is the reason which 143 (64.5%) of the 222 respondents gave for coming to the United States.[28] American university officials and scientists appear to be more concerned with integrating visitors into an efficient research process than with "educating" them.[29] Whatever the relative emphasis in the particular work situation, "research efficiency" and "training" take precedence over "education" in Boulding's sense, that is, improving the capacity to learn. The NAS study of foreign postdoctorals cited above concluded (as I did) that the visitor's experience is not designed to promote national development in "countries of origin." The NAS survey indicates that "individual development" receives primary emphasis; but this is misleading, not only in terms of my findings, but in terms of the NAS data themselves. Indeed, the report raises the spectre of the "exploitation" of foreign postdoctorals. The report confirmed my conclusion that little effort has been made to adapt visitor experiences to home country needs. This is in part due to the fact that visitors participate in research that "is performed in response to American national needs."

One condition for Ecumene—world society, or world community— is the proper cultivation of science as an expression of human creative and critical intelligence. Science can be viewed as the process underlying progress, which Lenski has defined as raising the upper limit of the capacity "to mobilize energy and information in the adaptive process."[30] The concept "third culture of science" is critical because it emphasizes the link between human inquiry, cooperation, and progress. It can be viewed as the system within which science develops and diffuses in the process of ecumenization. Ideally, the third culture of science turns out scientists "with an enlarged outlook and heightened self-confidence in what they expect to accomplish, with the latest knowledge and technical skills and with a zest to innovate."[31] But this is not a consequence of cross-cultural activity that can be taken for granted. I have noted the dysfunctional impact of professionalization and bureaucratization on the third culture of science. It appears that cross-cultural participation in science (as in other human activities) can increase in scale without facilitating scientific growth, developmental processes, or the emergence of a world society.

The emergence and development of an international system of activities can stimulate a concern among participants for their system and their roles independent of national, international, and global issues and problems. Professional commitments can change from "local" to "cosmopolitan" as the locus of the profession becomes more global, without stimulating ecumenical commitments. It thus becomes possible for scientists under such conditions to respond to practical, applied, or technological problems of control and coordination in an interdependent world by simplifying, specializing, and standardizing in the context of increasingly narrow commitments to work, professional advancements and status, and national interest. The loss of diversity entailed in such a process poses a threat to the evolutionary potential of human culture.[32]

More optimistically, the experiences of the visitors may stimulate a commitment to work and profession that transcends conventional commitments to neighborhood, community, and society. Such a commitment, with the marginal status it entails, may be a precondition for arousing a post-modern, ecumenical orientation.

Toward an Anthropology of Science

In retrospect, my survey research on the third culture of science was also a prelude to appreciating, advocating and undertaking more fully anthropological field studies of science. In this chapter, I sketch the rationale for and the nature of an ethnographic or anthropological approach to science. The significance of this approach lies not merely in the obvious fact that it puts us in touch with scientific practice but that it helps to reveal the social nature of scientific knowledge. The importance of the anthropology of science for the sociology of objectivity cannot be exaggerated. A hands-off approach to science could never give us the kind of understanding we need in order to pursue what Marx called "human science." Dealienation, demythification, and demystification are keys to this kind of understanding, and the anthropology of science is the key to dealienating, demythifying, and demystifying science, and especially scientific knowledge. In order to set the stage for an introduction to the anthropology of science, I will have to travel briefly (but I hope constructively) over some old ground.

For some observers and practitioners of science, the scientist is an objective, rational, disinterested, dispassionate person who has been trained and educated to crystallize direct encounters with "things in the world" into "terms that refer." This is a portrait of the scientist as a naive realist. The naive realist has been described in somewhat greater detail by Mary Hesse; for such a scientist,

> . . . there is an external world which can in principle be exhaustively described in scientific language. The scientist, as both an observer and a language-user, can capture the external facts of the world in propositions that are true if they correspond to the facts and false if they do not. Science is ideally a linguistic system in which true propositions are in a one-to-one relation to facts, including facts that are not directly observed because they involve hidden entities or properties or past events or far distant events. These hidden events are described in theories, and theories can be inferred from observation, that is, the hidden explanatory mechanism of the world can be discovered from what is open to observation. Man as scientist is regarded as standing apart from the world and able to experiment and theorize about it objectively and dispassionately.[33]

The naive realist scientist "stands apart from the world." Implicitly or explicitly, such a scientist is placed or places him/herself "outside of" and "above" ordinary mortals. In such a scientist's world, all acts and thoughts are pure and value-neutral or value-free. But even though this scientist is portrayed as someone who transcends earthly categories of good and bad or right and wrong, an aura of benevolence is cast upon him/her. The scientist's work is value-neutral, but it is carried out in the interest of furthering human knowledge and contributing to the development of civilization.

The naive realist is painted in the Heavenly Discourse of observers such as worshipful philosophers, awed journalists and loving biographers. The scientists who portray themselves in naive realist terms are generally "elder statesmen" who confidently interpolate across memory gaps, and romanticize youthful exploits. Outsiders and insiders in this realm of story-telling ritually cater to the public's and the scientific community's need for heroic figures. This leads to the Ivory Snow picture of science and scientists. But some observers (insiders and outsiders) have seen a darker side of science. G. K. Chesterton got a glimpse of this darker side and he wrote:

> I find it extremely difficult to believe that a man who is obviously uprooting mountains and dividing seas, tearing down temples and stretching out hands to the stars, is really a quiet old gentleman who only asks to indulge his harmless old habit and follow his harmless old nose.[34]

A 1618 engraving by Johann Theodore de Bry portrays the hermetic philosopher, soon to trade in his robes for the laboratory coat of the modern scientist, following in the footsteps of Nature. Nature is a woman; not incidentally, she is not old, or disfigured, or disabled; she is mature, attractive, healthy in appearance. The hermetic philosopher appears to be older, and is less handsome. He carries a staff and a lamp. These are useful tools for finding and following Nature's path. But, as Carolyn Merchant has pointed out, the staff can also be used to prod her, and the lamp to probe her. And, clearly, those tools could also be used to beat and burn her. The seduction-rape theory of science suggested here is more explicitly expressed in the work of the nineteenth century sculptor Louis-Ernest Barrias (1841–1905). Barrias has produced a number of statues of women baring their breasts or lifting their skirts. One of these statues, located in L'École de Médecine, Rue de la Sorbonne, Paris, bears the inscription: "la Nature se devoilant devant la Science." Sooner or later, these artistic representations suggest, the scientist persuades Nature to bare secrets, or coerces her into revealing herself.[35]

Historically, the "lighter" side of tales of science has tended to overshadow the "darker" side; and from that "lighter" side, social scientists inherited "obvious" notions that strongly influenced the development of the sociology of science from the 1930s to the early 1970s. The most important idea in this inheritance—the central dogma—was that scientific *knowledge* is based on the direct representation of the external world. (There was some willingness to modify this notion for the *social* world; but the dogma was strictly adhered to for the *physical* world). The central dogma effectively barred a sociology of scientific knowledge. Associated with the central dogma was a set of taken-for-granted dichotomies: social and cognitive factors are separated aspects of scientific practice; so are facts and theories, facts and values, descriptions and interpretations, subjects and objects. More generally, the idea that there are internal and external influences on science was widely accepted, along with the notion that these influences were mutually exclusive. External factors included social and cultural variables and conditions that could facilitate or obstruct scientific progress. But scientific progress itself was allegedly dependent on *non-social* internal influences—the inner logic of conceptual development, rationality, and deduction.

The important point about the view of science I have been rehearsing was not that it was clearly right or wrong, true or false—but rather that it was not grounded in *empirical studies* of scientific practice. The movement away from armchair and anecdotal reconstructions of science that served worshipful and ideological interests disguised as interest-free "epistemology" or "metascience" began in the early 1970s with critiques of idealistic and heroic histories of science, positivist philosophies of science, and functionalist sociologies of science. The intellectual roots of this movement can be traced to neglected or little known works and remarks by Marx, Durkheim, Spengler, and Ludwik Fleck. Important contemporary influences include Mary Douglas and Mary Hesse. Misreadings of Kuhn made his work a dominant influence on the development of a critical, empirical sociology of science. By the late 1970s, the movement from critiques to new modes of research and theory in science studies had spawned ethnographic and anthropological approaches to the study of scientific practice; it also stimulated the development of empirical philosophies of science and sociological histories of science. This chapter is concerned with what ethnographers and anthropologists of science have observed in the laboratory, and what they have concluded about science as a social and cultural process, and about scientific knowledge as a social product and a social construct.

As we explore the scientists' laboratories with our anthropological tools and perspectives, it will be useful to keep two things in mind. First, the anthropology of science, like the old sociology of science, deals with the social system and social relations of science. But, as a part of the new sociology of science, it tends to draw attention to the relatively neglected area of scientific knowledge. In this sense, it could be considered an exercise in empirical epistemology. Second, the anthropology of science does not necessarily lead to relativism. It does, however, relate knowledge claims to the social practices and situations of scientists in "thought collectives;" and anything that makes us suspicious or distrustful of a group, organization, or profession will tend to make us suspicious or distrustful of the things they produce and the claims they make for their products. This suggests at the very least the need to adopt a cautious and critical stance in relation to even the most self-evident claims and products of science.

From a slightly different perspective, the anthropology of science sharpens our awareness and understanding of the context within which "self-evident truths" are born and bred, and of the ways in which knowledge claims are grounded in particular levels of reality (or experience) and localities.

Laboratory Studies

Laboratory studies are widely referred to as *ethnographic* studies. The term "ethnography" tends to focus attention on the *methodological* aspects of studying laboratory life, and implies that the goals of the research are *primarily descriptive*. There is a long-standing tension among students of culture between the ethnographer as a scientist who describes and translates customs and the anthropologist as a general theorist of culture and humanity.[36] In order to foster an appreciation for the *cultural* focus of laboratory studies, and to avoid associating these studies with the untenable notion of pure descriptions, I will from here on refer to them as *anthropological* studies of science. This term also captures the diversity of on-site studies of scientific knowledge, practice, and culture.

"On-site studies" is probably a better shorthand description of "anthropology of science" than "laboratory studies." Some researchers do literally focus on life in a laboratory. Others treat the laboratory as one part of a larger cultural environment that may include professional meetings, seminar discussions, home life, and parties. Still others study settings which we can recognize as sites of scientific practice but not as "laboratories." All of these studies are based on the use of more or less standard ethnographic or broadly anthropological methods—observation (including participant observation), interviews, the analysis of conversations and written materials, and the description and analysis of tools, techniques and materials.

The degree of intimacy between the anthropologists and their sites and subjects varies. Latour and Woolgar's detached "Observer" (a heuristic device) is a fictional anthropologist who is ignorant of scientific culture; their study thus represents the low intimacy extreme. High intimacy is a feature of McKegney's "participant-observer" approach, and the "hermeneutic circle" created by Zenzen, myself, and the laboratory scientists we worked with. Researchers in this field also vary in terms of the degree to which they conform to paradigmatic notions about how anthropologists work and how they report their findings. Sharon Traweek, on the one hand, is the model anthropologist. She has spent several years "in the field" studying the culture of high energy physicists. Karin Knorr-Cetina's work, on the other hand, is less readily recognized as an example of traditional anthropology; she herself describes her work as "empirical epistemology."[37]

Latour and Woolgar use the term "anthropology of science" to draw attention to the following "distinctive features" of their work:

> Firstly, the term anthropology is intended to denote the preliminary presentation of accumulated empirical material . . . we aim to provide a monograph of ethnographic investigation of one specific group of scientist . . . Secondly . . . , we attach particular importance to the collection and description of observations of scientific activity obtained in a *particular setting* . . . .Thirdly, our use of "anthropology" denotes the importance of bracketing our familiarity with the object of our study.[38]

The important issue Latour and Woolgar raise is the significance of "strangeness." They make an argument for strangeness as a crucial source of insights about insiders by outsiders. But other anthropologists of science, such as McKegney, adopt an "insider" or "acquainted" approach to understanding science. These are differences found in more traditional arenas of anthropological discourse and point to a general problem of interpretative and explanatory authority.

Anthropological Authority

Three stages in the development of anthropological authority can be identified by examining the development of the *role* of anthropologist/ethnographer: the nineteenth century *amateur* (missionaries, adventurers); the early twentieth century *professional vanguard* (natural scientists who created the *anthropologist role*); and the later *professional specialists*.[39]   The professional vanguard actually stressed an *ethnographic* approach to the study of culture. This vanguard was made up of men like Alfred Hadden, a zoologist, Franz Boas, a physicist, Walter Spencer, another zoologist, and Rivers, an experimental psychologist. They conceived ethnography as a scientific approach to cultural analysis. The first generation of full-fledged anthropologists who followed in the footsteps of Boas and others retained this orientation to a science of culture based on a physical science model.

The most prominent specialist in the first generation of anthropologists trained as social scientists was Bronislaw Malinowski. (Still, he also had a background in chemistry and physics.) I have before me a photograph showing Malinowski the "anthropologist of science" posing with the "head" of the "laboratory" he studied. Actually, he is posing with his informant, a sorcerer. His dominating presence and stance is representative of his exploitative relationships with his "native subjects." In another photograph (circa 1917), we see "the ethnographer at work." It is Malinowski in Omarakana, writing in his tent while the "natives" observe from outside.[40]

Malinowski had a feeling of ownership about "his natives." He has not discovered their island but he will be the first to experience it artistically and master it intellectually. The limitations of Malinowski's "go native" approach are revealed in his diary. He writes about longing for white civilization and white womanhood; and the "niggers" who surrounded him received the "outpourings of aggression" with which he relieved his frustrations. Here again is the darker side of science; it lurks beneath the lighter side that invests Malinowski's reports with authority. Here, authority rests on claims about being *scientific*.

Two other not always distinct traditional sources of anthropological authority are *experience* and *interpretation*. Experiential authority is based on having "been there" and participated in the native culture. This is the basis, for example, of Margaret Mead's anthropological authority. The extent of participation varies. It can include initiation into the culture. In order to establish their experiential authority, Marcel Griaule and Michel Leins sacrificed chickens before the Kono altar at Kemeni, Africa (on September 6, 1931) as a condition for entering a sanctuary.

Interpretive authority is based on the philological model of "reading a text." Following Ricoeur's philological model, for example,

Clifford Geertz approached the study of culture as a problem in reading a text and giving an expert interpretation.

Traditional anthropological authority is based on an essentially exploitative relationship between expert and subject. And no matter how friendly or intimate the anthropologist becomes with his/her subjects, in the end one voice—the expert's voice—speaks in the lecture, article, or monograph that describes and interprets "native life."

Traditional anthropological authority has been challenged in the "new" ethnography/anthropology by arguments for *discursive* and *polyphonic authority*. Discursive authority recognizes the intersubjectivity of all speech, and the significance of the immediate performative context. This can still, however, lead in the end to one expert voice telling the story of a culture. Polyphonic authority provides a forum for many voices and many authors as outsiders and insiders together describe and interpret a culture.

The conflicts over interpretive and explanatory authority in general anthropology are reproduced in the anthropology of science. While the conflicts in the latter case are not as well defined or articulated as in the former, they are reflected in the variety of approaches used (from outsider/stranger to insider/intimate roles), and in the tension between ethnomethodological orientations and other forms of participant observation.

A quasi-ethnographic study brought June Goodfield, a philosopher and historian, into the laboratory of an "anonymous" scientist named "Anna."[41] The photograph on the cover of the paperback edition of Goodfield's book shows her perched on a laboratory bench looking down at her subject. "Anna" is seated, is wearing a white lab coat, and has her back to the camera. Erving Goffman might see some suggestive parallels in this photograph and the photographs of Malinowski "at work." One parallel, certainly, is that in both cases it seems pretty clear to us who is the "anthropologist" and who is the "informant."

In anthropology of science, as in contemporary anthropology in general, this is not always the case. For in addition to the points I raised earlier about anthropological authority, anthropology of science raises issues about the nature of the relationship between anthropologists and "natives" who are members of the same culture, the same social stratum, and even the same profession. Finally, anthropologists must always deal with the interaction between "folk sociologies/anthropologies" and their own "professional sociologies/ anthropologies." Some anthropologists of science have approached "their natives" in a traditional, even Malinowskian, manner. Others have not so much "gone native" as sought to establish a "hermeneutic circle" in which the roles of "anthropologist" and "native" become inextricably intertwined, anthropology and native scientific practice become interlaced, and anthropologist and native develop a shared interest in telling the story of laboratory life.

A Note on Anthropological Epistemology

There are three basic theories about the nature of ethnographic or anthropological inquiry. Implicitly or explicitly, they all have to manage a double-bias situation: anthropological inquiry has to manage the bias of the observer's cultural perspective; and the bias associated with the role he/she is given within the group under study. They also have to deal with the emic-etic distinction: try to see the world as the "native" sees it (emic), or "objectively" through their own eyes (etic).

The *positivistic* approach assumes (a) the possibility of objectifying others, and (b) the ability to control and repeat observational procedures. The *phenomenological* approach assumes (a) the possibility of mutual identification of observer and observed ("becoming" the other in the process of observing him or her), and (b) recognition of the equivalence of the observer by the one observed. *Subjectivist positivism*, a frame of reference position proposed by Rik Pinxten, assumes that (a) observation is theory—and culture—laden; (b) observation is interaction; and (c) observation implies mutual confidence. In discussing research on the Dogon, Pinxten writes:

> What is presupposed on the part of the Dogon is a certain amount of information, built up gradually for sure on the personality and the culture of the ethnographer. It is with this information at hand that they allow the white man to gradually "observe more and more" of the cultural system . . .[42]

In this case, the reference is to giving the anthropologist access to higher and higher levels of symbolic knowledge systems.

Pinxten's "subjectivist-positivist" is compatible with the concept of a polyphonic anthropology; and these two notions are embodied in the idea of a *reflexive* anthropology. In the end, it is reflexive anthropology that promises to fundamentally reverse our notions about our own professional activities by *incorporating* the anthropological imagination within the world of everyday work.

The Social Construction of Facts

We now appreciate that a text can have as many readings as, if not *readers*, then reading *thought collectives*. So I will not argue that Malinowski anticipates or preempts current notions about the social construction of facts in the quotations to follow; but it is at least interesting to note certain parallels. At the same time, it will become clear that Malinowski, like Marx and many others, could not clearly resolve the tension between a sociological conception of knowledge, truth, and belief, and a conviction about the fundamental value of scientific methods.

Malinowski was one of the founders of scientific anthropology. But he was at the same time a strong critic of the cult of the "pure fact." It is not at all possible, he claimed, to go into the field, gather up some "facts as you find them," wrap them in a blanket, and carry them home to the theorist to use in constructing his/her generalizations and theories:

> . . . there is a social dimension to a belief, and this must be carefully studied as it moves along the social dimension; it must be examined in the light of diverse types of minds and of the diverse institutions in which it can be traced.[43]

The tension arises when Malinowski claims that belief "does not obey the laws of logic":

> . . . the contradictions, divergences, and all the general chaos pertaining to belief must be acknowledged as a fundamental fact.[44]

Furthermore, he writes:

> Science, even as represented by the primitive knowledge of savage man, is based on the normal universal experience of everyday life, experience won in man's struggle with nature for his subsistence and safety, founded on observation, fixed by reason. Magic is based on specific experience of emotional states in which man observes not nature but himself, in which the truth is revealed not by reason but by the play of emotions upon the human organism. Science is founded on the conviction that experience, effort, and reason are valid; magic in the belief that hope cannot fail nor desire deceive. The theories of knowledge are dictated by logic, those of magic by the association of ideas under the influence of desire. As a matter of empirical fact the body of rational knowledge and the body of magical lore are incorporated each in a different tradition, in a different social setting and in a different type of activ-

ity, and all these differences are clearly recognized by the savages. The one constitutes the domain of the profane; the other, hedged round by observances, mysteries, and taboos, makes up half of the domain of the sacred.[45]

Durkheim argues that even the so-called "laws of logic" are social through and through. Is there a contradiction here between Durkheim and Malinowski? I would say yes, although this is in a sense a moot point. Durkheim and Malinowski both express constructivist viewpoints. But Durkheim seems better prepared to make the leap to contemporary constructivism than Malinowski.[46]

Laboratory Life

The stress laboratory life researchers place on *social practice* has led them to challenge a number of traditional ideas in science studies: The separation of social and cognitive factors, the internal/external dichotomy, the characterization of scientific knowledge as purely descriptive or cognitive, and the relevance of concepts such as "scientific community," "invisible college," and "specialty group." Instead, they portray science as a constructive, socially-situated (contextual, indexical), discursive enterprise. In what follows, I review these ideas and discuss other aspects of the lab studies reported to date. This "paradigm" completes the portrait of the contemporary science studies landscape I sketched in earlier chapters.

The Constructivist Paradigm. Constructivism focuses attention on how scientific objects are produced and reproduced at research sites. There are five features of social production that have been identified in the lab studies. First, the reality scientists operate on is *artifactual.* That is, scientists themselves manufacture the reality they study. They create conditions, select materials, and rely on conceptual and instrumental tools constructed by other scientists to "observe and analyze" their manufactured reality. Thus, they do not—and in principle, cannot—observe naked nature directly.

Second, laboratory activity is *decision-impregnated*: scientists are constantly selecting courses of action, instruments, chemical compounds, and so on from among sets of alternatives.[47] But earlier selections also reappear later as tools, methods, and interpretations; thus, scientific objects are *decision-impregnating* as well as decision-impregnated.

The third aspect of the social production of science is the *transformation* of "knowledge claims" into "facts." This is illustrated, for

example, in the transformation of statement types discussed by Latour and Woolgar. The laboratory "game" involves moving statements through five stages, effecting modality changes at each stage
until all traces of authorship have been deleted and the Type 5 statement stands as an unqualified "fact." Type 1 statements are "lin-
guistically marked conjectures;" knowledge claims by an author are
designated Type 2 statements; Type 3 statements are "qualified general assumptions" ("X is generally assumed to be . . ."); and Type 4
statements are "uncontroversial 'facts' still associated with an author."[48] Zenzen and I also show how various drafts of a report on a
set of experiments progressively incorporate statements that are
more technical, more general, more conclusive, and less controversial.[49] In brief, scientific rhetoric becomes progressively *objectified*
as we move from shop talk to published papers. Scientific work involves transforming selections into non-selections, the subjective
into the objective, and "the fabricated" into the "the found." Scientists separate the "natural" from the "social" by (temporarily) ruling
out certain selections and choosing others.[50]

The fourth aspect of the social production of science is that *social
and cognitive factors are inextricably intertwined*. The more closely
the "cognitive" core of science has been examined, the more it has
been revealed to be a thoroughly social accomplishment. The weak
form of this idea merely draws attention to the fact that knowledge is
produced by social groups. The strong form states that the type of social group that produces knowledge affects the type of knowledge
produced.

The fifth aspect of the social production of science is *self-reference*.
Scientists are concerned with the conditions for reproducing science
(specifically, scientific practice). In addition to "accomplishing" or
"constructing" their findings (e.g., the status of results as "facts" or
"artifacts") they also construct epistemological meanings for those
findings. The constructivist stress on the primacy of *social practice* is
based on the notion that issues about facts and artifacts, facts and
truths, and philosophical reconstructions of scientific work and objects are social accomplishments. Thus, constructivism is neither subjectivist (it does not focus on science as a psychological, individual, or
egoistic and idiosyncratic phenomenon), nor naturalist (in the sense
that it does not make science a "natural" phenomenon accessible only
to the methods and theories of the natural sciences), nor relativist (in
the sense that it does not make the construction of scientific objects
radically independent of an "external" or "pre-existing" and recalci-

trant physical or natural world). The focus on social practice, then, can be seen as an attempt to develop an empirical epistemology.[51]

Indexicality encompasses a variety of ideas that tie facts to social settings. The decisions (selections) scientists make are conditioned and constrained by social contexts, available resources, opportunities that present themselves ("opportunistic logic"), the circumstances and occasions of scientific work, variations in the criteria used to select methods and materials, and the negotiations leading up to the identification of a scientific finding.[52] Knowledge, according to the constructivist interpretation, is then the sum of these decisions, selections, and conditions.

Laboratory constructions are products of "discursive interactions" aimed at and sustained by arguments among scientists *and non-scientists* inside and outside of the laboratory proper. The locus of this discourse is referred to by Knorr-Cetina as the "transscientific field." I have used the term "transepistemic" to refer to the more general field of epistemic activity. The critical feature of scientific organization is not the shared characteristics of group members but what gets *transmitted* between and among scientists and non-scientists within the transscientific field.

Knorr-Cetina links indexicality to indeterminacy in social action.[53] She points out that in thermodynamics and information theory, indeterminacy, partial independence of variables, and chance interference are conjectured to "occasion" the emergence of information and progressive (re)-organization.[54] Indeterminacy in science arises from the fact that contingencies at the research site and in the transscientific field are important determinants of the products of scientific work. This means that we cannot predict the outcomes of scientific work based on knowledge of the characteristics of participants and circumstances at the research site, or in the transscientific field. This indeterminacy undermines the efforts of philosophers of science who seek to identify a small number of criteria that guide scientific selections. It also means that sociologists of science cannot hope to fully account for scientific productions by specifying a relevant set of social, cognitive, internal, and external *factors*. On the other hand, indeterminacy may be a necessary condition for successful scientific work and a force for scientific change.

Linguistic practices, according to ethnographers of science, are "constitutive of the objects of science." This is illustrated in the transformation of scientific reasoning as scientists move from the laboratory to the scientific paper, a process that is paralleled in the transformations of statement types, and expressed in subtle shifts of agreement during conversations in the lab. Knorr-Cetina writes:

> Written statements are constantly reconstructed (qualified, transformed, framed, selected) in practical discourse, which means that the significance of the properties of written discourse *apart from* practical discursive reconstruction remains doubtful.[55]

Indeed, it appears that scientists do not themselves take written statements at face value. They are not persuaded in a simple, straightforward way by rhetorical "objectification" strategies. Rather, they tend to reconstruct what they read in terms of personal and institutional contexts.

A number of additional conjectures have been formulated by ethnographers of science:

1. metaphor does not play a key role in the origin of ideas in the laboratory; *analogical transfer* is much more important.[56]
2. the dependence on local opportunities makes laboratory work very much a *tinkering* exercise.
3. *interest* and *success* (as opposed to "truth") are key driving forces in scientific practice. The scientist starts from a solution or an opportunity for success, and moves on from there with the objective of "making things work." Perceived solutions push the research forward, in whatever directions opportunities for success may lie. Thus, the logic of science rests on what scientists *do* with reality.
4. There are no rationalities unique to science; just like everyday reasoning, scientific reasoning is practical, indexical, analogical, socially-situated, literary, and symbolic. In Latour's words:

> Scientific fact is the product of average ordinary people and settings, linked to one another by no special norms or communications forms. . .[57]

   What *does* distinguish scientists from other people is their reliance on inscription devices. The inscription devices modify the scale of the things scientists want to talk about; complex and unwieldy phenomena become transformed into "the inscription on a flat surface written in simple forms and letters."[58]
5. Scientific work is a process of *simplification* in the presence of constraints; certain things that have been done are *ignored*, and certain things are just *not done*.[59]

6. Contingencies (social, material, and symbolic) are not merely "externalities;" they are "constitutive of" scientific facts.[60] That is, scientific facts are actually "made up of," or manufactured out of contingencies.

Ethnomethodology has played a significant role in ethnographic studies of science. Lynch, in particular, has explored the relevance of this approach for science studies. Ethnomethodologists assume that people who are not sociologists pose and deal with sociological questions as a matter of course in their day-to-day activities. Lynch agrees with other students of laboratory life that "the products of scientific activity are inextricable from the social contexts of their production . . ." But this raises the further question, Lynch argues, of "how the relevance of any of the potentially endless varieties of social contingency is to be established in concrete instances of scientific work:"

> Commonly, social studies of science specify such contingent relationships by relying on the established methods of the social science disciplines, while ignoring the fact that the natural scientific disciplines studied themselves include inquiries which specify such relationships as a necessary part of their ordinary practice.[61]

One of Lynch's papers reports an analysis of a conversation in the lab which, he argues, shows how "critical inquiry operates as a practical feature of natural science research rather than being a privilege of professional social scientists."[62] In general, then, Lynch concludes that a "sociological account" of laboratory life is an integral part of laboratory life itself, and is inseparable from the development of a "technical account" of the motives for, directions of, and results of scientific research. Scientific facts are constructed in terms of the discovery, articulation, and utilization of the social aspects of laboratory life.

Gil Peach has looked at how organizational processes and interests influence the production of "applied statistical products." Peach has studied the production and utilization of statistics in a governmental health and housing agency, a power company, a Public Interest Research Group, and a private foundation concerned with urban public services. He has worked as an applied statistician in these organizations. Participant observation has been guided by a theoretical approach that focuses on actual practice, Habermas' concept of cognitive interest, and Marx's views on work organization. Peach focuses on "the tension and interpenetration of professional and organizational interests in the creation and acceptance of applied statistics." According to Peach, the objectives, rules, and other characteristic features of statistics are cultural products, and the practice of statistics is a social practice.[63]

A Critical Look at the Lab Studies

Outsiders (non-anthropologists) have criticized the anthropologists for: (1) not writing "true" ethnographies; (2) overstating the "fictive" argument and conflating "facts" and "statements of facts;" (3) overdrawing the methodological and theoretical distinctiveness of lab studies relative to traditional and contemporary science studies; (4) taking science studies in the "wrong" direction (away from institutional studies, for example); and (5) supporting radical subjectivism and relativism.[64]

Insiders have also argued about whether given lab studies qualify as "ethnographies," and indeed whether they are even *sociological* (as opposed to, for example, *philosophical*) studies.[65] In addition, Woolgar has argued that the lab studies tend to be *instrumental*, that is, focused on producing surprising, ironic, demystifying news about science. He defends the alternative of a *reflexive* ethnography that may incidentally produce "news," but that is designed primarily as "an occasion for reflecting upon, and reaching a greater understanding of, those aspects of our own culture that we take for granted."

Knorr-Cetina has replied to Latour's criticisms by stressing that her work is "ethnography of *knowledge*;" she is not interested in doing ethnographies of what in orthodox sociology of science used to be referred to as "the social system of science." Her orientation to an *empirical* epistemology has, she claims, mistakenly been interpreted as "philosophy" of science.

Another area of contention between Latour and Knorr-Cetina is the utility of the "credibility model" proposed by Latour and Woolgar. Knorr-Cetina describes this as a quasi-economic exchange model: "Money is converted into arguments, arguments into articles, articles into recognition and recognition into (grant) money." But, she argues, like all earlier exchange models of science, this one ". . . insulates the content of scientific knowledge from the influence of society" except through *mediations*. Her book, *The Manufacture of Knowledge*, Knorr-Cetina writes, can be read as an implicit and explicit critique of *Laboratory Life* (which Latour co-authored); "the *making* of knowledge versus scientists' lab life, *reasoning and inter-*

pretation versus inscription, transscientific or *transepistemic fields* versus credibility cycles:"

> With my version of constructivism, I wanted to raise the possibility of dissolving reference into practices, the practices of fabricating bits and pieces of the world-to-be from, among other things, brute pre-interpreted matter. Antecedent "reality" continuously enters the picture, for example as the source material from which worlds-to-be are wrested. But these antecedent realities do not provide for the reference; rather they provide for material (matter-based) practices of achieving certain technical effects.[66]

Philosopher Thomas Nickles also tries to rein in relativism by arguing that there *is* an antecedent *reality*, but that there is no "antecedent description of the world (a *self*-description, as it were) which we are trying to approximate."[67]

Knorr-Cetina's remarks essentially capture my own reactions to the insider and outsider critics. I am, furthermore, aligned with Woolgar on the fundamental importance of a reflexive anthropology. In general, I view the lab studies and related "constructivist" approaches not as attempts to undermine realism but rather as ways of pursuing the full implications of the insight that facts are socially constructed and not *given* through a direct, privileged relationship between scientists and "things in the world." I am also concerned with not repeating the mistakes of earlier students of science by simply developing new stories about what science is "really" like without considering the human and value implications of doing science. That is, we need to develop ways of studying science *critically*; otherwise, all we can do is repeat old tales or tell new ones that turn out to be apologies for or worshipful psalms about science.[68]

What is the upshot of what we have observed in these laboratories? Students of laboratory life use terms such as *negotiation, circumstances, contingencies, opportunism, fiction, idiosyncrasy, rationalization, tinkering, common sense,* or *practical reasoning.* Their rhetoric can be (and sometimes is) a tool for criticizing science or trying to bring it down a peg or two. Sometimes it projects onto other scientists the ways of doing science and being a scientist that the anthropologist has internalized; or reflects common ways of doing and being that are characteristic of the contemporary scientific community. But the rhetoric doesn't have to be derogatory, merely projective, or relativistic. We can make sense out of our observations in the lab by seeing scientific practice as a process of creating order out of disorder. This idea is not so novel; it is used by François Jacob to describe natural selection and biological evolution, and by Ilya Prigogine and David

Bohm to describe happenings in the physical world. The point is that if we view scientific practice in this way (as opposed to seeing it as a simple process of *discovering* order), then the very words that seemed derogatory, to quote Bruno Latour, "start expressing the very nature of . . . scientific objects " or facts. We thus find ourselves on a path toward if still far from the goal of conceptualizing scientific facts as constitutively social because they embody a social history.

So we have at this point suspended a host of conventional dichotomies: social/technical, fact/artifact, internal/external, craftwork/ thought. We have come to view the scientist as a practical reasoner and thus suspended the distinction between common sense or everyday reasoning and scientific reasoning. And, reflexively, we ourselves have created order out of disorder; not in a lab like the scientists we studied but in a text. (Or perhaps, to some extent at least, we have been prompted to see disorder where we once saw order, and to create a new form of or level of order). We are on the threshold here of a revolutionary encounter with reflexivity. For in the end, we have been talking about scientists observing themselves. And it is this reflexive aspect of anthropology of science that will ultimately justify the methodology by helping us monitor changes in the social structure of inquiry that will facilitate or obstruct our activities as epistemic agents, and by helping us become conscious of hitherto unrecognized or unheralded dimensions of inquiry.

Constructivism, then, in a reflexive mode is not an outsider methodology or theory. It is not a "peep-show" epistemology. One does not, as Maslow put it,

> . . . look through the microscope or the telescope as through a keyhole, peering, peeping, from a distance, from outside.[69]

Such an "observer" has no right to be in the room "being peeped into." In reflexive constructivism, we are never "the enemy within."[70] It is at this stage of self-consciousness about ourselves as self-observers that we are best prepared to understand that indeed "Facts are a word of God" (as the anthropologist Maurice Leenhardt was reminded by his father, a pastor-cum-geologist). For, as Durkheim taught us, God is Society; and so, facts are the word of Society. Or, to follow Nietzsche:

> We are not thinking frogs, nor objectifying and registering mechanisms with their innards removed: constantly, we have to give birth to our thoughts out of our pain and, like mothers, endow them with all we have of blood, heart, fire, pleasure, passion, agony, conscience, fate, and catastrophe.[71]

6
Applied Science Studies and Science Policy

It seems inevitable that some students of science would sooner or later think about the "utility" of their research. In my case, opportunities and temperament have led me to consider the connection between science studies and science policy. In this chapter, I focus on the anthropology of science and science policy.

Anthropology of Science and Science Policy

The relevance of the anthropology of science for science policy is suggested by the intimate linkage between funding and the "essentials" of research revealed by on-site studies of working scientists. Consider, for example, the following dialogue reported by Law and Williams:

Watt.	What was interesting to you in our last discussion?
Williams.	What would be publishable, how that affects what you do.
Watt.	But I think it's the same question as what is valid and meaningful. I don't think it's a different question.
Morse.	I think they both occur when you reach a set of conclusions.
Gladstone.	They're a combination of results and . . . getting more money for the next research.[1]

Law and Williams argue that scientists do "market research" to assess the likely impact of their "products" on potential users. They use this market orientation in designing, packaging, and placing papers. Like other entrepreneurs, they combine resources to produce a paper that will optimize the return on their research investments.

The structure of a paper is influenced by "market conditions;" and this "helps to constitute the structure of knowledge, the status of the facts, and their relationship with other findings."

According to Latour and Woolgar, "grants" are one type of "capital" in the "cycle of creditability" through which all scientists move, converting one form of capital into another. Latour and Woolgar take seriously the fact that the scientists they interviewed discuss their work in quasi-economic terms:

> . . . scientists talked about data, policy and their careers almost in the same breath. They thus appeared to be working with a model of their own behavior which made no distinction between internal and external factors.[2]

Scientists' "calculations" about the direction they should take in their research and careers involve considerations about: (1) available funds; (2) the degree of positive feedback from colleagues and from "successes" in the laboratory; (3) general funding policies in different locations; and (4) the reception accorded publications. On the basis of this sort of evidence, Latour and Woolgar propose credit as a concept that makes it possible for sociologists to relate the various social relations of science. "Credit" refers to *rewards* (symbols of recognition by peers) and *credibility* (the ability to actually do science). "Credibility" seems to absorb "rewards;" the *cycle of credibility* then identifies ". . . the conversion between money, data, prestige, credentials, problem areas, argument, papers, and so on . . . each facet is but one part of an endless cycle of investment and conversion."[3] Listing grants on a curriculum vitae, for example, is a way of identifying how much of an investment has been made in the scientist to date. This reinforces other aspects of the scientist's credibility, such as his or her qualifications and position.

Scientists, then, are "investors of credibility." This leads to the "creation of a market:"

> Information now has value because . . . it allows the investigators to produce information which facilitates the return of invested capital.[4]

The "demand" side of the credibility market is the interest of "investors" in information which might increase the power of their inscription devices. The "supply" side is the information supplied by other investors. Supply and demand create value; the value of information commodities fluctuates in relation to supply and demand, the number of scientists in the market place, and producers' equipment.

The objective of scientific activity, according to the credibility hypothesis, is "to extend and *speed up the credibility cycle as a whole.*" The advantage of this model, according to Latour and Woolgar, is that it is independent of expressed motives. Scientists can *emphasize* one or another section of the cycle, they can consider any specific section to be the *objective* of their investment; but they have to go through *all* the sections of the cycle.

Funds can affect the research positions scientists find themselves in, and this in turn can influence the direction of research in a given field. Latour and Woolgar report numerous interviews in which scientists said that some experiment or line of inquiry "did not work," or that they were "getting nowhere." Such dead ends were followed by a period of "drifting" that continued until the scientist happened upon something—an instrument, method, collaborator, or idea—that worked:

> They were then able quickly to modify the situation in the field. Some statements which they discredited were never taken up by others. They be came strong, they gained weight. They obtained more funds, attracted more assistants, generated arguments. *The field was modified around their new position.*[5]

Latour and Woolgar stress that the "rational production of science" and the "political calculation of assets and investments" cannot be separated. Scientists are *strategists* and *politicians*; and the better they are at being strategists and politicians, "the better the science they produce." They are, however, always *employees*. Scientific capital cannot be sold or bequeathed, and only rarely can it be directly exchanged for monetary capital. Even if they achieve a certain amount of independence, or become "employers" themselves, they remain employees because they are always managing borrowed money from the private or public sector. The use of the term "borrowed" in this context seems inappropriate; but the alienation of scientists from the means of scientific production is a general feature of work in modern industrial societies.[6]

In spite of the fact that Knorr-Cetina is critical of "the credibility model," her work basically supports Latour and Woolgar's conclusion that scientists *as scientists* are *political strategists*. Thus while Latour and Woolgar do not get to the heart of scientific *knowledge* in the way that Knorr-Cetina wants to, their stress on the impossibility of separating *scientific* and *political* agendas seems to be consistent with Knorr-Cetina's objectives.

Knorr-Cetina focuses on *resource-relationships* rather than "credit:"

> Resource-relationships are at stake, for example, when money is to be distributed among scientists . . . when a speaker is to be chosen for a scientific lecture, or when a result produced by a scientist is incorporated into the research of others. The respective decisions usually relate to the value of the prospective resource (whether a candidate or a candidate's work) in the ongoing games of those who make the selections.[7]

The *transscientific field* is the locus of cooperation as well as conflict and competition over imposing, expanding, and monopolizing resource-relationships. These relationships are the same whether they link scientists to other scientists or to non-scientists.

A resource-relationship is a form of symbolic relationship. It has to be continuously and generally "accomplished" (created and sustained) in the reciprocal social practices of members of transscientific fields. There are three aspects to this reciprocal accomplishment. First, what is to count as a resource is negotiated and re-negotiated. Definitions are not stable but (more or less temporary) *stabilizations*. Second, resource relationships must be renewed:

> In its most vulgar version, this phenomenon can be seen in the disproportionate amount of effort which some research groups put into getting their grants and research projects renewed.[8]

Third, scientists must be continuously engaged in *"building, solidifying* and *expanding* resource-relationships."

The "oscillations between conflict and cooperation" are strikingly illustrated, according to Knorr-Cetina, in "the art of writing a grant proposal." Scientists seeking research support are faced with two opposing tasks: on the one hand, they must be "as concrete, substantial and precise as possible;" on the other hand, they must say as little as possible about their proposed research. The first task reflects the fact that there is "a surplus of proposals in relation to a diminishing supply of grants;" the second task arises "from the need to protect one's ideas from peer reviewers, who could well be the most dangerous competitors in the area:"

> Holding back a grant proposal for several months before accepting or rejecting it gives a competitor a significant advantage in time, particularly if the proposal provides a significant hint about the direction of research in question. Since there are often only two or three "strong" groups working on a given topic, such fears are by no means unwarranted (especially since the competitors are the ones most likely to conduct the review).[9]

The degree of consistency between the selections or discussions made at various levels and stages of laboratory life and the transscientific connections of science are actively constructed by scientists and non-scientists:

> Such effort is manifest in attempts to "figure" the sorts of results that would interest a financing agency, or efforts to work on "relevant" and "timely" (i.e., easily published) subjects. It crops up in the effort to keep abreast of new developments in order to stay on top of changing contextual conditions of research. It can be found in social control and the enforcement strategies (such as peer review procedures) used to assure consistency. And it appears, especially in recent years, in scientific policy or government regulations concerning science and scientific priorities.[10]

This idea has been expressed more generally in terms of the constant effort that is necessary on the part of members of any social group to reduce complexity as a condition of survival. Star has studied this process of "simplification" in scientific work. She interviewed neuroscientists in the course of her participant observation in a psychophysiological research laboratory.

Star's premises about the nature of scientific work are consistent with the constructivist stress on social practice. In order to understand *work*, she asserts, we *must* take the *products* of work into account; but we must do more. Work is *interactive* and *processual*—it involves "joint effort over time." The *meaning* of work is continuously negotiated and renegotiated by workers and consumers. This "joint work" results in the creation of products, the construction of meanings, and the delineation of a "social world."

Star, like other students of scientific practice, has been struck by the way certain kinds of contingencies she identifies as "constraints" direct the process of simplifying research findings.[11] There may not be enough *time* to examine all the details of the data. *Communicating* with scientists in other fields and non-scientists might require simplifying explanations in order to maximize intelligibility. Conclusions might have to be arrived at too quickly, or articulated sketchily, due to *pressures from granting agencies* or university departments. Confronted with these constraints, scientists regularly employ *formatting* and *deleting* in order to get the work done.

Simplification work involves: (1) telling your research story in a way that fits the demands of a target audience (formatting); and (2) editing in written presentations, and glossing over in oral presentations (deleting). A third form of simplification work occurs when one group in the research setting appropriates a set of tasks, then selects one aspect of the research to focus on and ignores other aspects.

Star found that in response to deadlines imposed by funding agencies, for example, the scientists she interviewed were able to produce "precise" results. But when questioned about why *particular* results were chosen from the multitude of results produced in a given research program, they became uneasy and unclear about their choices. They were "forced to act with certainty," but they were unaware of "the general context of choice." Researchers are often forced to, as one of Star's respondents put it, "pick a result, any result" in the face of pressure from granting agencies. For example, Star reports that one research group had initiated a funded project by collecting a large amount of data. The deadline for a continuation proposal, in their view, produced a "rather arbitrary selection of marketable conclusions" for the funding agency.

Similar pressures affect how science proceeds in the laboratory. Confronted with piles of "basic data" and lacking any "strong hypotheses," scientists reported feeling pressured "to specify relationships within the data, sometimes without obvious rationales." According to Star, funding agencies specify formats for presenting results that may not be congruent with the scientists' methodological and substantive requirements. This formatting pressure can be increased if the funding agency establishes a definite schedule for the presentation of results and for modes of presentation the scientists consider "over-simplified." Space limitations for proposals and research reports were another source of pressure to "format" and "delete."

One of Star's respondents distinguished between research designed to meet funding agency demands regarding topics and modes of presenting results ("opportunistic"), and research in which scientists set their own goals and adhere to them regardless of the "vicissitudes of funding."

When a research group has to deal with a number of funding agencies and funding trajectories at the same time, Star notes, there is inevitably "even more fitting, squeezing, and selecting to create compatible multiple formats;" most funding agency formats assume single-funding, single trajectory research. The simplest format among those required by various agencies tends to determine the nature of simplification work on research designs, objectives, and results in proposals and reports.

A Ph.D. candidate in the study Zenzen and I conducted referred to contractual obligations with funding agencies as "ropes attached to research funding." He discussed the many pressures he experienced as he sought directions for his research, including the pressure to choose fundable research. Laboratory life is an adaptation, and the characteristics of laboratories vary in accordance with whether adaptation occurs in an "environment of scarcity" or an "environment of abundance." Environments of scarcity are not necessarily poor environments for doing high quality science. But they clearly affect the kind of science that goes on. For example, the head of the laboratory we studied stressed "seeing," and "learning to look for something different." This phenomenological outlook is one sign of adaptation to an environment of scarcity:

> The interface between the laboratory scientist and his/her technology becomes more tightly bonded under conditions of scarcity than it is likely to become in a well-funded laboratory where state-of-the-art equipment can be taken for granted.[12]

Socialization in a laboratory environment of scarcity will produce a different type of scientist than socialization in an environment of abundance:

> The environment of scarcity seems more likely than the environment of abundance to put a premium on a keen awareness of, and intimacy with, a wide range of "things" which—in one form or another—can be drawn in to nourish the research process—and among these "things" one must count the five unaided senses.[13]

The identification and analysis of environments of scarcity and environments of abundance in laboratory life may be crucial for testing the limits of the constructivist hypothesis, namely, that there is a constitutive relationship between so-called "external factors" and the content of scientific ideas. A Hungarian physicist told one student of laboratory life (Professor Robert Anderson of the Communication Department at Simon Fraser University) that overfunding undermines ingenuity and elegance in thinking and in approaching problems. This suggests the corollary conjecture that overfunding may be reflected in less ingenious and less elegant statements and solutions. Both hypotheses entail the sort of constitutive relationship between funds and ideas posited by students of laboratory life.

At the very least, the ideas I have reviewed reinforce and complement more prosaic conclusions and speculations voiced in other areas of science studies regarding over-funding or unrestricted funding, and the increasing cost and scale of research technologies; for example:[14]

1. Increasingly expensive technologies and the associated development of research oligopolies can narrow the range of available research techniques, limit the number of problems scientists in given fields can address, and make the exploration of new problems and areas difficult or impossible.
2. Unrestricted funding cannot guarantee that scientists will be innovative, or even that they will be able to gather important information.
3. The social organization of what has generally been viewed as "pure research" (research not *directly*, *explicitly* or obviously guided by military, industrial, or more generally non-scientific interests) is changing and taking on the characteristics of the social organization of applied research. This has obvious implications for innovation and productivity in science if we assume that "pure" research is the wellspring of scientific progress.
4. Negotiations about resources determine "critical aspects of the scientific process."
5. Crude cost-benefit analyses are not effective in evaluating the performance and effectiveness of research units; human resources and the evaluation of human resources by members of research teams are more important.
6. Gatekeepers "help regulate the flow of information and fiscal resources through the community by directing, impeding, and expediting flows based upon judgments of quality and merit, allegiances and biases, and probably, on sheer caprice as well."
7. Funding sources have a disciplinary bias (interdisciplinary research is not competitive with disciplinary research in general).

In general, studies of science and funding suggest the need for paying more attention to the impact of funding on research. The lab studies underscore this need by suggesting an even more intimate connection between funding and science—a connection that affects scientific *knowledge* itself.

Anthropologists of science have linked funding and the direction of science using concepts such as credit, resource-relationship, formatting, and contingency. They have not uncovered anything surprising insofar as their studies simply document the generalization that the availability or scarcity of resources affects what scientists do, how they do it, and what they produce. In this sense, anthropological research can be viewed as a contribution to the literature on funding and science that includes studies of peer review, science policy, gatekeeping, and personal networks in science and science policy.[15]

More importantly, however, lab studies seem to have the potential for identifying with greater clarity and precision than possible in the past specific funding contingencies. In order to properly interpret this aspect of science, we have to relate it to the general social conditions of doing science. If it turns out, for example, that there has been and continues to be *an increase* in the speed with which scientists move through cycles of credit (to use Latour and Woolgar's terms), then the "realistic" taken-for-granted aspects of simplification take on more sinister implications. The faster and bigger science gets, the more we can anticipate multiplier effects that will raise the pragmatic choices of laboratory life to crucial status as determinants of the nature, content, and viability of scientific inquiry. That is, money and prestige may become more important than other factors in the credit cycle, and contaminate the influence of theory and experiment. One possible consequence of a change of this sort in the credit cycle is an increase in fraud.[16] Furthermore, the constructivist viewpoint seems to be leading us to a new understanding of what scientific *knowledge* is. In this respect, the lab studies can be expected to produce explanations that relate configurations of power in funding relationships to the form and content of scientific knowledge. It is already clear to some students of the social relations of science that money and equipment are not simply mediators of knowledge, but are, in some sense, constituents of knowledge.

Some caution is necessary in exploring the implications of the lab study findings on funding and science. Only a few anthropological studies of science have been carried out. Conjectures about the social construction of science tend to outrun empirical evidence. The evidence itself is often anecdotal. Theory statements are not always formulated clearly enough to facilitate productive communication and debate. And important assumptions and values in lab studies are implicit, unstated, and otherwise not readily accessible. Nonetheless, it seems clear that lab studies have been an important part of the science studies landscape, and that they have enhanced our understanding of all aspects of scientific work. The relationship between funding and science will get even more attention in these studies than it has received so far if "transscientific fields" become the focus of future lab studies.

In the broader context of science policy that includes industrial science policy, it is interesting to note that some years ago, executives of a Fortune 500 corporation expressed an interest in the anthropology of science. Directors of the corporation discussed the possibility of an anthropological study of scientific work on their corporate premises with two of my colleagues. It seems clear from my knowledge of the negotiations that the corporation directors were interested in more than having their company become another Salk Institute for anthropologists of science. They may have viewed the skills and knowledge of the anthropologist of science as an adjunct to or substitute for traditional academic tools and skills for managerial control such as those provided by industrial psychologists and sociologists, managerial economists, and other management-oriented consultants and advisors.

There is nothing novel about anthropologists becoming involved in the policy process. Indeed, the field of anthropology emerged in a context that tied it to "immediate public policy concerns." From the start, there were conservative as well as transformative aspects to this marriage between anthropology and public policy. The relationship between anthropology and colonialism is well-known. But in some cases, studies produced under the auspices of government agencies criticized agency practices among native populations. A classic example of this is James Mooney's *The Ghost Dance Religion and the Sioux Outbreak of 1890*. This study was based on fieldwork initiated in 1891 under the auspices of the Bureau of Ethnology and in the interest of United States Indian policy. Mooney was highly critical of the ways in which military and Indian service personnel conducted themselves in this affair.

Another study in which the anthropologist identifies more with the "immediate" welfare of the people he/she is studying than with the problems of the "dominant society" is F. E. Williams' *The Vailala Madness and the Destruction of Native Ceremonies in the Gulf Division*, published in 1923. Studies prompted by policy concerns can sometimes stimulate an awareness of new phenomena. Williams' study, for example, attracted attention to nativistic or revitalization movements which had not up to that time been of much theoretical interest to anthropologists.

In the post–World War II period, ties between anthropologists and public policymakers were established in the applied anthropology movement; and in the National Research Council's Committee on

Disaster Studies, and the Surgeon General's Scientific Advisory Committee on Television and Social Behavior. Some anthropologists have avoided policy engagements and adopted an "Ivory Tower" position. Some try to play the policy and ivory tower games simultaneously; this is the "Schizoid" position. "Activists" argue that participation in the policy process should be tied to a commitment to improving the conditions under which people live. In the "Research and Development" approach, anthropologists introduce changes into a social setting on their own instead of for a client. They then study the effects of those changes (e.g., the Cornell Project in Vicos, Peru). "Action anthropology" is represented by Sol Tax's participant interference approach. Groups are assisted in formulating their own plans for changes that will improve health and well-being among their members. The field of anthropology, then, offers a number of alternatives for dealing with the policy process. These options are in principle available to anthropologists of science. Anthropologists of science can operate in the interests of a variety of social groups, collectivities, and institutions, including the scientists they study, their own professional community, agents of governmental or private funding agencies, and corporate managers, and so on. In the final section of this chapter, I will explore some of the implications of the emergence of an anthropology of science for the anthropologists, the scientists, the science policy community, and the wider society.

The relationship between anthropology of science on the one hand and science and science policy on the other can be developed in at least three ways. The *conservative* program makes anthropology of science a tool of science policy. If we accept prevailing ideas about science policymaking, the development of a knowledge base for science policy, and the role of scientists in society, then there is a clear rationale for linking anthropology of science and science policy. Students of laboratory life have developed an approach that answers a variety of questions that science policymakers might consider:

1. How are research plans formulated and carried out? Anthropology of science provides a direct way of monitoring these processes;
2. How do funding sponsors influence problem choice in science? Anthropology of science contributes to our understanding of the influence of funding sponsors by recording what scientists themselves say about these influences, and how they operationalize these influences in day-to-day decisions;

3. Are standard ways of measuring scientific productivity and growth sufficient for producing insights about the impact of policy mechanisms and decisions on science? According to some students of science, the answer is no. This conclusion has been reached, for example, by students of the comparative organization of research units in different societies. The best insights as well as basic information about policy impacts cannot be produced without qualitative analyses, and especially without onsite observations;

4. How can we determine the consequences of innovations in science for the economy, and for the society at large, as well as for science? Anthropology of science is an important tool for this purpose because it not only can focus on particular sites but can broaden its focus to encompass what Karin Knorr-Cetina refers to as "transscientific fields," that is, the systems of scientists and non-scientists "outside" the laboratory that form the networks of communication and exchange that have the laboratories at their centers.

The anthropology of science can be more than a methodology for uncovering the dynamics of science. If it can be established as a standard approach in science studies, it could help policymakers monitor changes (for example, organizational changes, regressive as well as progressive changes) in science. This is an important advantage of the on-site approach, whether we are viewing it in conservative, radical, or reflexive terms. From a social and cultural perspective, science is not a static, unified, homogeneous, eternally healthy system. We cannot depend on historical studies or philosophical reconstructions to inform us about what is going on in science today. Neither can we substitute descriptive narrative histories of science, no matter how immersed they are in social and cultural details, for theoretical analyses of science as a social activity and social process.

The idea of institutionalizing anthropology of science as a science policy tool or more modestly as a source of information for science policymakers is fraught with problems. These include the impact of anthropological research on working scientists, who might be cooperative under some circumstances but might resist being "studied" by researchers who are being paid or encouraged by their employers or supervisors. This sort of resistance has developed within, for example, some native American groups.

Another issue is how the addition of one or more anthropologists to a research group will affect the research process itself and the products of scientific inquiry. There are related issues raised by considerations about informed consent, privacy rights, the effects of anthropological research on social reputations, and the publication of anthropological studies of science as advertisements for particular scientists and findings. Attention needs to be given to the unintended and uncontrolled consequences of anthropological studies of science. The bottom-line problem for scientists is that anthropological studies of science may be used to support policies that are not in the best interests of the scientists studied. From another perspective, however, such studies might serve broader social interests such as the public health.

A radical perspective on anthropology of science and science policy is suggested by the remarks of the late Margaret Mead, an anthropologist and former AAAS president. Mead conceived the anthropological method as one that systematically uses the role of stranger, but not to study "subjects," "objects," "respondents," "consumers," or "data producing animals." For Mead, anthropological activity (practiced by professional anthropologists or others who have learned the "art")—and in particular applied anthropology—

> . . . includes respect for those with whom one works, recognition of interdependence, purposive avoidance of lying and deceit, and the obligation to take into account the safety, sensitivities, and well-being of those with whom one works.[17]

Mead is here expressing a reorientation to the people who have traditionally come under anthropological scrutiny—the colonized, the oppressed, the dominated, the subjugated. She leaves open the question of how and whether we can "do" anthropology among people whose values we find to be what Mead would recognize as threats to human dignity and integrity.

Anthropology of science need not serve established science policy interests. It can be linked to "people's science" and "science shops," and so serve the interests of scientists as workers and as people working together with other members of the community to solve social problems, improve the public health, and so on. In this context, anthropology of science as an applied discipline can become a part of participatory self-management programs for scientists who cooperatively own their own means of production.

Finally, anthropology of science can play a role in the development of a reflexive science. Mead had an image of the anthropologist as an "investigator, research worker, or culture modifier" from one culture, sub-culture, occupational group, or class who studies another culture, sub-culture, occupational group, or class in collaboration with group members *"to produce a product that neither of them could produce alone."*[18] One such product of the collaboration of scientists and anthropologists of science might be a reflexive science. Ethnomethodologists of science argue that scientists "do social science" as a natural part of their everyday work. Their "social science" work should not be confused with the work of the social scientist. But the introduction into scientific work of the anthropologically trained stranger-collaborator might strengthen the "social science" practices of scientists. And this might eventually lead to the incorporation of anthropology into science as an integral part of everyday scientific practice. As a result, science would become (through the reflexive activities of scientists) "self-aware" or "conscious of itself." This sort of transformation of science would obviously have to be rooted in, and would in turn affect, parallel reflexive transformations in society at large.

The "reflexive ethnography" that Woolgar has argued for as an alternative to "instrumental ethnography" is a more realistic goal than the goal of *integral reflexivity* I have sketched. But Woolgar's form of reflexivity can be viewed as a step toward integral reflexivity. Woolgar argues that there should be more involved in our anthropology than telling stories about what laboratory life is "really like." Rather than merely producing "news" about science, anthropology of science should provide "an occasion for reflecting upon, and reaching a greater understanding of, those aspects of our own culture which we tend to take for granted:"

> Stories about scientific practice, just like stories about the Arawak, are most useful when they address the fundamentals of reasoning processes. Moreover, science is one social arena where we would expect to find special attention being paid to the form and currency of reasoning practices; science comprises various institutionalized procedures for "determining" the adequacy of reasoning. Hence the ethnographic study of the laboratory is an occasion for investigating scientific practices for what this can tell us about practical reasoning in general.[19]

It should be clear that the preceding remarks lead immediately to the idea of an anthropology of science policymaking. Indeed, the need for an anthropology of science policymaking arises in conservative and radical as well as reflexive approaches to science studies and science policy. It is a logical consequence of viewing the laboratory or scientific practice as a point in a transscientific field. In other words, the rationale for an anthropology of science is also a rationale for an anthropology of science policy.

We should, as I noted in my discussion of funding, be very cautious before drawing firm conclusions about science or science policy on the basis of research in anthropology of science. Anthropologists of science may be in a position to offer us some insights about science, and some ideas about science policy. But their work should not be looked to for unequivocal prescriptions for science policy. At the very least, however, anthropology of science has begun to give us a detailed portrait of the complexities and problems of scientific work: how and why research problems are formulated, why certain materials are selected for laboratory research, how laboratory practice is rhetorically transformed into objective fact, the social nature of replication, and so on. More than this, anthropology of science brings us in touch with science today, on-line science rather than science as it was, as an idealized reconstruction, or as a "once-and-for-all" phenomenon. The problem that looms large for us now is how to avoid Big Brother anthropology of science and promote reflexive science.

The Finalization Project

Few anthropologists of science have shown any interest in getting involved in the policy process, or in any sort of action for social change. This is not true of the science studies researchers who are the focus of this section. This section deals with three activist perspectives and agendas in applied science studies: finalization, the weak program, and the critical sociology of scientific validity. These cases reveal the strengths and weaknesses of various approaches to linking the search for knowledge and the search for reasoned ways of living.

In 1970, Carl Friedrich von Weizsäcker established the Max Planck Institute for the Study of the Conditions of Life in the Scientific-Technical World at Starnberg in West Germany. The institute was jointly directed by von Weizsäcker and Jürgen Habermas. Soon afterward, Gernot Böhme, Wolfgang van den Daele, and Wolfgang Krohn formed a research group at the Institute known as "Alternatives in Science." They were later joined by Wolf Schäfer, Rainer Hohlfeld, and Tilman Spengler. The perspective guiding the work of this group was sketched in a 1973 paper by Böhme, van den Daele, and Krohn titled "Die Finalisierung der Wissenschaft." In 1983, the "finalists" published *Finalization in Science*, the first document in English on their collective efforts.[20]

The finalists view science as a "collective utility." Their program is rooted in the development of ecology as a "normatized natural science" in which objectivity (scientific theory-formation) and values (the pursuit of social and political goals) are consciously and intentionally integrated. Nature (in broadest terms, the ecosphere) is viewed as a subject rather than a productive, juridical, or economic object. The finalists' commitment to grounding the pursuit of societal goals in scientific theories is designed to avoid "the instrumentalization of science;" and their effort to give "task communities" the responsibility for pursuing science and technology in the public interest is designed to avoid "the academicization of oriented research." Finalization thus seeks to integrate a theory of science (based on critical as opposed to positivist science studies) and a vision of a "reconstructed science." The reconstruction of science is aimed at turning it away from Faustian quests that threaten to destroy the natural environment in the process of pursuing knowledge of nature "for its own sake."

Three alternative approaches to the ecological and environmental crisis are identified and found to be inadequate. "Going Natural" is criticized for romanticizing the pastoral past and raising the spectre of a "Blood and Soil" agenda nourished by sociobiology. "Going Luddite" is described as working for the total abolition of science and technology as we know it, and criticized for going too far, that is, for being "hot" radicalism. "Going Technocrat" (basically the "technological fix" approach) is viewed as a perverse attempt to solve problems caused by a technological orientation by intensifying our commitment to technologism. The main ingredients of the finalization program are: (1) a conception of what the finalists simultaneously refer to as two "epochs" in the history of science, and two "alternatives" open to science—the Darwinistic epoch or alternative, in which useful knowledge is produced spontaneously, and the finalist epoch or alternative in which useful knowledge is produced strategically; (2) the thesis that science develops in three stages: pre-paradigmatic (explorative), paradigmatic, and post-paradigmatic; (3) the idea that as they "mature," sciences become stable and relatively complete, that is, theories become "closed" (in a sense suggested by Heisenberg); (4) the thesis (or perhaps the main plank in the finalists' political platform) that during the mature stage, when science can no longer be improved by small changes but only by major changes in the "paradigm" or the "entire theoretical structure," it becomes appropriate to replace the norm of "intra-scientific autonomy" (valid for the paradigmatic stage) by the norm of social and political planning for science. It is important to stress that the finalists contend that social and political planning for mature sciences is not merely a matter of social utility and social responsibility, but a way of furthering *theoretical* development. Finally, (5) the finalists offer a research prospectus that calls for (a) integrating natural and social sciences, pure and practical reasoning, facts and values; (b) a devaluation of natural science and an upward "revaluation" of social science; (c) the expansion of the social influence of political ecology; (d) making the societal reproduction of nature a central social objective; and (e) the conscious construction of natural environments.

The evidence for the finalists' theory of science is presented in Part I of their book in the form of case studies of agricultural chemistry and fluid mechanics (finalized sciences), cancer research (an instance of "sub-finalization"), and fermentation research (which became "autonomized" instead of "finalized"). The case studies raise two problems that haunt the entire finalization program. One is the problem of the referent for "science." The finalists implicitly adhere to a "once-and-for-all" view of a method of knowing that emerged in seventeenth century Europe (with classical Greek roots), and crystallized into the universal epistemic strategy we call "science" or "modern science." This ignores changes in the referent for "science" that follow historical, cultural, and social structural changes in the activities of "scientists." Is there any "science" before the seventeenth century? Do the epistemic strategies of the ancient Maya, or Chinese qualify as "science"? These sorts of questions emerge because the finalists adopt a basically asocial conception of science, a point I will discuss in more detail below. The second and related problem is that it is never clear whether the finalists believe that things might have been otherwise in the history of science. Do all sciences go through the three stages? Can a science be fixated at one stage, or regress to an earlier stage? The finalists are at best ambivalent on these sorts of queries.

Part II of their book deals with problems in the philosophy of science, science policy, the "scientification" of technology, and normative finalization. The crisis of legitimation in science, and the idea of a social science of nature (or a social natural science) are discussed in Part III. The appendix on the "finalization debate" gives the authors a chance to reply to their critics. This debate was for the most part confined to West Germany, colored by specific events and developments in contemporary West German politics and culture, and conditioned by the history of politics and intellectual life in Germany. Still, as I will note later, the debate reproduces recurring contests in the history of intellectual life.

The finalists trace their intellectual roots to a tradition of attempts to conceptualize a New Natural Science that stretches from Marx to Marcuse. Advocates of reconstructive, emancipatory, liberatory, and humanistic science often have difficulty steering a steady course between what they perceive to be the positive attributes of "Science" and the negative features of "Modern Science." This difficulty is inevitably reflected in their theories of science. The finalists are no exception. Their "three stages of science" thesis is vulnerable to a variety of well-known empirical and normative criticisms. Their use of the "paradigm" idea also exposes them to well-rehearsed criticisms; and they sometimes fall into the trap of using "paradigm" and "theory" interchangeably. But the Achilles heel of finalization is probably the notion of "closed theory."

"Closed theory" refers to the extreme case of theoretical stability in a given science. The use of the term "closed" should be considered in light of the status of "closed" and "open" as weapons in struggles over intellectual turf. Terms like "closed" and "finalization" have a volatile potential for irritating democratic intellectuals. But they are especially provocative among the self-appointed guardians of the norms of openness and freedom in modern science. The finalists do not seem to be very sensitive to the war of words. Their closed theory thesis is also problematic because it is based on the implicit idea that theories in general are free-standing, independent, look-alike objects. On the contrary, theories are not so substantial. They are more like fields than particles, more like networks than nodes. To the extent that we can identify particular sets of concepts, statements, hypotheses, theorems, laws, or equations and use them as theories, we will notice that theories vary in size, shape, density, and susceptibility to change. Theory construction and use, like scientific work in general, involves more tinkering and trial-and-error strategies than the finalists' developmental thesis allows for. Finally, since "closedness" or "theoretical maturity" entails "a notion of the completeness of the concepts the theory provides," according to the finalists, the idea is vulnerable to some form of Gödelian analysis or critique.

The idea of closure seems to be the main object of the attack by the finalists' critics. The anti-finalists defend scientific freedom on the grounds that it has produced "the fertile humus" for applied research and technology in the public interest. This "manure theory of science" is so potent that it contaminates even the finalists' view of the history of science. They make the unsupported (and unsupportable) claim, for example, that early modern science *automatically* promoted emancipatory interests. This sort of global claim, common among defenders of the Republic of Science, ignores the fact that interests are distributed throughout a system of social stratification, and that among those interests we must count the professional and related interests of the scientists themselves.

Many of the problematic aspects of finalization seem to stem from the rather narrow intellectual and political context within which the finalists work. They do not venture far from German and "Continental" quoting circles. And even within these limits, they seem to be attracted to conventional internalist treatments of scientific knowledge. The tension between Continental conventionalism and the finalists' orientation to a radical reconstruction of science is perhaps the source of the totalitarian implications some people read into their position. It may also be responsible for the finalists' tendency to veer off in scientistic directions in spite of their emancipatory goals. A more general source of the problems I have pointed out in the finalization program is that the finalists consciously adopt what can be called, given their opposition to the "hot" radicalism of the neo-Luddites, *cool radicalism*. The most important consequence of adopting this cool approach is a hesitancy about, if not an opposition to, "Going Sociological." It is telling that the discussion of the finalization thesis in Part II is explicitly carried out in *philosophy* of science terms. The finalists' booming silence on relativism and constructivism in contemporary social studies of science interferes with their efforts to communicate important emancipatory messages.

The finalists seek an explanation for the tendency toward isolation in the development of specialist terminologies and the differentiation of scientific discourse without considering the causal roots of these processes in social organization. Their argument that science contains the cognitive preconditions for both autonomization and finalization also fails to take account of social structural factors. They do, it is true, recognize that "neutral science" was a political and not a cognitive necessity for the institutionalization of science in seventeenth century Europe. But they do not seem to recognize that the autonomy they reify as "the paradigmatic stage" is no less a function of political and social factors, and that this makes asocial notions about "cognitive necessity" untenable.

Finalization rests upon a Kuhnian "theory" of science, and not studies of scientific specialties or the transscientific contexts of scientific work. As a result, the finalists do not explore the possibility that networks of one sort or another may have linked what appear from an internalist history or philosophy of science point of view to be completely independent intellectual events. The sociological vacuum in finalization means that the finalists have virtually nothing to say about the social structures and norms of institutionalized scientific activities. These "internal" social phenomena and the human interests associated with them are inseparable from cognitive objects and interests. The finalists' internalism also leads them to view the "classical" disciplines of physics, chemistry, and biology as homogeneous benchmarks for the comparative analysis of sciences such as agriculture chemistry. At the very least, the homogeneity of the benchmark disciplines should be supported by empirical studies and not simply assumed. In fact, these disciplines appear more complex and heterogeneous the more we turn our sociological field glasses upon them instead of relying on armchair cogitations about unseen worlds. Empirical and historical science studies also underscore the importance of exercising care when using ideas like "discipline" or "scientific community." The referents for such ideas are not only dynamic; sometimes they are mythical.

Schäfer seems readier than his colleagues to consider the possibility that sociological analyses could explain cognitive structures. But this idea plays no role in finalization. And in any case, Schäfer would restrict, a priori, sociological analysis to the pre- and post-paradigmatic stages of scientific development. The isolation of finalization from relativist and constructivist social studies of science helps explain why this program is subject to the same sociological criticisms today that were levelled against it in the early 1970s. This raises a related question regarding the hermetic treatment of the "autonomous paradigmatic phase" of scientific development. Why do the finalists restrict the minimum normative requirements of not damaging the natural environment or violating fundamental humanistic norms to those sciences "open to finalization"? This implies a readiness to tolerate deviations from those minimum requirements in sciences not open to finalization. What about the effects of such sciences on the environment, on society, and on the quality of the lives of working scientists?

The finalists' argument that it is no longer possible to distinguish between science and technology is not especially controversial. Most scholars in science studies would probably agree that the distinction has been blurred, if not obliterated, in this century. But the assumed historical separation of science and technology is not as clear or simple a matter as the finalists suppose. They ignore, for example, the social conditions that help explain why hand and brain are now separated and now integrated across time and culture—in myth as well as reality. Indeed, the debate between finalists and anti-finalists is partly a manifestation of that ancient tension between doing or making and thinking. A more precise formulation of the theme at issue here would recognize the conflict between "pure" thinkers and "practical" ones. Not too long ago, this theme surfaced in the debate between the advocates of a socialistic science led by J. D. Bernal, and the defenders of the Republic of Science led by Michael Polanyi.

The finalists implicate themselves in yet another recurring phenomenon of intellectual life when they suggest that normatizing science is merely giving to modern science what *early* modern science lost. There are echoes here of Roszak's affinity for gnosticism and Capra's infatuation with ancient mysticism.

In 1975, a Study Group, "Wissenschaftsforschuung in der BRD" was established by Kurt Hübner, Hermann Lübbe, and Gerard Radnitzky. In March of 1976, the Fritz Thyssen Foundation financed a conference in Munich at which the Study Group and allied colleagues attacked the finalists as Stalinists, neo-marxists, and dialectical ideologues. Some observers have argued that the media exaggerated the anti-finalists' criticisms of finalization. The finalists, however, do not agree. They point out that the anti-finalists accused them of seeking a "Final Solution," provoking a "1984 situation," practicing "Lysenkoism," and generally threatening scientific freedom. The flames of this epistemological war between finalists and anti-finalists (including prominent critical rationalists) were nonetheless fanned by the popular press, and engulfed the 1976 West German *Bundestag* election campaign. In a series of advertisements aimed against the finalists, the Christian Democratic Union urged voters to support the CDU and help keep science "free from ideology." As a result of these and related controversies, the Institute at Starnberg was closed in 1981, and the finalists went into diaspora at Bielefeld, Darmstadt, Erlangen, and Frankfurt.

There is a lot of theoretical reflection in their book. But the authors realize that a new legitimation for a new science will emerge out of the struggles among different interest groups and not out of ivory tower musings. I have criticized the finalists for ignoring important developments in social studies of science. They also ignore the wide variety of activities on behalf of liberatory science going on around the world. But their work points out and underscores the failure of the sciences and science studies to confront the social and political problems that are the focus of finalization. It has become increasingly difficult since Hiroshima and Nagasaki to defend the autonomy and purity of science. It is by now and at the very least reasonable to expect that the defense of or attacks on purity and autonomy in science will be based on empirical scrutiny instead of being grounded in wish-fulfillment and the a priori.

It is not irrational to worry about the implications of finalization and other liberatory or reconstructive programs for autonomy and freedom in inquiry. The autonomy of the medieval European schools seems to have been the main factor that distinguished them from their Islamic counterparts, and the factor that explains why the former prospered while the latter were destroyed—by orthodox religious attacks on Islamic intellectual life. There are many other examples, from the "schools" of Sumer, to the Napoleonic écoles, from the cathedral at Chartres in the early middle ages to the modern universities, that support the thesis of a positive relationship between autonomy and intellectual growth. However, the historical record reflects certain types of conflictful relationships among the varied activities of social life. Under those conditions—conflicts of interest, struggles for scarce resources, Faustian goals, and in general the unequal distribution of power—defending the autonomy of intellectuals and the free pursuit of inquiry is crucial for the growth of knowledge (even if the benefits of free inquiry generally accrue to the privileged classes). Under other cooperative, liberatory social arrangements the conventional notion of autonomy would become irrelevant. Indeed, the limitations of conventional autonomy are revealed by the impact of professionalization (a process of "autonomization") on freedom of inquiry, innovation, and the redistribution of knowledge wealth.

In the end, the value of their program is that it brings us face to face with the problem of whether we can design a mode or modes of inquiry, and ultimately modes of living and working, that are ecologically sound and supportive of humane, cooperative social arrangements. The cool radicalism and ethnocentrism of finalization fail to adequately address the social problems of contemporary science, technology, and society. And that failure is at the root of the worrisome features of finalization noted by the anti-finalists and other critics. There are no easy answers here, but my own view is that the social and political changes the finalists propose, in particular those that are aligned with Marx's vision of a "human science," require a hotter, more anarchistic radicalism than finalization offers. It is past the time when we should have realized the importance of challenging (with due regard for historical context) Robert Hooke's charge to the Royal Society, and to begin to "meddle" with "Divinity, Metaphysics,

Moralls, Politicks, Grammar Rhetoric or Logic" in pursuing the improvement of our "knowledge of natural things." For the moment, it is perhaps promising that there are tensions between finalists and anti-finalists, the Bernals and the Polanyis, pure thinkers and practical ones; for it is out of these tensions that a new science and a new society may yet emerge. My own "meddling" is the subject of the next two sections, episodes in my search for a way of integrating my politics, my life, and my inquiry.

The Weak Program (with Daryl Chubin)

In the early 1980s, Daryl Chubin and I articulated an alternative paradigm for science studies that we christened (with Bloor's strong program rhetoric in mind) "the weak program."[21] The weak program is characterized by a focus on process and product in science, a contextual perspective, an evolutionary epistemology, a future orientation, *and* an unremitting criticism of values in science, society, and policy making.

The first criterion embraces the decade-old admonition that science, like any other institutionalized activity, should not be studied as a "black box."[22] To the meta-analyst this means that what scientists say and do varies with their interests and the listening audience. Furthermore, the gulf between rhetoric and artifact is where the often unseen and untold negotiation unfolds. The scientometrician for example, fixes only on what goes into the box—the "received view" of resources, people, and problems—and what comes out the other end; papers, discoveries, citations, and prizes. Scientometricians celebrate these artifacts and grandly infer the processes they never observed. They feed the scientists' own mythology about rationality and progress. They therefore play into the policymaker's hands by delivering simplistic, manipulable findings of the "how much, how often" variety. Reaffirming the excellence of the few in science without specifying the conditions of their handiwork and the science meccas whence they came just perpetuates elitist science policy. Stratification becomes the operating principle of grandeur. Meta-analysts are out to open and analyze the black box of science as process and product.

A contextual perspective places *scientists-as-workers* into organizations, institutions, and material cultures.[23] Unlike the strong program for example, the weak program does not identify legitimate actors in science, and more generally, in technical controversies on the basis of credentials. The culture helps define: (1) who is an interested party; (2) the scope of that interest; (3) the struggle of all parties to demarcate their expertise; and (4) dependence of the parties on other institutions to validate and support their practice. In the contextual perspective, identifying the "transepistemic" connections that link scientists to patrons and adversaries alike is the key to understanding why and how negotiations occur. Representing this process, from the lab bench to the courtroom to the policy-maker is the task of the meta-inquirer. The sheer multiplicity of actors, views, and interests militates against elegant synopses and quick-fix policy recommendations concerning careers, research programs, and national funding priorities in R&D.[24] Infusing scepticism about organizational goals and efficiency, given targeted missions or the search for short-term applications, just compounds the policymaker's problem.

An evolutionary epistemology underlies the aforementioned focus on practice. From the mundane to the controversial, science—depending on one's historical allegiances—has moved inexorably for some time. While philosophers debate the "progressive" content of science, others argue for the inherently adaptive mechanisms that propel research.[25] Whether or not the "natural selection"—"survival-of-the-fittest" metaphors have been stretched beyond current biological science license, the meta-analyst rejoices in the restoration of science to its "proper" place as a cultural activity. In it, the scientist is again seen as a tinkerer, a creative craftsperson who proceeds not by methodological rigour alone, but by curiosity, luck, serendipity, and yes, a well-endowed chair or long term research grant. Such a picture of resourceful and timely creativity, however, gives small comfort to the policymaker who must light a few "research trails" among many with the benefit of limited allocations.[26] Predicting the pay-off in knowledge, discovery, and invention is a risky business, so risky that it fuels the interminable "basic-applied" debate.[27] This merely justifies certain policy decisions and precludes others. In times of fiscal restraint, it jerks policy towards conservatism—greater centralization of resources and support of proven investigators, programs, and institutions.[28] Evolutionary epistemology reminds us of the politics of life, not just science. A future orientation denotes that the weak program goes beyond platitudes about "policy-relevance," and pledges a commitment to interventionist or activist science. Futurists, evaluation researchers, social forecasters, impact assessors, and the like, all anticipate the future.[29] Their pronouncements are prescriptive, sometimes doomsaying, and always provocative. Typically, these prognosticators disdain interrogations of the past through either documents or first-person recollections. They could learn something from the strong programmers about reconstructing the past; the strong programmers could take heed about projecting the future. We do not endorse the methods of the futurist, such as Delphi, scenarios, and mathematical modelling, but we urge those most predisposed to predicting developments in science and technology—the scientometricians—to augment their pedestrian positivism with methods that introduce new variables, data sources, and interpretive possibilities.[30] Methods that allow the "case study" to be seen as more than a stereotyped exploratory tool, and ethics as a vital policy consideration (instead of a nuisance, or at best, an afterthought), need to be recognized as timeless inputs to the policy process. One makes this case, however, with examples in hand, not studies in preparation. The meta-analyst must compile them, digest them, and beseech the policy-maker with them. To influence the future of policy, we must leave the confines of our disciplinary, and even multidisciplinary, moot courts, and walk the corridors of power.[31]

Once in these corridors, the meta-analyst's role is to challenge conventional policy wisdom and jar the policymaker into perceiving a complex (and if our efforts succeed unexpectedly, a "multiple") reality. We do that through an unremitting commitment to value-criticism—an examination of our own and others' values and interests. This self-consciousness is an intellectual check on our politics, if you will. It thrusts us into partisan struggles within the culture *as partisans*—with a difference. The difference is our realization that those struggles are value clashes over value-laden problems. In seeking to understand the process by which the clashes came to be, and the values underpinning them, we also seek to influence outcomes. More specifically, we desire resolution with "due process"—with an airing of viewpoints, of all available information, of all the uncertainty that accompanies the views of the experts, the policy-makers, the interested public, and the social institutions entrusted with mediation and resolution.

Scepticism is our chief ally, for claims-making is a political act. Research "protocols" for dissecting this act may assist in our meta-inquiry.[32] But more crucial perhaps is the decision to be on-site, to tackle the messy problem, to function as a meta-scientist.[33] To decide this is to become a factor in the problem, not to recoil in horror as an intellectual issue graduates to the status of social problem or public controversy. The decision is a personal and professional one (though the meta-scientist sees no difference). But how does one explain the value of value-critical meta-analysis to one charged with the formulation or implementation of policy? How does one communicate that values are the *policymaker's* ally, or at worst, an ineluctable (albeit uninvited) companion? How can the meta-analyst challenge the authority of science, which according to Nelkin, "must give way to a more open understanding of the social, political, and ideological values that have always influenced its own development?"[34] A "more open understanding" of values prescribes inquiry into what has always been there. By removing the mantle of privilege, the shroud of mystery, that science has enjoyed for decades, the meta-analyst makes explicit to the policymaker that which both self-interested scientists and commentators on their unique cultures have endeavored to describe—on their own terms. That is, their values have been immune from those who move in other arenas, attached to other programs that seldom intersect their own. For them, intellectual self-sufficiency within a hallowed social institution safeguards the practice of science unfettered by the politics of the "rest" of the world. For the meta-analyst, science is politics, and the rest of the world, however conceptualized, is programmatically inseparable from research on science and technology. Value-criticism is the message and the science policy-maker is presumed to be listening. The future of meta-analysis is staked on this presumption and the confidence that listening makes a difference.

Picture the scene in Wittgenstein's *On Certainty*; he and a philosopher are sitting in a garden. In recalling this scene, we take the liberty of joining Wittgenstein and the philosopher. Now the philosopher says again and again, "I know that's a tree," pointing to a nearby tree. We say again and again, "I know that's a social construction," pointing to the same tree. A woman arrives and hears all this. Wittgenstein tells her: "These fellows aren't insane. We are only doing philosophy (and sociology)."[35] This garden dialogue is effectively interminable. In order to address the agenda of a relevant epistemology, we must leave the garden and muck about in a different sort of environment: Outside of the garden, human beings are everywhere. They implicate themselves in, and thereby realize the causal (and other) connections between what philosophers distinguish as "things in the world" and "terms that refer." Humans constantly (and perversely, some intellectuals believe) interfere with attempts to treat aims such as "truth" or "success" without reference to their existence. The recognition that we cannot eradicate the human and social element in discourse, inquiry, and knowledge is a prerequisite to advancing any epistemological program in science studies.

"Epistemology" disguises theological, apologetic, and ideological quests. Epistemologies shorn of theology and apology can be classi-fied as critical or conformist ideologies of knowledge and science. A critical epistemology is not based on the a priori assumption that "sci-ence" is the paradigmatic mode of inquiry. It is resistant to the idea that the best way to study science is to use "scientific methods." This resistance is a necessary condition for the *critical* study of science. A conformist epistemology is based on the notion that science is the paradigmatic mode of inquiry, and that the best way to study science *is* to use scientific methods. The objective of a conformist epistemol-ogy is to nourish and faithfully reproduce science-as-it-is along with its social trappings. A critical epistemology creates the possibility for a transformation of science-as-it-is and its social trappings.

There are some dangers, too, of which we should beware in our ef-forts to work out a changed vocabulary. (1) Science is a specific and delimited epistemic activity; it is one type of inquiry. Anything epis-temologically relevant for science will not necessarily transfer to other modes and will be irrelevant for an *evolutionary* epistemology. (2) While science with its social trappings is *one* type of inquiry, it is not *monolithic*. (3) Since epistemic activities exist within transepis-temic fields it is impossible to get an accurate portrait of a science by focusing exclusively *on* "science."

If we are willing to leave Wittgenstein's garden and construct a critical epistemology, we will have to engage in criticism and re-newal with respect to "facts," technological processes, specific theo-ries, types of theory, and conceptual frameworks.[36] We will have to assess critically the allocation of resources among different arenas of criticism. And we will have to confront currently institutional-ized structures of research and criticism. We will be actively en-gaged in designing and experimenting with social structures; the tinkerer principle will, if adhered to, help to appraise programs of design, implementation, and expectation in science studies. Any program, after all, is constituted of its subjects, goals, and audi-ences. The strength of the weak program is a consciousness about these very expectations. I will show in Chapter 7 that the weak pro-gram leads beyond critical epistemology to *the end of epistemology* and even of science studies.

Donald Campbell has argued for a sociology of scientific validity and has stressed the importance of applying the results of sociologi-cal studies of science in applied social science research. In the next section, Julia Loughlin and I offer a counterpoint to Campbell's con-ception of validity, a policy-relevant sociology of science grounded in the weak program.

Sociology of Science, Validity, and Applied Social Science Research (with Julia Loughlin)

The question of scientific validity is important in the sense that valid findings are persuasive. They compel acceptance, at least provisional acceptance, and the most well-designed and well-implemented research programs will have no impact if they are not understood to have produced accurate and useful information.[37] However, the definitions of validity used by various scientists, audiences, clients, and subjects differ; while this is not an unusual phenomenon in science, it is pervasive in applied social science research. Moreover, each validity community is complex and an arena for competing views on validity. The diverse positions of policymakers and the public may be seen as essentially and patently political or as the result of the fact that the scientists have not yet spoken clearly. Scientists, by contrast, are assumed to be exempt from a politics of validity. But scientists do not always and automatically agree about validity, and their views are in part influenced by their memberships in social groups outside of "science." Research decisions, interpretations of findings, and willingness to accept results achieved by other researchers are influenced by, for example, the methodological conventions of the physical scientists, commitments to what is already "known," and a willingness to protect the society or the public from the perceived consequences of gifting them with knowledge that they cannot use properly.

The term validity is used in the discussion of research on public policy in at least three ways. Ideally, these aspects of validity would coincide, and improved validity would provide greater coincidence. First, validity is often understood to mean conformity to a set of methodological conventions. Second, validity is used in the sense of scientific truth, information that will be recognized as in some way new, and a basis for further work. Campbell tends to use the term validity in this sense. Third, in policy research, data are accepted as valid when they are understood to be useful, accurate, and obvious once one follows the analysis. Such internal validity is often resorted to in the course of making research decisions, and thus may be inevitably built into the conclusions. For example, in a study of "Drugs and Delinquency: A Search for Causal Connections," the authors review the validity of the data and note that "there are consistent and reasonable relationships between the drug-use and delinquency items on the one hand, and other variables dealing with attitudes and behaviors on the other."[38] In any discussion of validity that relies on imitating the structure of research in the physical sciences there is an implicit assumption that following certain methodological canons, including here the broad conventions for selecting problems dictated by the reward structure, and concentrating on questions important for the development of theory, will result in findings that are readily persuasive to the science community and that can be translated either by logic or demonstration into results that will persuade clients, including the public.

Campbell's proposals are based primarily on the prestige of the physical sciences. It is not clear, however, that social scientists can achieve the status of the physical scientists by imitating their social organization or methods. In addition, they may unnecessarily restrict their own research in a naive commitment to narrowly conceived methodologies. It is precisely because of their understanding of the complexities of social worlds that social scientists should reverse the methodological hierarchy. The discussion below of the relative validity of social, medical, and epidemiological studies of drug use will illustrate this point. A return to the sociological imagination, the ability to explicate the juncture of individual and historical experience, is needed to inform effective policy-oriented social science research.[39]

There is no reason to suppose that we cannot apply sociological theory to the problem of enhancing validity or producing objective knowledge. But the idea that validity and objectivity are community products—social constructs—means that valid knowledge has a *qualitative* aspect. Critical sociology of science parts company here with those sociologies of science that do not address the *quality* of valid knowledge. This does not merely mean that we need to be concerned with the ways in which the intersection of various standards of validity might affect our evaluation of knowledge claims. It means that there is no form of valid knowledge that does not carry with it cultural content. The problem for sociologists of science, then, is to contribute to clarifying this thoroughly social conception of validity, and the development of new standards for evaluating knowledge claims.

THE NARROW PROBLEM AND QUALITATIVE METHODS

Campbell offers two suggestions for improving validity that appear to be directed more toward useful research than valid research. These are: (1) the emphasis on narrowly defined research problems (and an insistence that researchers not be allowed to diverge from such definitions); and (2) the encouragement of qualitative research.

While Campbell insists that qualitative research addressed to the same conclusions should usually accompany quantitative research, clinical, humanistic, ethnographic, or qualitative approaches are always complementary to the main research enterprise: "We need these *not* because the social sciences seek a different kind of validity than do other sciences, but rather because *to stay with our problems*, we must use techniques which, while improving the validity of our research, nonetheless provide less clarity of causal inference than would a retreat to narrowly specified variables under laboratory control."[40]

Campbell's concern with ensuring that researchers stick to the "problem" ignores the fact that it is in the formulation of the question that we find science. The very identification of a topic as a social policy concern constrains the definition of the research problem. It seems reasonable to suggest that, from the perspective of policy advocates, more "scientific" research would have the advantage of being less likely to be critical of the formulation of the question and more likely to proceed with identifying and operationalizing the variables. From the perspective of a sociology of validity, however, validity is of only hypothetical interest when the wrong question (one based on a misunderstanding of data or biased assumptions) is asked. It is precisely in the formulation of questions that social science is essential when informed social policy is the desired outcome of the research.

RESEARCH ON ILLEGAL DRUGS

Research on the use of illegal drugs has a long history and has included a variety of traditions: behavioral, social, epidemiological, and biomedical. This history is useful as a complement to the preventive-intervention programs that Campbell uses to illustrate his proposals for improving the validity of applied social science research. In the field of social policy research there are many competing professional interests, and these interests must be taken into account in order to understand the social dynamics of validity. The two professions that for historical reasons compete for authority in research and social policy on deviance are medicine and law enforcement; in economic and foreign policy areas, political ideologies are also clearly relevant, although played out between the social sciences and the government service professions. Here the question becomes: Can we conceive of validity in such a way that the audience to be enlightened is not simply the physical sciences or competing professions but the public?

Competing explanations of drug use have developed in the context of changing social policies, but all have been inevitably affected by the criminal status of drug distribution and the ideology that legitimates drug legislation. Since drug sales and possession are illegal, drug use is by definition "deviant behavior." Since drugs are illegal because they are defined as physically and psychologically harmful, people who use drugs are easily defined as "sick." Thus, the research on drug use that has been logically consistent with social policy has been epidemiological research based on the public health model. Research that is critical of social policy on drugs has emphasized the political nature of drug legislation and enforcement and argued that such policy was, at least in part, an attempt to control cultural minorities. A third type of research on drug-use patterns has explored drug taking as "normal behavior," that is, as behavior that can be understood only by observing actors in specific social contexts and by paying attention to their own definitions of motive and response. These three research traditions have been different not only in their assumptions, but also in the types of data used and the conclusions reached about the causes and consequences of drug use.

We might take as an example the invention of the concept of drug abuse. When it was generally clear that the powerful term *addiction* could no longer be used for a variety of illegal drugs, such as marijuana and LSD, *abuse*, which sounded like addiction but made less easily defeated claims, was developed and backed by authority. As Goode notes,

> the scientists and physicians who created the new terminology of dependence were being employed as propagandists to convince the lay public that nonaddicting substances were just as "bad" for them, that they could be just as "dependent" on them as on the truly "addicting" drugs, and that the continued use of both arose out of a compulsion . . . as abuse is used in context, however, it conveys the distinct impression that something quite measurable is being referred to, something very much like a disease, a medical pathology, a sickness in need of a cure. Thus the term simultaneously served two functions: it claims clinical objectivity, and it discredits the phenomenon it categorizes.[41]

Major changes in the definition of the seriousness, extent, and appropriate control of drug use have followed changes in the perception of the social status of drug users. The most recent such change, of course, has been the response to changes in the social characteristics of marijuana users in the 1970s. As Bonnie and Whitebread note, "when the consensus against marijuana lost its sociological support it inevitably lost its scientific support as well."[42]

Perhaps the critical question here is whether there is a difference between validity and persuasiveness. In the case of drug research, where the audiences are clearly different communities, it appears that it is not the conduct of research as such, or even those dimensions of funding that Campbell has selected for comment, but the multiplicity of problem definitions and competing value commitments that have limited both research and the impact of research findings. There are at least four characteristics of this applied research tradition that are useful to examine.

Myths about drugs. First, we find a series of myths about drugs that persist despite clear and repeated disconfirmation. These include the central role of pushers in initiating drug use, the inevitability of addiction as a result of drug use (especially heroin), the criminogenic effects of drug use, and the primacy of pharmacology in explaining drug effects.[43] We might also add a myth that is important in legitimating recurrent waves of social concern with and action on drugs, although it is beyond the scope of most sponsored policy research, the myth that greedy or malevolent foreign powers are deliberately infecting American society with drugs.[44] These are myths that legitimate policy and are therefore enshrined in official pronouncements and educational materials.[45] To threaten these myths is to threaten and discredit the work of government agencies, therapists, treatment programs, curricula, and voluntary-service organizations. Perhaps the controversy over methadone maintenance provides the most telling example; evaluations of methadone maintenance are crippled by commitments to certain kinds of treatment and against certain others, especially the provision of all "demonized drugs," as well as by the persistence of the myths discussed above.[46]

The medicalization of deviance. Second, in research on drugs, as in many other areas of public policy research, we need to deal with the special position of the medical profession. The disease model that has been applied so widely to deviant behavior has suggested both an expert profession, that is, physicians, and a dominant method, epidemiology.[47] While the medical professionals have been successful in achieving recognition as biological scientists, they have also been successful in achieving recognition as *de facto* social scientists. Their pronouncements on social problems and social policies have not been as carefully examined for their ideological biases as have those of other social scientists, in part because of their prestige as natural scientists and in part because their scientific training does not provide them with a basis for a critical understanding of their society. Thus, we find both that attention can be obtained easily by clearly inadequate research if it appears in a medical journal, and that the "scientific" model of epidemiology is dominant in research, although it remains fairly sterile and descriptive. Because of the dramatic changes in policy that followed changes in the social class of drug users, the controversy over marijuana has been best reviewed and documented. It provides any number of cases in which clearly inadequate research published in medical journals was accepted by the public and the policymakers as valid. For example, a December 1971 article on cerebral atrophy in marijuana users has continued to be influential: "even though the *Lancet* editors published a lengthy caveat in the same issue and the authors' attribution of cause was questioned, disputed, or ridiculed by virtually every American authority, this study was widely publicized and has remained in the forefront of antimarijuana rhetoric."[48]

While articles in medical journals that received such public attention were primarily clinical studies, the public health model for research was often adopted by interdisciplinary teams and was strongly supported by government agencies. The epidemiological model implies carriers (who do not necessarily display symptoms), risk factors either in terms of exposure or susceptibility, and an orientation toward cure or prevention. As Ball and Chambers note when comparing their work to classical studies of tuberculosis, smallpox, syphilis, hypertension, and leukemia, the emphasis in such research is on the "etiology, incidence and prevalence of addiction."[49] While the shift from special studies of Puerto Ricans, Negroes, Mexican Americans, and inmates of the federal hospitals to surveys of the "normal" population was supported by widespread concern over what was perceived as increasing drug use among middle-class adolescents, there has been a continued emphasis on pathology; terms like "inadequate personality," "inept," "adolescent hedonism," and "poorly adjusted" appear routinely in the literature.[50] There are attempts to find a model of behavior that will predict such diverse "problem" phenomena as drug use, sexual experience, and activist protest.[51]

Such individualistic approaches miss the crucial role of social patterns and interaction. Social networks are defined in terms of exposure rates, and attempts to identify the progress of the disease lead to the search for the statistically normal case and neglect of important alternative patterns of behavior. Drug use is primarily a social activity, not an expression of individual pathology.

Trebach makes an interesting observation about the reciprocal impact of social theories of drug use on medical practice. Fears of addiction and assumed links between addiction and other moral consequences may affect prescribing practices and reduce the dosage of narcotics below the level required for appropriate relief of pain:

> The failures in the medical arena go beyond the choice or legality of certain drugs and into the inappropriate use of the drugs available. [Sacher and Marks found] "a general pattern of undertreatment of pain with narcotic analgesics, leading to widespread and significant patient distress."[52]

Trebach also quotes an editorial in the *New England Journal of Medicine* by Louis Lasagna, a leading spokesperson for the medical-research professionals: "Individual patients might be better off with heroin than morphine, and vice versa, yet with so many morphine surrogates legally available and the potential problems in regard to storage, theft, and diversion, the legalization of heroin for medical use does not seem to be socially responsible."[53]

The status of qualitative research. Third, we find that qualitative work has been and continues to be treated as supplementary or complementary and evaluated in terms of its agreement with policy, not in terms of method or findings. In part, this may have been related to the relatively successful adoption by social scientists of the epidemiological methods, and the relative convergence of their findings; they were more widely accepted than social science findings in general. Medical and behavioral research remained dominant for other types of drug use even after the special case of marijuana use was reexamined and social science findings were accepted as a basis for policy. The fact that qualitative findings were ignored, or paid attention to only when they confirmed more quantitative approaches, however, may also have been related to the often dramatic differences between the understandings of drug use that emerged from the two traditions. For example, Beschner and Feldman, reviewing the major ethnographies of heroin use, note that they "observed that the addict was sharply different when viewed within a context of his own culture. Rather than the psychopathic personality so often presented in the psychiatric literature, the addict was characterized with positive as well as the usual reprehensible traits. Within the street culture, the addict could be seen as resourceful and clever, enjoying pursuits that gave his life meaning and adventure."[54] The use of the medical model includes an individualistic approach, an assumption of intrinsic deviance, cure, contagion, and the clinical tradition of ignoring negative findings. How do we evaluate validity apart from the judgment of the sponsoring community?

One might, in fact, argue that the major advances in understanding drug use and abuse, especially the role of policy itself in shaping the problems, have been contributions of qualitative research often supported by researchers themselves, universities, or foundations—but seldom by the government. These contributions may not, however, be recognized until "complementary" or "supplementary" quantitative studies are completed.

Program evaluation. When we move from social policy research in general to evaluation research, suggestions for validity enhancement come to sound much like suggestions for efficient problem solving. In an attempt to replicate what he sees as the relevant scientific structures in this context, Campbell favors *selection* of ideas for support rather than the encouragement of novelty:

> Do we need more novel ideas? Or do we need most to better winnow out among the plethora of intelligent and creative ideas those that are most valid, most worthy of building upon? Contrasting the unsuccessful social sciences, pure and applied, with the successful physical sciences, leads this essay to favor emphasizing the latter . . . we should be funding fewer topics more densely.[55]

However, even when the findings of policy research, especially evaluation research, meet all methodological canons of validity, the programs evaluated may achieve their results in ways that are inaccessible to correlational research. Unless we wish to restrict social science to efficiency criteria we should be wary of narrow designs that fail to look for spurious relationships or the unanticipated consequences of well-intended programs. For example, effective programs may succeed because they are based on effective *control* of deviants rather than the elimination of the "causes" of deviance, that is, punishing reasonable responses to inhumane conditions rather than changing conditions to permit real alternatives. The development and evaluation of methadone-maintenance programs is a good example of such a case. These programs are innovations that reflect an effective alliance of the medical and criminal-justice models, relying on a "new" and legally prescribed drug to "cure" addiction. The question of whether methadone is in fact different from heroin in its effects can hardly be asked without threatening the program. Meanwhile methadone has been added to the repertoire of street drugs.[56]

Concentration on formal control also leads to neglect of important resources for support and control in unprogrammed groups. One of the most dramatic findings of participant observation with drug users is the nature and extent of structured abstinence, controlled dosage and ordered effects. These phenomena tend to be ignored because the drug users' sources of information and sanction are not formal and legitimated by outside criteria. An important comparative study of patterns of PCP use, for example, finds dramatic differences between groups in the use and effects of the drug. Cleckner notes that "many individuals have resources in their environments which allow them to control and limit the negative effects of drugs . . . As with other drugs that have been problematic in the past, the solution may lie in working with social environments that encourage abusive behavior regardless of the substance ingested."[57]

ENHANCING VALIDITY?

Optimizing validity can become a narrow organizational and administrative goal, and not the best way to ensure that we are getting high quality results in our research. Validity (internal and external) is a concept rooted in a quantitative, measurement-oriented conception of science. In this sense, it can be an especially appealing criterion for legitimating research findings from the point of view of governmental or other administrative and social control agents and agencies. A focus on validity in this narrow sense separates the research community from its audiences, clients, and subjects and reinforces the notion of a social system of science that is immune to "external" social forces and values. The concern for establishing, sustaining, and reinforcing a research community producing knowledge that is "useful" from a humanistic and ecological point of view is better served by focusing on the social *relations* of science, and on the problem of generating a sense of the social nature and value of valid knowledge among researchers and users alike. It is important in this regard to understand that validity (or more generally, objectivity) is a social process, and that there are degrees of validity. The quality of the validity generated by any given community is a function of the degree to which the social interests of the community are general and diffuse rather than specific and focused.

As informal modes of consensus formation become stabilized and institutionalized, they become transformed into "truth tests" that appear to be independent of social forces. These tests can then be used as official guarantors of the validity of research results. More specifically, professionalization and bureaucratization cause creative and innovative ideas and actions to be devalued.[58] Such ideas and actions are a threat to the internal stability of the scientific profession. They also threaten the established social order, and the position of science in that social order. This is why Campbell's "social system of science" approach is so problematic. It is a theory about science that is not merely grounded in the findings of science but is also (and not incidentally) congruent with the conservative requirements of scientific ideology. A critical sociology of science cannot for any reason ignore the fact that epistemic communities develop "self-validating knowledge-use systems," and that the claims, predictions, recommendations, and theories of a prestigious epistemic community can be taken as warnings, become self-fulfilling prophecies, and facilitate social control.[59] Ignoring these social realities can only undermine efforts to apply social science knowledge in ways that are both effective and humane.

Standards of rigor and validity are historically and culturally situated. Moreover, the loosening of canons of rigor is often a condition for solving intractable problems, developing new approaches to get around obstacles, and generally for "getting things done." *Standards* of rigor, rationality, validity, and related notions are generally established by or associated with orthodoxy and authority. And, we should not forget the stake scientists have as *professionals*—as *workers*—in demarcationist strategies.[60] Admitting that scientists have ideological and professional interests and goals, but ignoring these factors in the interest of some sort of normative model of inquiry, only veils the complex social realities that link discovery and validation with issues of status, power, and prestige, make cognitive "correctness" context dependent, and link theories, methods, and social organization.[61]

The results of research in the sociology of science tend to undermine the tendency by some sociologists, historians, and philosophers of science (as well as some scientists and science watchers) to take physics as the paradigmatic (and for some the only "true") science, and to make hard distinctions between the methods, concepts, and findings of the physical and social sciences. The relevance of *practice* in physics as opposed to *theory* at the level of laws—the distinction between phenomenological and fundamental laws—is widely overlooked, as is the centrality of *qualitative* methods such as dimensional analysis, symmetry considerations, and perturbation theory.[62]

Just as *science* can be a label for the general problem-solving activities of humans and the variety of cultural, organizational, and institutional manifestations of epistemic work, so *enhancing or optimizing validity* can be viewed as a label for routines in the realm of argument, demonstration, and proof that are standard features of a culture that is self-sustaining and in some sense "growing" or "progressing." We do not object to the idea that we can analytically and socially isolate science in the above sense and develop the epistemic potential of human beings through the study and application of principles of social organization. And while we find the focus on enhancing or optimizing validity too narrow, we do not object to the more general idea that it is possible to enhance or optimize the human capacity for generating objective knowledge. But we must at the same time be concerned with developing *forms* of science and validity that embody and express humanistic values and social relations.

There are often overlooked social costs that have accompanied scientific "progress." It is thus important to develop an approach to enhancing validity or promoting objectivity that explicitly incorporates means for assessing and minimizing the social costs—such as alienation and the reification of research results—of scientific work.

What can be done to enhance validity and, more generally, what factors do we need to consider in our efforts to connect science studies and social policy? In the sense of achieving consensus and vigor within specialties, Campbell's suggestions for the organization of research groups, the encouragement of secondary analysis, and support of a variety of methods are challenging and important. In the sense of continuing to develop accurate, objective knowledge of society— real social science—breadth not narrowness is needed. The outlines for the communities that may eventually emerge as powerful sciences are not clear. Formal policy research is inevitably ideological; freedom needs to be built in by broadening the base of research support. Clients, including the public and the deviants themselves, need to be empowered as research sponsors, not merely consulted as control agents, moral entrepreneurs, or potential subjects of the cure for a social disease. Finally, research on policymaking and its consequences needs to elucidate the processes that restrict support for objective research, encourage narrow questions, and lead to the too ready acceptance of ideologically consistent findings.[63]

What is the "scientific" community? In the case of drug research there are several scientific communities, each asking different questions. Two factors prevent these communities from becoming more integrated. The first is the narrow problem definitions of the more quantitative tradition, and the second is the more critical implications of the findings of the qualitative tradition. This suggests that we might learn from the conduct of social science research something interesting about the conditions under which resistance, fraud, and failure may be experienced in the physical sciences.

There is indeed a dilemma in selecting methods. Quantitative methods are more persuasive, in part because of the specificity of the questions that are asked, and in part because they appear to duplicate the methods of the physical sciences. However, they may also be more likely to lead to erroneous conclusions precisely because of their narrowness; they are difficult to generalize from in a social setting without the use of untested but politically congenial assumptions. They also are less vulnerable to revision through interaction with the subjects of research; to the extent that quantitative methods provide contact with the perspective of the subjects themselves they involve the important potential corrective of contact with alternative experiences in the phenomenon under study. The search for valid knowledge will be enhanced to the extent that social science research is based upon, and legitimated by, broad and accurate knowledge of the potential for social development and change of the capacities and interests of relatively powerless individuals and groups. This requires improving opportunities for education and upgrading the literacy of the general population in all areas of human knowledge.

The more knowledgeable and involved a citizenry is, the more democratic a society is. And if the process of democratization is carried out to the extent that it becomes participatory, the social structure of society (as we know it in the United States, for example) will have been dramatically refashioned. Science will then be a new institution. Not only will it be more closely integrated with the interests of society as a whole; it will be a new mode of inquiry guided by the values of equality, cooperation, and participatory democracy. Enhanced validity (and objectivity) will be an inherent result of such a structural change. At the very least, this will realize some of the basic goals of the various "science for the people" movements. A more radical result would be the realization of a "human science" *of and for* the people fully integrated into everyday social life. A critical sociology of science can help to bring this alternative into focus by challenging taken-for-granted ideas about "successful science" and "social progress." More important, critical sociology of science can help to validate the organizational and cultural ideas that underlie the program for a human science.[64]

In the next chapter, I explore the general program for a sociology of objectivity that I have been developing since 1974. Chapter 7 includes a brief introduction to the sociology of mathematics and an argument for sociologizing epistemology.

7

The Sociology of Objectivity

At some point in the early 1970s, it occurred to me that the various interests I had in the sociology of science were all means to one end: to understand the sociological foundations of my and others' convictions about reality. My *basic* interest, then, was in understanding *scientific objectivity* as a social and cultural phenomenon. I would eventually realize that focusing on *scientific* objectivity committed me to the claims and realities of modern science as a social institution. I have already indicated why this is a problem. The alternative was to begin to think in terms of inquiry, and to focus on exploring "best possible" epistemic strategies. This eventually led me to conclusions I have adumbrated earlier in this book. I began thinking about objectivity as a social fact in the course of examining definitions of objectivity and how the concept was used.

The concept of "objectivity" has been described as "slippery," and burdened by a history of interminable and inconclusive discussions and contradictory usages.[1] It has been described as a value and an ideology that embodies and expresses detachment and alienation from self and society.[2] But objectivity as a troublesome philosophical concept, a value, and an ideology should not be confused with objectivity as the affirmation of an "objective reality." This affirmation is based on the fact that human beings do not and cannot know anything a priori. They must exert mental, physical, and social effort to gain knowledge. This is the basis of the general view of objectivity as the product of a social process widely referred to as "intersubjective testing."[3] Related views ground objectivity in the public and communal nature of science and scientific evidence.[4] Traditionally, then, there has been a generally accepted "social theory" of objectivity. It rests on the assumption that communication and exchange in a public forum or community of scientists are necessary and effective means for insuring that we admit to science only statements that are valid approximations to objective reality and not products of abnormal perceptions, selective and unique subjective cognitions, or "uncontrollable and unverified introspection."[5] This idea, superceded by a more sophisticated sociology of science, is still nonetheless considered viable, especially in philosophical circles.

In his *Critique of Pure Reason*, Kant used the term "objective" to refer to knowledge that could be justified independently of any individual's whim. If a justification can, in principle, be tested and understood by anyone, it is objective. Modern philosophers have followed Kant in labelling statements objective if they can be corroborated in intersubjective tests. Notice that while objectivity is sometimes referred to the potential for universal consensus, in practice we rely on corroboration by a limited number of people invested with the authority to establish "truth" by virtue of their qualifications and credentials.[6]

The extent to which a given definition of objectivity expresses its social nature varies from the use of such phrases as "universal agreement" and "the cooperative nature of scientific research" to Popper's conception of "social institutions" (e.g., laboratories, scientific periodicals, and congresses) as the collective bases for generating objective (scientific) statements.[7] Popper argues that an individual cannot simply decide to be "objective." Objectivity is a product of cooperation among scientists.

Assume, Popper proposes, that an individual, trained in science but now alone and isolated from communication with others, succeeds in building laboratories and observatories. This Robinson Crusoe writes numerous papers based on his experiments and observations. He has unlimited time, and ultimately succeeds in developing scientific systems that coincide with those accepted by "our own scientists." This, says Popper, would be as much an accident and a miracle as the case of science being revealed to a clairvoyant. There is, first of all, no one who can check this Crusoe's results, and correct the prejudices that are unavoidable consequences of his peculiar experiences. No one can help him exploit the inherent possibilities of his results because such possibilities are often recognized in the course of adopting "comparatively irrelevant approaches" to the results. There is no one for him to explain his work to. He is therefore unable to develop the ability to communicate his results in clear and reasoned ways. This is a discipline, Popper argues, that one learns only by having to explain one's work to people who have not done that work. Finally, he can only discover his "personal equation" in a revealed way, by noticing changes in his reaction time, for example, and learning to compensate. In "public" or "objective" science, reaction time is discovered by analyzing contradictions in the results of various observers. Popper concludes that objectivity is a social product and not a matter of an individual's impartiality. To the extent that it exists, the impartiality of an individual scientist is not the basis but the consequence of the "social or institutionally organized objectivity of Science."

In summary, Popper contends that scientific criticism, progress, and objectivity depend on cooperation, intersubjectivity, and public method. In a similar philosophical exercise, Norman Campbell concluded that a scientific Crusoe *could* develop science even though the criterion of universal assent could not be applied.[8] Campbell's Crusoe could replace the intersubjective criterion with "the criterion of the satisfactoriness and coherence of the laws which could be derived from the subject matter." This is interesting. If it is meaningful to consider social factors that facilitate objectivity, then it should also be meaningful to try to identify psychological (and biological) factors that facilitate objectivity. But Campbell's Crusoe would have to be socialized in some form of "scientific community" in order to be able to later carry out his work in isolation. It is with the nature of such a community that the sociology of objectivity is concerned.

Having accepted a social theory of objectivity, some students of science have gone on to ask what it is about the organization and values of science that accounts for its objective and progressive nature. One response to this query is that science is an adventure in rugged individualism. Michael Polanyi has been the most articulate defender of this *laissez-étudier* position. He argues that there is an "invisible hand" that coordinates the independent activities of individual scientists and leads to "unpremeditated" scientific discoveries. Goodall's view of science as a "genuinely democratic" system with "largely built-in guarantees that it is not going to get spoilt" is another version of the *laissez-étudier* (*laissez-faire*) position. Stated in its crudest and most sociologically vulnerable form, this position requires scientists to simply act in terms of their perceived self-interest; the "invisible hand" is then responsible for the "beneficial" social outcomes of these independent acts of self-interest. But *laissez-étudier* often gets linked to altruism and humanism so that scientists get portrayed as individuals whose self-interests *happen* to be "broadly humanisitic."[9]

The social theory of objectivity, based on the concepts of intersubjectivity and consensus was, generally speaking, formulated and systematically developed by philosophers of science. It was a theory that on the surface seemed to conform to the canons of the sociology of science. And indeed it was an uncritically accepted "theory" in the old sociology of science. Joseph Ben-David, for example, concluded that public test, logic, experiments, and empirical observations gradually eliminate *personal* biases and mistakes.[10] Kuhn's assumption that the individual rigidity caused by normal science is compatible with scientific progress is also part of a "social theory" of science. But these "sociological" and quasi-sociological viewpoints, like their parent philosophies of science, cover up a problematic psychology of science with an *unproblematic* sociology of science. Why, for example, doesn't Ben-David consider the identification and elimination of *social* biases and mistakes to be as much an issue as the identification and elimination of *personal* biases? Why doesn't Kuhn consider *rigidity* to be as much a problem for social institutions as for individuals? A sociologist *should*, in fact, consider intersubjectivity and consensus problematic; they are social processes and activities, and therefore precisely the sorts of phenomena sociologists take for their subject matter rather than for granted.

Popper's three world hypothesis poses a somewhat subtler but related problem. Dewitt, for example, interprets Popper's discussion of Worlds 1, 2, and 3 (the physical world, the mental world, and the world of intelligibles, or objective ideas) as implying that one head can, in principle, perceive World 3 accurately. (Sociologists should become instantly alert whenever someone attaches the phrase "in principle" to a form of human thought or action; it is often, if not always, a sign that the behavior at issue is realistically impossible). DeWitt's interpretation follows from his assumptions that objective knowledge transcends even intersubjectivity, and that World 3, the world of abstract entities, is not part of what we usually think of as culture. Admitting that we are still struggling to make sociological sense out of higher level abstractions (in, for example, the sociology of mathematics), it is still fair to point out that DeWitt fails to show how a cultural process can generate what he conceives to be an acultural, extra-cultural, or trans-cultural domain.

What DeWitt does is compound the sociological difficulties of Popper's World 3 concept by introducing a non-social "one head."[11] The sociology of objectivity ultimately aims at making World 3 a sociocultural phenomenon.

The Sociological Problem of Objectivity

One of the basic objectives of sociologists of knowledge is establishing relationships between types of social structures and types of knowledge. This idea had occurred to Francis Bacon:

That monarchies incline wits to profit and pleasure, and commonwealths to glory and vanity. That universities incline wits to sophistry and affectation, cloisters to fables and unprofitable subtilty, study at large to variety; and that it is hard to say, whether mixture of contemplations with an active life, or returning wholly to contemplation, do disable and hinder the mind more.[12]

The systematic development of the sociology of knowledge in the late nineteenth and early twentieth centuries is associated with names such as Marx, Mannheim, and Scheler. Scheler, for example, associated Plato's theory of ideas with the organization of the Platonic academy; he followed Troeltsch in arguing that Protestant beliefs determined and could only exist in the form of organization of the Protestant churches and sects; and he argued that *Gemeinschaft* societies generate a traditional, conclusive fund of knowledge rather than a form of knowledge which is continuously subject to discoveries and extensions.[13] The generalization of these types of hypotheses led to an intolerable relativism in the sociology of knowledge. For, it was argued, if "scientific theories" are rooted in social milieux, then the prospect of obtaining warranted knowledge appears utterly futile. Objectivity then appears to be "an arbitrary emulsion of social conditions, regarded as proper in its time as soothsaying was by the Greeks who once stood before the gleaming towers of Troy."[14] Indeed, if we accept this perspective, what warrant is there for the sociology of knowledge, which must itself be "nothing but" a product of its particular social milieu?

The problem can be resolved as follows. First, as Mannheim recognized, the sociology of knowledge can trace the emergence of different types of knowledge to different social milieux, but it cannot judge the truth-value of these systems. Secondly, if types of knowledge are rooted in types of social milieux, we can set ourselves the task of discovering the social conditions under which "scientific" or "objective" knowledge is generated. The literature on science and society illustrates a number of approaches to this task. The facilitative relationship between science and democracy has been commented on by Tocqueville, Sigerist, and Merton among others. Merton sees some basis for the provisional assumption that science flourishes in democratic milieux.[15] He notes that science in some form has existed in all kinds of societies; but the crucial question is which societal type(s) facilitate(s) the "fullest measure of development" in science. The emphasis in these and related inquiries is on external "social forces" that facilitate or obstruct scientific activity and scientific progress. Internal social forces that affect science as a social activity, process, organization, or institution are treated incidentally if at all. To fully comprehend science as a social fact, we must attend to internal social forces. Professionalization and bureaucratization are examples of such forces. Both processes have been associated with the emergence of science as an autonomous, progressive social activity. Their continuing impact on science has stimulated some concern about dysfunctional consequences.

Richard LaPiere argues that the adaptivity of the universities and of the professions has decreased as they have become increasingly bureaucratized:

1. *Rewards for bureaucratic conformity* tend to be higher than rewards for innovative behavior.
2. *Bureaucracies tend to exercise some control*, directly or indirectly, over nonmembers; thus scientists often have to design their work in accordance with the "rules and prejudices" of bureaucratic organizations; and
3. *Established, or "mature" bureaucracies tend to resist adaptation* to changes in external conditions and to resist adopting available innovations.[16]

Bureaucratization, according to LaPiere, tends to subordinate individual to collective decision-making, dividing responsibility for a given decision. This can easily lead to the negation of responsibility, and then to a failure to act effectively with regard to internal organizational problems, or broader "external" societal problems.

The dysfunctions of bureaucratization are reinforced by and reinforce the dysfunctions of professionalization. The two processes are linked at least to the extent that they are concomitant in the modern history of industrializing nations. Professionalization has been associated with the increasing specialization in the division of labor, the knowledge explosion, and the increasing demand for management expertise in highly technical and bureaucratized societies. In the process of professionalization, an occupation becomes "relatively colleague-oriented," with practitioners seeking exclusive rights over naming and judging their mistakes.[17] The goals of professionalization include standardizing, specializing, gaining status for occupational roles and services to society, and "objectivizing," that is, limiting the impact of subjective elements on performance and service.

One of the first, and among the foremost, students of professionalization, Carr-Saunders concluded that:

> . . . taking all in all the growth of professionalism is one of the hopeful features of the time.[18]

The dysfunctions of professionalization, however, arise precisely from the "hopeful" tendency toward occupational demarcation. This creates a volatile potential for subordinating reason to dogma:

> . . . once given its special status, the profession quite naturally forms a perspective of its own, a perspective all the more distorted and narrow by its source in a status answerable to no one but itself.[19]

In his analysis of the medical profession, Friedson argues that while professional autonomy may have facilitated significant increments in knowledge about disease and treatment, it "seems to have impeded the improvements of the social modes of applying that knowledge." Horowitz affirms this aspect of professionalization:

> The professional can, by virtue of his professionalism, exempt himself as a scientist from responsibility for the ends to which his scientific findings are put.[20]

The negation of responsibility, as I noted earlier, has also been associated by LaPiere with bureaucratization.

The literature on professionals and complex organizations has traditionally stressed the conflicts inherent in linking the roles "professional" and "bureaucrat" based on differences between "professions" and "bureaucracies."[21] This research focuses on the independent professional's resistance to bureaucratic rules and supervisors, rejection of bureaucratic standards, and conditional loyalty to the bureaucracy. But Scott notes an increasing convergence of bureaucracies and professions, as bureaucrats become professionalized and professionals become bureaucratized. In this convergence, the dysfunctions of the two processes are likely to reinforce one another.[22] Bureaucratization, for example, may reinforce tendencies in professionalization toward occupational closure and dogma with its demands for "reliability of response and strict devotion to regulation."[23] To the extent that the dysfunctions of bureaucratization and professionalization become increasingly salient and converge, we can expect a tendency toward occupational closure, an ethnocentrism of work, and a decrease in the capacity of individuals and organizations to respond to problems in critical and creative ways. Horowitz has remarked that the ultimate consequence of this process may be the "loss of objectivity."[24]

The important point to consider in reviewing the literature on the dysfunctions of professionalization and bureaucratization is not so much what it reflects about particular empirical realities, but the fact that it illustrates the mutability of social facts and the potential that exists in all social phenomena for dysfunctional or pathological transformation. Philosophers and other students of science have acknowledged the potential for evolutionary change in science, but they have not given adequate attention to the potential for devolutionary change inherent in science as a social phenomenon.

Consensus and Intersubjectivity

Objectivity is associated with truth, or true belief. In other words, objectivity is a relationship between human beings and "objects of inquiry" that leads to truth. Meynell argues that truth is trans-social; it is a product of the capacity for self-transcendence, that is, of the capacity "to come to know what actually is so, and not just 'so for me' or 'so for the members of my society'." But persons who have what Meynell refers to as the basic mental faculties necessary for ascertaining truth, and who live in societies which stimulate the development and facilitate the use of those faculties, may develop radically distinct and conflicting beliefs. Meynell contends that in such cases there must "tend to be at least a *convergence towards agreement* (my emphasis) so far as the parties concerned attempt attentively, intelligently, and reasonably to pool their resources." There must be a movement toward *consensus*. But this is part of the social theory of objectivity and raises again the problem of appealing to an unproblematic social activity and process.[25]

What constitutes consensus? Is it the "universal agreement" referred to sometimes in the rhetoric of science? In fact, objectivity is not a matter of universal consensus but of a certain type of restrictive consensus. *Intersubjective consensus*, for example, could be used to refer to the type of consensus that occurs among properly certified human beings whose sensory apparatuses are in "proper working order" and who in modern times have become known as scientists. They rely on this type of consensus in deciding whether given statements about reality are "objective." But there are other types of consensus, all of them restricted in one way or another. *Special consensus* is associated with the so-called "man-of-knowledge," his apprentice, and his associates; the case of Castaneda and Don Juan (fictional or not) is exemplary.[26] *Individual consensus* might be used to describe the result of achieving cognitive consistency; this type of consensus is the basis of idiosyncratic, personal, or subjective knowledge. Types of consensus develop on personal, group, and sociocultural levels. They are the result of specific kinds of relationships between people and environments (physical, biological, and social), and they lead to the construction of distinguishable realities. It is important to note that all types of consensus involve some sort of intersubjective testing (even individual consensus, which can be conceived as a product of internal dialogue). This should not be obscured by the fact that the term, "intersubjectivity," has to some extent been preempted by science and is not readily appropriated for more general usage. Schutz and others have, of course, discussed the intersubjectivity of everyday life. Schutz's analysis of intersubjectivity can be viewed as a model for the transformation of intersubjectivity in science from the taken-for-granted into the problematic.[27] Incidentally, it is conceivable that an advocate of the distinctive nature of intersubjective testing in science might argue that science is the only mode of knowing in which egalitarian and communal norms are operative. This argument would have to be rejected given the social stratification of the scientific community.

Intersubjectivity and consensus do not solve the problem of the demarcation of scientific and non-scientific knowledge and do not guarantee objectivity. The failure arises not because intersubjectivity and consensus have nothing to do with objectivity, but because they are treated as unproblematic. The awareness that intersubjectivity and consensus are problematic leads to the following problem: assuming that it is, in the first place, possible to define objectivity as a social fact, what type of intersubjectivity and what mode of consensus are most likely to stimulate the creation of objective statements about reality? To solve this problem, it is necessary first to examine the ideas of reality and objectivity.

Reality or Realities?

In recent years, we have become accustomed to such terms as "alternate-," "alternative-," "separate-," and "multiple-realities" in many areas of intellectual life. These terms are kin to such terms as "paradigms," "glosses," and "language games." They pose a challenge to the idea that there is "one reality"—an idea central to some viewpoints as the necessary condition for scientific inquiry. Storer, for example, assumes that there is "but a single physical reality 'out there';" Meynell contends that true belief "is about the one real world."[28] In such cases, the pluralist view of reality may appear to undermine the program for the scientific pursuit of truth (or objectivity). Consider, for example, LeShan's view. He distinguishes an ordinary reality of separate objects, simultaneous happenings, and simple cause and effect relations from a relativistic reality of flowing events. He treats "firewalking" as an activity that takes place in an alternate reality. Some people can walk on white-hot coals without burning their feet. Those of us who can't walk on hot coals operate in a different reality. LeShan argues that there are a number of "equally valid definitions of reality, and in one of these . . . firewalking is possible."[29]

There are different views of what alternate realities refer to. Don Juan's argument that he was "deglossing" Castaneda (as opposed to Castaneda's view that he was being "reglossed") and introducing him to a "pure wondering perception" has been interpreted by J. C. Pearce as an argument for separate but equal realities. For Carl Oglesby, the message is "that realities, although they may be various, are not discontinuous, are *not* separate from one another."[30]

William James and Alfred Schutz offer another perspective on alternate realities. In his *Principles of Psychology*, James suggested that there are several, perhaps an infinite number of, realities; he called them "sub-universes." He distinguished the worlds of (i) sense (physical things, the paramount reality), (ii) science, (iii) ideal relations, (iv) "idols of the tribe," (v) mythology and religion (the supernatural), and (vi) individual opinion, sheer madness, and vagary. Schutz seized on James's suggestion as an important insight but freed it from its psychological context by developing the idea of *finite provinces of meaning*, each of which may be given "the accent of reality."[31]

The property of finiteness implies that provinces of meaning— each characterized by a specific cognitive style and consistent set of experiences—are not mutually referable via transformation formulae. One "gets" from one province to another through what Kierkegaard called a "leap." Such a leap is subjectively experienced as a "shock," and is accomplished by modifying the tension of consciousness, that is, by changing one's *attention à la vie*. Following Bergson, Schutz argues that there are an infinite number of planes in conscious life, ranging from the plane of action to the plane of dream. The tension of consciousness is highest on the *plane of action*: "our interest in meeting reality and its requirements" is at its highest. This is the realm of "wide-awakedness"—attention is active and directed. The tension of consciousness is lowest on the *plane of dream*—there, attention is passive. Here Schutz's meaning is congruent with contemporary theories of attention and consciousness such a C. O. Evans's theory of absorptive and deflective attention, and Erika Bourguignon's theory of states of consciousness and degrees of nervous system arousal.[32]

Each finite province of meaning has a specific tension, *epoch* (suspension of doubt), spontaneity, self-experience, socialty, and time perspective. The world of everyday life is the archetypal reality; all other finite provinces of meaning are modifications of it. Schutz suggested that we try to systematically group finite provinces of meaning in terms of their constitutive principle, their degree of consciousness-tension. It is reasonable to conclude, if we accept Schutz's point of view, that each finite province of meaning could be associated with a type of intersubjective testing and a mode of consensus.

The idea of alternate realities informs the dialogue on the relationships between science and other modes of knowing. One way of dealing with the problem of science and religion as alternate realities, for example, is to distinguish between the *hypotheses* of science and the *dogma* of a church, a more or less political distinction if we consider the early history of modern science. Duhem separated the two realities along more intellectual lines (though the distinction between political and intellectual here may be spurious). The Roman Catholic physicist argued that physical theory can neither support nor oppose *any* metaphysical assertion or religious dogma. More recently, scientists and theologians have argued for convergence or complementarity between science and religion. Furthermore, LeShan and Capra have proposed that ancient mysticism parallels, converges with, and is analogous to modern physics. Arguments relating ancient wisdom and contemporary knowledge are not unusual in the history of ideas, and there are notable parallels between the views and rhetoric of LeShan and Capra and those of earlier thinkers, such as Ficino, Pico, Bruno, and others in the Renaissance period.[33]

The conflicts and contradictions between the "one reality" and "many realities" views can, I think, be resolved. This resolution may be achieved by, first, accepting physicist David Bohm's view of reality as "an inexhaustible diversity and multiplicity of things (e.g., entities, properties, qualities, systems, levels), all of them reciprocally related and all of them necessarily taking part in the process of becoming, in which exist an unlimited number of relatively autonomous and contradictory kinds of motion." Second, the resolution of the conflicts between the "one reality" and "many realities" views requires following the implication of the "bootstrap hypothesis" in elementary particle physics, the hypothesis that the universe is a self-consistent whole, or in Helier Robinson's words, a "singular possibility" and a "single polyadic relation" (i.e., a single structure which *can* be conceptually divided into substructures, and *is* so divided in, for example, the rational mode of thought).[34]

This proposed resolution is consistent with both the existence of an "objective reality" *and* the existence of "multiple realities." It is consistent with the existence of an "objective reality" at least in the negative sense that it does not contradict or preclude "lawful relationships" or the possibility of their discovery. This in part follows from our experience that actions and their consequences are not arbitrary. With regard to multiple realities, our ability to take different *perspectives* on reality in given states of consciousness and to have different *experiences* of reality in altered states of consciousness may be a *manifestation* of inexhaustibility and polyadicism and the *source* of notions about other realities besides so-called everyday reality. That is, a given phenomenon (a chair, for example) can be examined from different points of view in terms of (i) spatial relations, and (ii) disciplinary or perspectival orientations. The different viewpoints and interests of an artist, a carpenter, a person looking for a place to sit, and a physicist will lead each of them to "see" something beyond what each of them in an *ordinary* (normophrenic) state of consciousness will describe as a "chair." This is not the same as experiencing the chair differently than others do (as a glowing, flowing set of lines, for example) because you have altered ordinary perception-consciousness by ingesting a drug, or by any other means.

The reality we experience is always (constituted in) a *relationship* between ourselves, others, and things. The experience of reality always contains some "objective content" that transcends (but is not alienated from) the various unique qualities of self, setting, and time. The relationships between self, others, and things are adaptations; thus *"realities"* are *adaptations*. More generally, each reality is a worldview. Later I will generalize this to "theories."

If there is, in the Bohmian sense, an "objective reality," does this mean that the problem of demarcating different modes of knowing is indeed one which we must solve? In a sense the answer is yes; but this does not imply that we know or can discover a demarcation rule in any conventional sense. The reason is that the Bohmian conception of reality leads to an unconventional conception of objectivity.

Objectivity as a Social Fact in a Bohmian Universe

There is an objective reality in the following sense; (i) our experiences can be summarized in "lawful relationships" (not necessarily "causal" ones), and (ii) there are "things" that existed before you and I were born, and that will continue to exist when we are dead, but that can never be experienced as "things-in-themselves." Objective reality is a relationship between inquirers and objects-of-inquiry; it is ever-changing, infinite in breadth and depth, and, as a whole, incomprehensible. It is an open-ended system. *Information* in a Bohmian universe is always increasing (syntropy overrides entropy).

If we want to find out as much as we can about open-ended, ever-changing reality, we must behave and think in an open-ended, ever-changing way. If objectivity is a social fact, it must be an open-ended, ever-changing social fact. Individuals who want to be objective (engage in the *process* of objectivity) must strive to become open-ended, self-actualizing epistemic agents. We are, from this point of view, inquiring, self-reflective organisms (epistemic agents). Survival, and beyond that, the growth, expansion, and evolution of the quality of life and consciousness depend on our abilities to tap the effectively infinite capacity we have (individually and collectively) for critical, creative inquiry. The degree to which the societies we live in and the processes of socialization we experience are open-ended will determine the degree to which we will be able to achieve open-ended living and thinking.[35] Open-endedness entails the continual generation of new information in the universe; in conjunction with inexhaustibility and polyadicism, this insures the continual generation of new ways of comprehending our experiences. Whether this in any sense could be interpreted in terms of "closer and closer approximations to the true nature of things" is indeterminate and probably irrelevant. Values, lifestyles, and the conditions for objectivity are intimately interrelated and interdependent. In fact, the process of objectivity from this perspective appears as the process of human beings adapting to, transforming, and evolving in the world: the search for the conditions of objectivity is the search for the conditions of survival, adaptation, and evolution.

It should be obvious that there is no way to decide *a priori* whether reality is singular or plural; nor can we anticipate constructing a basis for such a decision in the future. However, on the basis of our negative experiences to date with finite and finalistic systems of thought and explanation, in the light of the various tendencies to rigidity which we encounter in the physical, biological, and social realms, and given the wide range of cases in which contemporary thinkers in intellectual and practical settings have turned to or come upon open-ended solutions and theories in response to a wide variety of problems, it seems *reasonable* to act as *if* reality were Bohmian.[36]

The Rejection of Relativism,
the Privileged Status of Science, and the Strong Program

The acceptance of the notion of many realities and the acceptance of the notion of an objective reality lead to the rejection of relativism. In its extreme form, relativism implies that the privileged status of a mode of knowing can only be established by virtue of, for example, its association with a center of political-economic power, its power of persuasion (independent of "universally" applicable standards of logic or rationality), and/or its power of prediction. But there is, or so I am assuming, a reality that is infinitely unfolding, polyadic, and re-lational. The problematic nature of intersubjectivity and consensus thus comes to mean in this context that some types of intersubjectiv-ity and consensus may be more fruitful than others for any given time and place in the unfolding of human inquiry. The open-ended view I have sketched is an imperative for incorporating the full range of modes of inquiry in the pursuit of objectivity. This should be done without giving a priori preference to one mode or another and without assuming that the sociology of scientific knowledge, or truth, or ob-jectivity, must be a theory of rationality. In either case, the restric-tion of an a priori preference would interfere with the possibility of developing a full-fledged *critique* of science as a whole.[37] This strat-egy would apply in the case of any prevailing mode of knowing; for the moment, it is the basis for rejecting the *strong program* proposed by Bloor.

Bloor argues that the best strategy to follow if we want to give an account of scientific knowledge is "to adopt the scientific method it-self."[38] This might be a reasonable position if there were some rea-son to believe that the "scientific method" is, first of all, a method and, furthermore, that it is a finished, universally valid method of in-quiry whose levels of complexity are well-known and whose applica-tion is entirely straightforward.[39] From the assumption of a Bohmian reality, it follows that the study of science using its own methods ex-clusively can never reveal the limitations of science or new horizons of inquiry. Even if reality is in some sense static, it is so extensive and complex that it is difficult to imagine how we would go about convincing ourselves that we have discovered a universally valid and unchanging mode of inquiry.

The problem of the limits of the sociology of knowledge may arise in part on account of an implicit imperialism, that is, on account of the assumption or implication that a given statement or idea (in science, but also in mysticism or in any other given knowledge system) is solely, or ultimately, a social product. This assumption should be rejected on the grounds that sociology attends to limited aspects of human experience, and that the full range of factors in human experience must be drawn on to account for human creations. This does not resolve the problem of what "proportion of any given thing" can be accounted for by this or that discipline. But this is a matter of testing the explanatory powers of different disciplinary orientations and combinations thereof; and the problem may, in fact, change radically or disappear altogether if the disciplinary strategy is transformed or transcended (by some form of holistic inquiry, for example). Contrary to Meynell, who seems to advocate a rather orderly pursuit of truth, I conceive truth or objectivity as a process firmly rooted in intellectual conflict. The conflict need not be violent or combative in the conventional sense; it can be of the kind which is constructive and based on mutual respect.[40] But struggle and conflict are in any case conditions of social and intellectual change, and permanent features of Bohmian reality.

The Sociology of Objectivity

The sociology of knowledge can contribute to identifying the conditions under which knowledge systems undergo closure and stagnate. It can also help to identify the conditions under which knowledge systems resist closure. But resistance to closure implies open-endedness. Thus, the sociology of knowledge can help to identify the conditions under which human inquiry is most likely to resist stagnation, or, in other words, to be developmental, progressive, or evolutionary. This, given the Bohmian view of reality, must be considered a perpetual problem which allows only limited and regional solutions. The introduction of the general term, "inquiry," is necessary in order to avoid the two-pronged problem that science is (i) a culturebound term, activity, and process, and (ii) subject to the stagnating and stifling effects of social processes such as bureaucratization.

The perspective I have sketched changes the nature of the problem of bias, whether personal or social. Bias is unavoidable. Inquiry in the best sense, that is, open-ended, developmental, progressive, or evolving, is characterized by the presence of a *certain type* of bias, *not* the absence of bias. This can perhaps be better appreciated if we recognize that knowledge systems can be construed as worldviews: Clifford Hooker has shown that philosophies of science such as empiricism and realism can be so construed; and similarly, sociologies of knowledge and science under labels such as "Mertonian" and "neo-Marxist" can in the same way be construed as worldviews. Revealing worldviews in science, or in philosophies and sociologies of science, involves a meta-inquiry into, for example, theories of reality, consciousness, and social action.[41] If a knowledge system can be construed as a worldview, it cannot be free of bias since by definition it contains ideological and political dimensions, and is hence a value-laden system. Value-free and value-neutral inquiry is, from this point of view, impossible.

Modes of knowing, including those of science, are worldviews and, therefore, as worldviews, are value-laden. They are biased, but they vary in their capacity to (i) generate, over time, statements consistent with our changing experience of reality, and (ii) stimulate our involvement in reality as a dynamic process. These capacities are related to organizational and value aspects of modes of knowing.

The *sociology of objectivity* is the study of the social and cultural conditions of inquiry and how these conditions affect our individual and collective abilities to construct objective statements and develop objective knowledge. There is a need to conceptualize objectivity in a way that (i) avoids absolutism and relativism, and (ii) links commitment to truths (substantive, methodological, and theoretical) with perpetual openness to signals that may alter that commitment (which includes the possibility of becoming aware of new sensory apparatuses). The notion of ideal or transcendental truths may reflect the relative stability of *substantive* truths; *methodological* truths may be somewhat less stable but not as unstable as *theoretical* truths. However, since all three types of truths are interrelated and interdependent, it should be clear, even if somewhat paradoxical, why even the most obvious so-called truth or objective statements must be considered problematic. More generally, it might be useful to distinguish between *informational* and *comprehensional* objectivity. An objective statement might then be defined as one which is consistent with the full range of information possessed by the human species at a given time and "known" to a single ideal intelligence. Information exists to the degree that it is possible for human beings to achieve certain effects by carrying out certain actions in accordance with certain principles and to be able to do so repeatedly. Information tends to accumulate into relatively stable and increasingly universal "bundles" which can be pressed into operation in appropriate circumstances (e.g., the objectivity of selecting and eating edible mushrooms). At this level, objectivity approaches limits defined by the boundaries of information niches. But the ability to be objective about mushrooms is not simply a matter of the "facts" about mushrooms; the ability is dependent on intersubjectivity and consensus probabilities.

Objectivity has a second dimension which I refer to as comprehension. It is in this sense that the concept of objectivity as a process is most clearly established. For we can learn to do things, and once we learn to do them, repeat them over and over, generation after generation, with the same degree of success: in this sense, we can say that we "know" something. But our comprehension of what we do can and does change; our theories change. They change because of new information in the form of new signals, new configurations of old information, or new sensory apparatuses which tune us in to new realms of information. Our theories become new worldviews, so that so-called "eternal" truths change in terms of how we "see" or comprehend them.

The degree of objectivity (objective content) in any given statement is determined by ascertaining the scope and depth of the information available to, or "in," a given individual, group, or community. Thus, the most objective statements that can be made at present about *any* human experience, can be made by the people, groups, and communities who, or which, have had the widest psychic and physical exposure to human experience as a whole, that is, in the present and in the past through exposure to historical accounts. The most objective statement possible about the nature of, for example, a star (the statement with the highest possible objective content) is constrained by the range of experiences it is possible to have as a human being on this planet. The most objective mode of inquiry at any given time is the mode of inquiry practiced by those who have access to the widest possible range of human experiences, and who are oriented to exploring the limits of those experiences in order to expand their range. Note that while objective statements are referred to an ideal system (the omniscient knower), they are not themselves conceived as "existing" in an ideal or transcendental form or realm.

Objectivity is more than just a matter of "statements:" it is a complex, unfolding process of relationships, feelings, thoughts, intuitions, "imponderables and ineffables." A sociological theory of objectivity must take into account, for example, the prominence of "unreasonable" modes and motives in the history of science. Discoveries in science can be: (i) the result of "hardwork and luck" even when the driving force *appears* to be mathematical or theoretical "reasonableness" (as in the case of, it now appears, the discovery of Pluto); (ii) stimulated by unusual or bizarre experiences (as in the case of Poisson, whose interest in pendulums may derive from his childhood experiences of swinging to and fro on a nail upon which he was sometimes hung for safety by a nurse who had to leave him alone for short periods): (iii) indirectly by personal traumas (the young Newton, for example, seems to have been stimulated to pursue his studies with greater dedication in order to overtake a boy who stood ahead of him in class—after that boy had kicked him in the stomach); and (iv) achieved by the suspension or alteration of conventional canons of logic and rigor (as in Wallis's treatment of infinitesimals).[42] Once we get past positivistic and idealistic reconstructions of science, it becomes easy enough to read the history of science as a record of irrationalities, bizarre incidents, and improbable events. However, that history can also be read as an argument for establishing and sustaining conditions of open-endedness and pluralism.

The sociology of objectivity as I conceive it operates on the assumptions that (i) no objective statement or truth can ever be final or absolute; (ii) no system for arriving at truth can be universally valid and unchanging in its foundations; and (iii) a broader context for establishing truth always exists than that of any system of knowledge which is given or which is dominant. By definition, the first assumption is not an objective statement or truth; this, then, avoids a classical paradox! By virtue of these assumptions, the sociology of objectivity should contribute to generating new contexts and meanings for truth or objectivity. This perspective, incidentally, tends to dissolve the distinction DeGre made years ago between gnosio-sociology and the sociological theory of knowledge.[43] Perhaps the most important substantive problem that a sociologist of objectivity must face is the traditional recalcitrance of mathematics in the light of the sociology of knowledge. This recalcitrance has been slowly undermined over the past fifty years, and especially in the last fifteen years or so through the efforts of Bloor, MacKenzie, and myself and Randall Collins. In the following section, I highlight some of the main achievements and problems in the sociology of mathematics in ways that carry forward the idea of a sociology of objectivity.[44]

The Sociology of Mathematics

The sociology of mathematics has grown slowly on the periphery of developments in mainstream sociology of knowledge and science. Spengler, Hessen, Wittgenstein, Struik, and Needham were among the small group of important contributors to the sociology of mathematics between 1920 and 1970. But their contributions were overshadowed by the development of functional analyses of the social system of science that virtually excluded studies of mathematical activities and knowledge. Mannheim explicitly exempted mathematical knowledge from sociological inquiry. During the past twenty years, new directions in the sociology of knowledge and science have helped to stimulate interest in and research on mathematics as a social phenomenon. The renaissance in Marxist science studies, the "strong program" in the sociology of knowledge, and ethnographic studies of science have helped to break down the traditional barriers to sociological studies of mathematics. This is a critical development because among all systems of knowledge, mathematics has been the most resistant to sociological incursions and the ultimate arbiter of the limits of the sociology of knowledge.[45]

Consider the statement "$2 \times 2 = 4$." This is a condensation of thousands of years of human experience *within* a particular community of consensus. This community is virtually universal, but earthbound. There are situations and communities of consensus (especially in higher mathematics) for which "$2 \times 2 = 4$" in its conventional sense is not meaningful, (e.g., Kline 1962, 582, 661, 665; cf. Gasking 1956, 1710). It cannot *mean* the same thing (in the semantic sense) to a pre-Socratic and to a modern mathematician familiar with modular algebras.[46]

Given the statement "$2 \times 2 = 4$," one would have to establish a whole set of conditions that are usually taken-for-granted (e.g., the existence of certain prerequisites for arithmetic manipulations such as "normal" cognitive functioning) before its meaning could be specified. The fact that most if not all humans and cultures live under those conditions *does not* make "$2 \times 2 = 4$" a "pure" or "transcendental" truth. Nor does the fact that certain experiences and statements may *bridge* worldviews or that worldviews may overlap, contradict the idea that numbers are parts of worldviews. All knowledge is simultaneously mediated by mental-and-physical activities, culture, and history. Mediation entails that we are integral with, not separate from, "external reality."

We cannot separate even "obvious" statements such as "$2 \times 2 = 4$" from the mediation process and assert that they represent a universal, eternal, ultimate reality, or that they represent the one-and-only "true," "objective" reality, as opposed, for example, to a Dostoevskian reality in which "$2 \times 2 = 5$."[47] Certainly, there is a "reality" that exists independently of the lives and deaths of individual human beings and the rise and fall of civilizations; but it is a reality human beings are part of, a reality that can only be known through mediating activities of human beings, and a reality that is more or less common to us all to the extent that we participate in the same or overlapping communities of consensus. But the novelty that arises at the intersection of unique individuals and cultures, and the universals of human experience, makes it inevitable that such similarities or overlaps must eventually give ground to incommensurable differences between worldviews.

There is no a priori reason to bar sociological analyses of numbers and number relations. This does not mean that "social causes" can explain everything about everything, but rather that there is a social component in every mathematical entity, and in every unit of knowledge, and that therefore, sociology can help to explain at least some aspect of any given knowledge phenomenon.

Alternative Mathematics, Relativism, and Realism

Bloor (1976) and Wittgenstein (1978, 1976) have discussed alternative mathematics and alternative arithmetics, respectively.[48] But they have not demonstrated that their alternative number worlds are incompatible with some form of realism.

Wittgenstein suggests two types of alternative arithmetics. First, he asks us to consider two communities: in one (our own, for example), $7 + 5 = 12$; in the other $7 + 5 = 13$. His argument here is not convincing to realists primarily because the "other" community simply cannot be made to appear a "fair" alternative. The people Wittgenstein makes up are just not "real." This alternative arithmetic leaves realism unscathed in the sense that it is not a case for relativism unless we are ready to accept imaginative alternatives as a basis for relativistic arguments.

The second "alternative arithmetic" arises in the case of *errors* that, for *practical* reasons, are too subtle for us to discern. This is contrasted with the case of *miscounts* (on what Wright refers to as the "best possible perceptual evidence") in cases where objects are perceptually accessible.[49] An alternative rooted in practical limitations and exigencies clearly cannot qualify as an alternative arithmetic in any radically relativistic sense.

Bloor leads us down the same path. He considers, for example, the case of the syllogism: All A is B; C is A; therefore, C is B. He sets the limits of the sociology of knowledge at the threshold of the *rule* of the syllogism; that rule is not questioned. What *can* be questioned and negotiated—and what, therefore, can have social causes—is any particular *application* of the syllogism. Is C really an A? Are all things counted as A's really B's? It is clear from this example that Bloor's "alternative mathematics" is not at all incompatible with the "real" mathematics (and logic), in which the syllogistic rule holds.

It appears from these examples that alternative arithmetics and mathematics are not a basis for relativism. They leave intact a recalcitrant reality that constrains our number worlds and serves as a basis for ascertaining errors, miscounts, philosophical games, literary license, and so on. There is some sort of relativism suggested by variations in mathematical ideas and some sort of realism suggested by recalcitrant phenomena. Can this dilemma be resolved?

The Relativism-Realism Dilemma

Spengler was alert to the relativism-realism dilemma prompted by a "naturalistic" interpretation of mathematics. He identified two different kinds of a priori thought content. First, there are certain things that seem to be valid across Cultures, centuries, and individuals. Then there are "necessities of form" characteristic of given Cultures. These two kinds of thought are associated, respectively, with realism and relativism. Spengler argues that there is no way to define a boundary between these two kinds of thought content; indeed, there is no way even to demonstrate the existence of such a boundary. As a consequence we must press our inquiries forward without any a priori restrictions based on the demarcation of truths or facts that are and are not independent of human contexts. In other words, since the demarcation problem is insoluble, we must proceed *as if* no boundaries exist. Specifically, Spengler argues as follows:

> So far, no one has dared to assume that the supposed constant structure of the intellect is an illusion and that the history spread out before us contains more than one *style of knowing*. But we must not forget that unanimity about things that have not yet become problems may just as well imply universal error as universal truth . . . Conclusions on the deep and final things

are to be reached not by predicating constants but by studying differentiae and developing the *organic logic* of differences.[50]

Wright, in his critical analysis of Wittgenstein's remarks on mathematics, concludes his discussion of relativism and realism on a note that is harmonious with the views of Spengler, but perhaps clearer as a strategic dictum: We must be prepared to act on the possibility that things might be otherwise—regardless of the strength of our conviction about "necessary truths." What Wright does (and here, I think, he helps to clarify Wittgenstein's program) is to show that the relativism-realism dilemma is a political dilemma:

> The decision involved when we accept new necessary statements not by way of adopting an explicit convention but as the result of, in the widest sense, proof would be one of policy.[51]

The principle of Caution, according to Wright, prompts us to grant the acceptability of a *necessary* statement and grant the weight of "whatever" prompts us to accept the statement as necessary—including appeals to imaginability and the like—but in the end we will only agree that the statement is "well founded." This Cautious attitude, more than anything else, is essentially political; it expresses an *unwillingness* to participate in linguistic institutions such as the institution of proof.

Hooker resolves the relativism-realism dilemma as follows: He admits, to begin with, that some form of skeptical relativism is a reasonable response to the results of research on the social and historical dimensions of science. Such research clearly suggests that science is relative to sociopolitical interests, values, culture, and history. On the other hand, we experience the recalcitrance of the world daily in the nonrandom relationships between actions and reactions, acts and consequences. Hooker writes that he sees no better way of dealing with the positive features of relativism *and* realism than:

> to construe cognition as the exploration of possibility structures, to construe theories as hierarchically organized conjectures concerning possibility structures, and to construe systems of norms (expressing values) as conjectural theories.[52]

Like Wright, Hooker wants to be a realist, but not the kind of realist who becomes trapped by seeking binding necessities that may prematurely stifle inquiry or close information pathways. Elsewhere, Hooker takes the position that there is no justification for investing a conjecture with positive or absolute belief.[53]

Spengler, Wright (along with Wittgenstein), and Hooker try to avoid the *pathologies* of realism and the *absurdities* of radical relativism. So too, Feyerabend separates himself from the radical relativist and the naive realist by distinguishing between philosophical and Protagorean relativism—and adopting the latter position:

> It is not asserted, for example, that Aristotle is as good as Einstein; it is asserted and argued that "Aristotle is true" is a judgment that presupposes a certain tradition; it is a *relational* judgment that *may* change when the underlying tradition is changed.[54]

Relativism and realism are polar intellectual strategies. Individuals and cultures seem to swing between these extremes.[55] Spengler, Wright, Wittgenstein, Hooker, and Feyerabend all seem to agree that the best way to deal with the relativism-realism dilemma is to recognize that it involves a policy decision and to adopt a strategy (policy) of "conjecturing." This is just one of many strategies that can be adopted. Each strategy reflects a particular stance, more or less advantageous or disadvantageous, in the arena of intellectual conflicts over scarce material and symbolic resources.

In the case of the sociology of mathematics, it makes sense to pursue the notion that every mathematical statement is socially determined not because that seems to be an ultimate truth but because it may lead to some insights. This orientation is compatible with the paradoxical query Gregory Bateson once posed about whether there are any "true ideologies."[56] Number worlds are embedded in and reflect worldviews. Worldviews are products of social structures created by people as they strive to determine and utilize patterns and regularities in the world. The success of these structures and their accompanying worldviews in the struggle for survival and development is a measure of the extent to which they give us access to the world in all of its fullness, multiplicity, and depth and not to an illusory "flat earth" reality or a narrow (for example, ethnocentric) vision of the real world.

Mathematics and Rationality

It has become fashionable to argue that science is not a privileged mode of inquiry. Science, mysticism, witchcraft, astrology, and "primitive" belief systems cannot, according to some authors, be distinguished by any "rationality criteria." Barry Barnes, for example, writes:

> We possess no rationality criteria which universally constrain the operation of human reason, and which also discriminate existing belief systems, or their components, into rational and irrational groups. Variability in institutionalized beliefs cannot be explained by a conception of external causes producing deviations from rationality. Likewise, the culture of neutral science cannot be distinctive because of its rationality, in a universal rather than a conventional sense.[57]

Hooker argues that how epistemic agents and communities work, whether some are "better" than others, and so on are open questions:

> (Are we really historically in a position to decide between a Zen Buddhist or Tibetan culture and our own?—even with respect to exploration of the real nature of the universe?) Certainly it will typically require temporal spans much longer than an individual lifetime. The more so, since there is scarcely an extant (or past) culture that has tolerated critical inquiry to any significant degree yet (one of the reasons why we have never attempted a "metacultural" rapport with Zen Buddhist or Tibetan Culture in the spirit of critical, comparative exploration).[58]

Not even the *achievements* of mathematics are incontestable. Thus, Morris Kline argues that "the developments in the foundations of mathematics since 1900 are bewildering and the present state of mathematics is anomalous and deplorable," that mathematics is not always as rigorous as outsiders are led to believe, and that proofs are not as important as intuitions, even though mathematics is our "chief accomplishment, the product of man's own reason . . . (and) our most effective link with the world of sense perceptions."[59]

That mathematics is not as rational as some people think, or that it is no more rational than the Azande "poison oracle," does not mean that all modes of inquiry are equally valid. Some modes of inquiry *are* better than others. One basic error the relativists *and* the realists make is that they compare what are assumed to be monolithic belief systems. But belief systems are not monolithic; in fact, every belief system probably contains elements of every other belief system. The elements associated with the most successful strategies for adapting to and transforming the world are, for many scholars, associated with mathematics and science. But mathematics and science are human activities subject to all sorts of organizational and psychological pathologies. Perhaps idealized versions of mathematics and science *symbolize* the best adaptive and transformative strategies humans have developed in their struggles for survival and development. Mathematics clearly warrants careful scrutiny in the search for the "best possible" ("most rational") intellectual strategies for gaining and accumulating knowledge. But an uncritical a priori commitment to mathematics is *not* warranted if the commitment must be based on a monolithic view of mathematics and ignoring the social roots and social trappings of mathematics-as-it-is.

If mathematics gives the appearance of being paradigmatically rational—in the sense of "successful" *and* in the sense of being based on "sufficient," "reasonable" grounds—it is perhaps because it has not only been developed under social conditions that foster the construction of general principles "valued for themselves" but also that it has carved out as its subject matter the most general language for systematically talking about the world. And if "success" seems too pragmatic as a rationality criterion, it might do well to consider David Hilbert's 1925 remark: "In mathematics as elsewhere success is the supreme court to whose decisions everyone submits."[60] It is important to consider changing fashions in mathematical proofs and the cycles of rigor and loss of rigor in the unfolding of the history of mathematics in our search for "the rational."[61] In order to come to terms with the recognition that there is a recalcitrant reality *and* that human beings socially construct reality, we can perhaps do no better than follow Fleck. "Truth," according to Fleck, is neither "subjective" nor "relative," nor simply a matter of "convention." At least, the words "subjective," "relative," and "convention" are misleading if they obscure truth as "a stylized solution." Truth is "an event in the history of thought," "stylized through constraint" in its contemporary context.[62]

It *is* possible to discriminate among knowledge systems in terms of some sort of "rationality" paradigm. But the paradigm cannot be rigid, and it must be rooted in success and the contexts for defining and ascertaining success. The paradigm might be strengthened by examining the scale and scope of past successes and the probability of future successes on a large scale and with increasing scope as we review different strategies for knowing.

Finally I would like to explore the implication that I read into the idea of a sociology of objectivity concerning the end of epistemology. I carry out this reading initially by way of a critical discussion of Richard Rorty's program in the philosophy of science.

The End of Epistemology

Rorty's aim is to extend the line of thought in analytic philosophy represented by Quine, Sellars, and the later Wittgenstein, and including Dewey, James, and Heidigger.[63] In particular, he is concerned with developing the implications of their common commitment to holism and pragmatism. Holism is associated with the thesis that justification is a matter of conversation or social practice rather than of a special relation between words or ideas, and objects. Pragmatism makes truth a matter of "what it is better for us to believe" (James) rather than of "accurate representation." Rorty's crucial premise is that if we understand "the social justification of belief," or the rules of a language game, we "understand knowledge;" there is then no need for a theory of "accurate representations." In other words, there is no need for epistemology as we understand that discipline from Locke and Descartes to Kant; there is no need for a discipline that "grounds" knowledge-claims. This does not imply that once we understand social justification or the language game we understand all that there is to understand about knowledge. But any "extra understanding" cannot be furnished by epistemology; rather, it would derive from studies of the history of language, brain structure, evolution, and society and culture.

Rorty argues that the idea that there can be something called "foundations of knowledge" or a "theory of representations" depends on the sorts of a priori constraints imposed by the Cartesian claim that "ineluctable truth" can be found by "turning inward" and the Kantian claim that truth "imposes limits" on what can be arrived at through empirical inquiry. This reduces to the Kantian need for a universal, neutral framework within which all past, present, and future inquiry can be anchored and criticized. In summary, the idea of "foundations of knowledge" rests on a metaphor about beliefs and objects:

1. Beliefs are determined by being brought face-to-face with objects of beliefs.
2. Understanding how to know better means understanding how to improve the activity of the Mirror of Nature, a "quasi-visual faculty." This entails thinking of knowledge as "an assemblage of accurate representations."
3. It is possible to find within the Mirror of Nature a privileged class of representations. This class is distinguished by its being

formed from representations of compelling truth. The indubitable accuracy of these representations justifies us in considering them accurate representations. The privileged class of representations is the privileged foundation of knowledge.
4. The theory of knowledge through which we identify privileged representations is the foundation of culture.
5. The neo-Kantian consensus is the final product of substituting *confrontation* for *conversation* as the determinant of what we believe.

Rorty's reply to the foregoing principles is:

If we have a Deweyan conception of knowledge as what we are justified in believing, then we will not imagine that there are enduring constraints on what can count as knowledge, since we will see "justification" as a social phenomenon rather than a transaction between "the knowing subject" and "reality." If we have a Wittgensteinian notion of language as tool rather than mirror, we will not look for necessary conditions of the possibility of linguistic representations. If we have a Heidiggerian conception of philosophy, we will see the attempt to make the nature of the knowing subject a source of necessary truths as one more self-deceptive attempt to substitute a "technical" and determinate question for that openness to strangeness which initially tempted us to begin thinking.[64]

Certainty is not a product of a special relation between human and non-human realities but of conversations between persons. If we want to understand knowledge, we must attend to social contexts, not to the relationships between inner representations.

Rorty thus urges us to renounce Plato's invention, "philosophical thinking," and the search for unshakeable foundations. Instead, we should rejoin the Sophists in their quest for an "airtight case." In brief: drop the idea that language is the source of a priori knowledge, along with the Kantian self-image of philosophy—and decide the issue of understanding knowledge in favor of the pragmatists; choose pragmatism, not relativism, in opposition to realism.[65]

Rorty suggests two major roles for philosophers of knowledge, a hermeneutic one and an epistemological one. The former involves viewing inquiry as routine conversation; the latter involves viewing conversation as implicit inquiry. The hermeneutic philosopher is an "informed dilettante," a "polypragmatic, Socratic intermediary between various discourses." He/she charms "hermetic thinkers out of their self-enclosed practices." Disagreements are compromised or transcended through conversation. Hermeneuticists are united in a *societas*—they are people united by civility, rather than by a common good, much less a common ground. This is in dramatic contrast to the epistemologist, the Platonic philosopher-king, the cultural over-seer who has access to the "ultimate context" of Form, Mind, and Language. In this Platonic world, participants are united in *universitas*, sharing interests and a common goal.[66]

Sociology is at the heart of Rorty's argument for the hermeneutic option. He presses us to focus on conversations, social practice, social bases for belief, our "interlocutors" rather than our "faculties:"

> ... if we have psychophysiology to cover causal mechanisms, and the sociology and history of science to note the occasions on which observation sentences are invoked or dodged in constructing and dismantling theories, then epistemology has nothing to do.[67]

Quine renounces the conceptual-empirical, analytic-synthetic, and language-fact antinomies. But he does not give up the distinction between the postulated and the given. Sellars renounces the latter and holds to the former. Rorty is right to claim that in each case the argument is prevented from reaching its conclusion by a lingering Kantian commitment. He presses the argument forcefully, and seems to be on the brink of transforming philosophy into sociology by destroying the mirror metaphor. But he reaches a limit too. On the brink, he turns back, and revives epistemology. In arguing for abnormal and "existential" discourse, he concludes by stating that such discourse is "always parasitic upon normal discourse." So in the end it turns out that hermeneutics is "always parasitic upon the possibility (and perhaps upon the actuality) of epistemology."[68]

Another limitation emerges in his closing remarks:

> The only point on which I would insist is that philosophers' moral concern should be with continuing the conversation of the West, rather than with insisting upon a place for the traditional problems of modern philosophy within that conversation.[69]

This explicit restriction of moral concern to "the conversation of the West" is a serious limitation on Rorty's argument and is, ultimately, the same sort of limitation he criticizes in Sellars and Quine. On the brink of a radical social construction conjecture on the nature of knowledge, he is prevented from stepping over by several factors: (1) his stress on the ideal of polite conversation and his failure to deal with the more militant and even violent forms of social practice in science and the wider culture; (2) his Western bias, manifested in his intellectual and cultural debts; (3) his ultimately saving critique of epistemology (which, in a crude sense, saves the jobs of the philosophers who do epistemology out loud); here he ends up in the Kuhnian camp—hermeneutics is revolutionary science, epistemology is normal science. This lands us in a Kuhnian model that serves science-as-it-is, and that cannot produce an in-depth critique of science nor an alternative in social structural terms; (4) his focus on justification. Beyond the brink Rorty reaches, constructivist sociologists of science are arguing that justification *and* discovery (or invention as some people prefer to call it) are both through and through social processes. Rorty is a little better than Kuhn only in the sense that his social rhetoric has a little more sociological substance (mostly imaginative rather than empirical, however).

The dialogue between sociology of knowledge and epistemology has flirted with a radical sociological reconstruction of our understanding of knowledge and culture. To some extent the dialogue has been polite academic conversation; to some extent it has bordered on disciplinary imperialism; and to some extent it has introduced issues of everyday life and moral concerns into otherwise hermetic exercises. I want to urge that the excursion into sociology by epistemologists be extended; and argue the futility of an epistemologically relevant sociology that falls short of a full-fledged worldview analysis, critique, and reconstruction of science. It is my continuing objective to work toward a liberatory social practice that takes priority over orthodox notions about the value of science-as-it-is, pure and applied; at the same time, I defend the value of epistemic activity and epistemic agency. These are not aims that can be set forth systematically and rationally defended; they are statements about what I think it is worth our while to strive and struggle for.

Three ideas stand out for me in the sociology-epistemology dialogue: (1) knowledge as a social construction; (2) knowledge as a coping mechanism; (3) knowledge as a moral issue. Rorty entertains all three ideas. Suppose then we approach Rorty the way Rorty approaches Sellars and Quine: by identifying areas of agreement, identifying limits, and then pressing past these limits in the interest of completing the argument. If Rorty is going to bring in conversation and social practice, then why not full-fledged social construction? If he's going to view justification as a social process, then why not carry discovery along too? If he wants to think in terms of moral concerns, coping, and civility, why not think in terms of a full-scale sociological theory of knowledge that expresses an explicit value-commitment and that is grounded in the everyday realities of power and conflict rather than in the pseudo-civil discourse of the academic world? If we're going to leave Plato behind, then why not articulate an agenda that not only declares our commitment to egalitarian and democratic values but also our readiness to combat fascism, oligarchism, elitism? If we are going to defend abnormal discourse, or revolutionary science, then let's not be complacent about normal discourse and normal science. Let's recognize the degradation and alienation in normal modes and commit ourselves not to accepting the inevitability of a circulation of modes but to seeing if we can create and sustain social structures and worldviews that de-alienate and de-fetishize cognitions, knowledge, and representations. Instead of following Kuhn, let's join Bohm, Feyerabend, Hooker and others who have sought to develop a self-critical inquiry grounded in a well-articulated but flexible worldview.

I suggest the following extensions of Rorty's arguments; first: extension of his notion of knowledge as conversation or social practice to the social construction conjecture; second: extension of his notion of hermeneutics as a coping mechanism dependent on epistemology to a general hermeneutics that reduces to an agenda for knowledge in permanent revolution; third: extension of his weak notion of "moral concern" to a full-fledged political agenda. The first extension is summarized in "A," and the second and third extensions are in "B" at the end of this chapter. These extensions imply the end of epistemology. But they imply much more too. For as Rorty suggests, the end of epistemology is an end to a certain way of doing philosophy. If we interpret this conclusion in terms of its broadest implications, we will find ourselves confronted with the end of a certain way of doing inquiry, and finally with the end of a certain way of living. In order to stop doing philosophy or sociology as usual, we must stop "doing life" as usual. The obstacles we encounter or erect to prevent subverting normal discourse, normal science, normal life may ultimately limit or end our conversations and our conflicts. But they can never be deterrents (rational, logical, or otherwise) to the search for more humane ways of doing inquiry and wiser ways of living than prevail in the normal world. What follows are rationales for the conjectures I conclude with.

The social construction conjecture ("A" below) is that all forms of knowledge, representations, and cognitions are *constitutively* social. The history of this conjecture is coincident with the history of the sociology of knowledge and science. For most of this history, it has been defended for social studies, not for the natural sciences and mathematics. In recent years, studies of scientific practice and knowledge have contributed to generalizing and strengthening the social construction conjecture. I should like to give a brief example of what this conjecture implies for studies that rely primarily or entirely on cognitive approaches.

McClain and others have given substance to the conjectures of thinkers from Archytas to Leibniz and Spengler on audial cultures and mathematical musicology. Spengler's views are especially interesting. He pointed out the centrality of music in ancient culture, suggested that Pythagorean numerology was derived from music, and noted that the music of the ch'in was a "path to wisdom." But he also stressed that ancient music was linked to morals, religion, and other areas of social life. The significance of Spengler's remarks on the relationship between mathematics and religion (cf. Stieglitz's comments on numbers and gods) has yet to be fully appreciated in scholarly and lay circles.[70]

Studies of music and culture in China provide additional materials for a "political economy of music." Musical notes were connected with directions for ritual dancing and military activity; magic squares were correlated with musical symbols; and mathematical harmonics was linked to dynastic legitimacy.

If Platonic wisdom cannot be understood apart from the audial and mathematical musicology conjectures, neither can it be understood by removing it from its elitist and oligarchic contexts. Benjamin Farrington illustrates the importance of social and political contexts for understanding Greek thought in his studies of science and mathematics in Greek society. More generally, the theme of harmony and order that links those who composed the ancient texts and those who now analyze them is often associated with conservative responses to the problem of evil, social disorder, and threats to political legitimacy. In its extreme form, the theme is an outgrowth and a component of law and order political economies. Similarly, some forms of holism are associated with totalitarian policies. It is also important to consider the *social* significance of the algorithmic imperative in the wisdom texts, especially in relation to issues of social power and social control. Pribram, for example, seems to accept the machine-like qualities of logarithms and Fourier transforms uncritically. Are these mathematical devices *simply* neutral tools for dealing imaginatively with complexity?

The "journey eastward" and the glorification of ancient wisdom as the source, the pure form, or the salvation of modern knowledge and culture are not unique features of the current epistemic climate. In the Weimar period, Richard von Mises defended "speculative natural science," and argued that relativity and atomic physics recalled the ideas of the Pythagoreans and Cabbalists. The Cambridge Platonist More contended that Moses had Cartesian mechanics. In the wake of the Hermetic tradition, Newton described himself as a "rediscoverer" rather than an "innovator." Campanella wrote a letter to Galileo in which he claimed that heliocentricity is "a return to ancient truth" and portends "a new age." Medieval scholars searching for a *prisca theologia* "discovered" Pythagorean and Platonic anticipations in Moses and the Biblical prophets. The nineteenth century did not produce a "tao of physics" but it did produce a "religion of geology." The description of Bohmian physics as "mystical science" echoes Sommerfeld's concept of "Atomystik," the eighteenth century idea of *physica sacra* (which expressed the belief that Newtonian physics and Genesis are in "perfect harmony"), and various systems of *physiktheologie*. I rehearse these near and far antiquities because they suggest that the "return" and the "harmony and holism" of today's so-called "mystical sciences" are stock features of an intellectual strategy that gains strength and prominence recurrently when one or more of the following situations arise: (1) prevailing, established, and more or less rationalized modes of thought lose their potency; (2) prevailing modes provoke attacks from intellectuals who feel that the modes' unqualified successes *or* massive failures threaten to subordinate *or* suffocate alternatives; (3) a favorable shift in the opportunity structure and newly available resources for intellectual activity improves the position of peripheral modes of thought, more or less independently of the power and status of prevailing modes.

Haunted by the Holocaust and in the shadow of the Bomb, it is not surprising that people turn to ancient wisdom and the "east" for solace and renewal, to escape from science as well as to save it. I put "east" in quotation marks because once someone settles on an "alternatives" or "parallels" strategy, he or she can discover alternatives to Western science in Jesus as well as Lao Tze, or find quantum and relativistic parallels in Aristotle as readily as in Buddha. I consider the argument that the ancient (and especially the eastern) mystics *had*, in some sense, modern science or privileged access to the nature of reality to be unwarranted. However, the argument has historically been and may still be a useful strategy for challenging and rejuvenating routinized and rigid rationalities.

Historical sociology adds a reflexive dimension to arguments that link knowledge systems across time and space through analogies or homologies. Reflexivity is not a central feature of discussions about ancient wisdom. As a result, the arguments tend to fit the "swing of the pendulum" model suggested by Pribram in his remarks on the need to provide a "counterweight" to offset the "current overweighting of one mode of thought." This model may describe movements between opposing cognitive themes; but it offers no pathways to *new* cognitive themes. For that, to pursue the metaphor, we would have to think in terms of swings through a wider than normal arc, and swings in a different plane of thought.

The use of analogies to establish parallels between ancient and modern knowledge systems is subject to a variety of semantic, ideological, and sociological pitfalls. Homological analysis is a more sophisticated enterprise. But homological studies can become quests for the least interesting universal structures, or for elusive "essences," "foundations," or "grounds." In the former case, the danger is that we will identify structures whose very universality makes them useless as frameworks for constructing radically innovative patterns of culture and cognition. In the latter case, structural analysis can align itself with such intellectual strategies as Platonism, Kantianism, positivism, and phenomenology. This set of God-surrogate strategies tends to close off what Richard Rorty calls the "conversations" of humankind (thought, criticism, curiosity) at the thresholds of Truth, Objectivity, and Reality, transformed into altars of Faith. I cannot say for certain that this orientation motivates some or all of the discussions and arguments about ancient wisdom. My feeling that it does play a part stems from the rhetoric of mystery, glory, spirituality, and holism the authors use. This is not the path to wisdom I recommend we follow. I prefer (with the reservations noted above) Rorty's notion of wisdom as "the ability to sustain a conversation;" this means viewing humans "as generators of new descriptions rather than beings one hopes to be able to describe accurately." This orientation is not entirely absent from the sorts of analsyses I am criticizing; it tends to be overshadowed, however, by a more orthodox posture about which I have reservations.

Structural parallels are not surprising in ancient cultures which were still relatively undifferentiated and culturally intimate with highly undifferentiated prehistoric and contemporary societies. In a structurally undifferentiated society, parts and wholes tend to interpenetrate with little or no mediation. This situation is not clarified by invoking holographic metaphors or the holistic paradigm as much as by examining available resources, communications networks, the social practices of everyday life, and the distribution of power.

Perception and cognition are multi-modal; they are simultaneously visual, aural, emotional, and more. More importantly, they cannot be separated from social relations. This is probably the single most important conclusion to emerge from the empirical sociology of knowledge and science during the past twenty years. Once we recognize that knowledge is socially constructed—in the radical sense that all forms of knowledge are constitutively social—it becomes easier to root ideas in social contexts. There is no romance and nothing to glorify, for example, in Farrington's analysis of the *social* function of the Noble Lie. A sociological perspective can help us avoid the danger of viewing history as the province of heroes and elites; historical figures (Plato, for example) who *do* stand out are more likely to appear as exemplars of cultural patterns to someone studying history with a sociological eye than as minds for all seasons and arbiters of all future modes of thought and discourse.

Wheeler views the mathematical musicology conjecture as part of the explanation for the "sudden" emergence or invention of "the sciential animal." In my view, the sciential animal was a social product, and the "suddenness" was a social-cognitive and not a purely cognitive revolution. That is, certain "sciential" intellectual strategies that had already crystallized came into prominence as social institutions. In the Greek case, this process is rooted in the Ionian commercial revolution, the emergence of a slave-based economy, and other social developments. One problem with telling the sciential animal story in purely cognitive terms is that legacies such as "Platonic wisdom" are stripped of their social trappings, and the representations of social institutions are disguised as free-floating mental constructs.

The hermeneutic strategy should be generalized methodologically and theoretically. This will, for one thing, allow us to see *science* for the hermeneutic strategy it is and make us more effective in addressing the abuses of science and creating humane alternative forms of inquiry and culture. It will also make it easier for us to abandon the quest for Essentials and privileged representations.

The laboratory studies, mathematics studies, and other developments in social studies of science provide a rationale for a social construction conjecture. A second set of conjectures extends and modifies Hooker's world view analysis of philosophies of science, and earlier work on this problem by Zenzen, Chubin, and myself.[71]

Constructivist and Emancipatory Conjectures—
Paradigm for a Sociology of Objectivity

The following summaries are preliminary and exploratory. They are designed to be starting points for discussion and debate. My minimal claim about these conjectures is that they can help us defend ourselves against the alienation bred by normal discourse and normal social practice. If it helps, the reader can think of what follows as an experiment in abnormal discourse.

    A. The Social Construction Conjecture: The following conjectures owe much to the works of Bloor, Hooker, Barnes, Fleck, Knorr-Cetina, and Douglas.[72]

1. Societies, communities, and thought collectives are sustained through discursive practice, and more generally social practice.
2. Social practice integrates psychological and biological states and processes, social relations and activities, and material things and processes.
3. Thoughts (cognitions, knowledge) are products of, sustained by, and embody social practice.
4. Predicates, classifications, and representations are organized into rules, laws, or norms. Rules, laws, or norms are organized into networks. These "rule networks" are associated with and guide behavior and thought in every social context. Rule networks are metaphorically interconnected; meaning "flows" or "leaks" from one context to another between structural similarities. Every social act therefore tends to be laden with meaning overflowing from the rest of the concerns of social life.
5. Representations (etc.) are therefore products of, sustained by, and embody social practice. They are socially constructed assemblages of cultural resources whose meaning is given by their role in social practice and their location in rule networks, or more broadly networks of meaning (worldviews being the most comprehensive networks of meaning).
6. Representations arise out of social practice; they carry within themselves the social forms of the settings within which they are produced, diffused or distributed, and utilized. They are locally and historically stylized solutions in the service of social interests.
7. Representations "re-present" social practice and social interests.

8. Social interests are any material or symbolic resources perceived to be relevant for a group's survival and for gaining advantages in relative power, privilege, and prestige. Attributed interests are social interests perceived to be relevant for a group by "outsiders," and may be more or less congruent with group perceptions (interest attribution is a social interest).

9. Social interests are manifested in the claims individuals make on cultural resources on behalf of the groups they represent, are members of, or aspire to membership in or association with.

10. Social interests are always relevant to a particular arena of competitive social practices.

11. Representations are multi-dimensional tools (or adaptive mechanisms, or strategies) for adapting to and transforming the world. They are designed within agonistic arenas of diverse social practices, and with the objective of developing, furthering, or protecting social interests. The degree to which their original production renders them "generalizable" varies.

12. Depending on the level and intensity of competitive social practice, representations will act, more or less, as remonstrances, protests, expostulations, calls to battle, or slogans.

13. Because representations embody social practice and social interests, they carry within themselves the particular social locations of their production, diffusion, or distribution, and utilization; and they become located in the structure of the sacred and profane, conservative and radical values, and purity and danger.

14. Some of the representations of dominant groups are likely to be labeled "self-evident," and put in use to enforce conformity, put a subject beyond dispute, and deal with ambiguous and anomalous events. These representations will be prime targets for those who want to criticize, change, or demolish the reigning social order.

15. In general, the wider and more diffuse the social interests embodied in a representation, the more it qualifies as "objective." Objectivity, in other words, is a variable, and it is a function of the generality of social interests.

16. Aesthetic and truth motives are not denied, but they are viewed as rooted in individual and social interests ranging from making one's way in the world through tension management, to exercising control over a cultural environment; there are no "pure" motives, cognitions, representations, or modes of thought.

B. An Emancipatory Epistemic Strategy: The following conjectures are components of a self-articulating, self-critical worldview.

1. Action conjecture. An epistemic agent's current states are functions of imagined states, of preferred, probable, and possible future states, as well as (as in the case of epistemic *engines*) of past states and current environments. (this is the first major modification of Hooker, that is, shifting the analysis from an engine metaphor to an agency model).

2. Value conjecture. The Free Inquiry program is subordinated to the Free Society-Free Person program (following Feyerabend).

3. The Well-Being conjecture. The healthy or viable epistemic agent has the following characteristics: (a) *cautious*—prepared to act on—regardless of the strength of his/her convictions—the possibility that things might be otherwise (in keeping with Naess' Possibilism Slogan, "Anything is Possible"); willing to accept that certain things are well-founded, but refuses to participate in linguistic communities which harbor "necessary truths," "proofs," etc. (after Crispin Wright's principle of caution).[73] (b) *practices a mode of inquiry that sings, sizzles, and sighs*—after Nietzsche; (c) sees the search for "a reality shareable by all knowers" (D. T. Campbell) as a *search for a community of consensus*, not a search for "reality;" (d) is *anarchist/ dadaist* in Feyerabend's sense; (e) accepts *theories-in-use,* not theories-as-truth: (f) accepts a modified (perhaps transformed) version of Nicholas Goodman's *principle of objectivity*—". . . anything which is *practically* real should be taken as objectively real"; understands that anything that is practically real is real for a community of consensus; it is socially real, that is, it is socially constructed; (g) speculates on–Godel: fundamental limitations to consistent formal systems with self-images; Church: no infallible method for telling theorems of the predicate calculus from non-theorems; Turing: a termination tester is impossible (such a decision procedure would allow all problems of number theory to be solved in a uniform way; Tarski: no decision procedure for arithmetical truth; speculation leads to the conjecture that there is a *general limitative theorem* that transforms metamathematics into a strategy for everyday life. The GLT is operative on every level of reality, but also implies the existence of "jumps." Thus the GLT is not a barrier, but a motive for jumping to a bird's-eye view of science; this is a necessary condition for critique and renewal in science and more generally in

inquiry. There are limits to self-representation, but they may be inherently asymptotic in practice or it may be possible to transcend them through some social equivalent to a Kierkegaardian leap. The *capacity to live with contradictions* is crucial in this respect.[74]

4. Practice conjecture. The best possible epistemic strategies are *tinkering strategies*. A range of "dominant utilities" should be available in any given culture to maximize the potential for problem-solving, i.e., for survival and development.

5. Rationality conjecture. A rational act maximizes the probability of actualizing problem-solving potentials; this includes but is not limited to becoming a maximally efficient information processor. It is important to note that a theory of rationality (if one is needed) is not a theory of science.

6. Language conjecture. Language is a surface abstraction of a complex, rich set of cortically localized information processes; these processes are transformed and simplified from the "total stimuli" inputs of experience.

7. Demarcation conjecture. It is possible to tell the difference between an amoeba and a Zande, and between a Zande and an evolutionary epistemologist. But this is not a rationale for pursuing a traditional demarcationist strategy for distinguishing science and non-science. It reflects an expansion of the notion of a best possible epistemic strategy. A best possible epistemic strategy is determined by the scope of the schema of criticism, and the capacity for critical, reflexive meta-inquiry; and by the scale, level, scope, and depth of past successes, and the probability of future successes on a larger scale, higher level, with greater scope, and/or with greater depth.

8. Critical culture conjecture. The determinant of the general patterns of evolution and devolution is the "shape" (Hooker) of the total net of individual and collective ecologies and its accrued wisdom.

9. Reality conjecture. Reality is a never-ending process of unfolding in which new "things" are continually emerging; it is complexly determined—lawful but indeterminate. "Discoverable" laws, etc. are indicators of mechanisms which produce the phenomenal stabilities, irregularities, and fluxes we experience. It is a multi-level, heterarchical, open, and infinitely decomposable system (that is, there is no effective limit to the ways in which we can experience the world, trace causal chains, etc.). Local- or micro-sites can generate statements of wide (macro-)

applicability because of isomorphism and coupling. Locality is manifested in and at the intersection of nature, biography, and culture.

10. Comprehension, consciousness, and communication conjecture. The comprehension of any given thing is a dialectically changing configuration of rational, intuitive, and trans- or sub-rational/intuitive modes of knowing and consciousness. The domain of "rationality" is always changing; it is not restricted forever to what we now consider the best mode of inquiry (for example, "modern science"), or to realms accessible to conventional symbols or language. Language, ordinary or formal, is not preferred a priori as the medium of communication and comprehension. Comprehension encompasses information, explanation, understanding, knowledge, and appreciation. There are no statements or systems in philosophy, meta-philosophy, meta-inquiry, or any other self-styled foundational disciplines that are logically, ontologically, or epistemologically prior to or independent of social practice. There is no God, there is no First Philosophy, there are no Ultimate Grounds (phenomena-logical [sic] or otherwise), etc.

11. Pathology conjecture. Any conjecture can be pathologized. Pathologies may lead to irreversible damage, death, etc. A candidate for "best possible conjecture" (strategy) must deal with health and well-being as well as pathology. A preventive approach is inherent in the self-conscious, reflexive approach, but doctoring is not ruled out. Labeling a potentially useful change a pathology and aborting it is a risk of the first kind (Type 1); not taking evidence of a pathology seriously, or delaying action because of uncertainty or for other reasons in the presence of a pathology is a risk of the second kind (Type 2). Systems tend to get into ruts and to lose adaptive/transformative potential. The concern with well-being and pathology extends to an experiment designed to determine whether we can "jump" to a new epistemic strategy without losing local and phylogenetic continuity.

12. Possibilism conjecture. "Anything Goes" (Feyerabend) and "Anything is Possible" (Naess) are adopted as *policies* designed to prevent and doctor pathologies, and to foster open inquiry.

13. Adaptation conjecture. There are numerous and overlapping contexts of adaptation. They are not necessarily coordinated or compatible, and their spatial and temporal boundaries vary. Selection processes in these contexts are competitive.

14. Truth conjecture. All truth claims reflect "real" intersections of nature, biography, and culture. The world is an arena of competing truth claims; the competition is carried out in various contexts of adaptation. Success accrues in ways that do not necessarily lead to adaptation on the macro-level (society, species). More than likely, exploiting local opportunities will foster devolution on the larger scale of life. Conjecture 11 is a policy designed to change this connection in favor of micro- and macro-level integrations. Following Fleck, truth is viewed as a stylized thought constraint.

15. Rigor mortis conjecture. Rigor and predictability are not positively correlated; they are therefore not useful criteria for good "science" or good inquiry.

16. Dis-uniformity conjecture. Interesting things may happen when we abandon the assumption of uniformity in nature, or when the assumption breaks down.

Addenda

History is conceived to a reservoir of strategies, successes, failures, etc. which we can survey and draw from in our present; these are not things of the past, but things of the present, not things to respect but things to scan, play with, succeed and fail with, discard, reclaim, transform . . . It is necessary to ask about every strategy: what good is it, in what context, within what boundaries, for whom, with what costs, risks, and so on for individuals, classes, societies . . .

Science is subject to all the pathologies and perversions that can transfigure and misdirect social organization and its value-correlates—over-specialization, bureaucratization, ecclesiasticism, elitism, co-optation, etc. Science is particularly susceptible to algorithmitis (giving us Gresham's Law for Science: Successful procedural rules–bad science drive out understanding–good science), numberitis, and scientism.

Tinkering: The tinkering principle is that similar problems tackled by different people in different environments will yield different solutions. But the "limited possibilities principle" constrains solutions to different degrees and in different ways. The constraints operate at more or less general levels, and may apply to materials, forms, or principles.

The Hooker Fail-Safe Theorem: There is no justification for investing any of the above conjectures with positive or absolute belief.

Conclusion

Objectivity is a social fact. The achievement of closer, more detailed, and more exact approximations to objective reality in a universe of infinite diversity cannot be taken for granted. This has been recognized by students of the crisis in science. The crisis in science is a species-level crisis, one that reflects the emergence of ecological and evolutionary challenges that are new in type and scale. I do not believe that a new biological response is necessary for dealing with these challenges. New value orientations and new forms of social organization are necessary in order to survive in ways that enhance the lives of individuals and communities. New levels of consciousness concerning the physical, natural, and social worlds must be achieved. This applies to our consciousness of science as a social reality. Our conception of science must be broadened to include all inquiry pursued indefatigably, identifying and encompassing more and more of reality. The facilitation of science—or, inquiry—depends on developing an integrated perspective on (and, ultimately, theory of) the nature of reality, the psychology of inquiry, and the relationship between inquiry, values, and social organization. The primary concern of the sociologist of science in this endeavor is with social organization and how it facilitates and/or obstructs inquiry.

Notes

Chapter 1. Introduction: The Sociology of Science

1. Karl Marx's ideas on the social nature of science are scattered throughout his writings; see especially, *Economic and Philosophic Manuscripts of 1844* (Moscow: Foreign Languages Publishing House, 1956) p. 104. Emile Durkheim's speculations on the sociology of logic occur in the widely ignored conclusion to *The Elementary Forms of the Religious Life* (New York: Collier, 1961), originally published in 1912. Max Weber's *The Protestant Ethic and the Spirit of Capitalism* (New York: Charles Scribner's Sons, 1958), originally published in 1904–5, is the source of the widely debated Puritan ethic theses. And see his essay, "Science as a Vocation," pp. 129–56 in H. H. Gerth and C. W. Mills (eds.), *From Max Weber* (New York: Oxford University Press, 1946); the essay, originally published in 1904–5, is the topic of a book, P. Lassman and I. Velody, with H. Martins (eds.), *Max Weber's 'Science as a Vocation'* (Boston: Unwin and Hyman, 1989). And see F. Nietzsche, *Twilight of the Idols/The Anti-Christ* (New York: Penguin Classics), 1968, and *The Gay Science* (New York: Vintage, 1974); and O. Spengler, *The Decline of the West,* in two volumes (New York: Knopf, 1926, 1928), especially Chapter 2 of the 1926 volume, on numbers and culture.

2. See Norman Storer's editorial notes on page 281 of R. K. Merton, *The Sociology of Science* (Chicago: University of Chicago Press, 1973); for the basic ingredients of the Mertonian paradigm, see pp. 136, 139 (editor's notes), 175, 270, 559, 270ff., 340, 204, 209, 357, 446, 442, and 444.

3. R. Collins and S. Restivo, "Development, Diversity, and Conflict in the Sociology of Science," *Sociological Quarterly 24* (1983): 185–200.

4. K. Marx and F. Engels, *The German Ideology* (New York: International Publishers, 1947), p. 35; and K. Marx, *Manuscripts,* pp. 110–11, and *Grundrisse* (New York: Vintage, 1973), pp. 699ff.

5. See the introduction to Marxist sociology of mathematics in S. Restivo, *The Social Relations of Physics, Mysticism, and Mathematics* (Dordrecht: D. Reidel, 1983), pp. 179–207.

6. Spengler, *Decline,* pp. 56–70; and see the introduction to Spengler's views on numbers and culture in Restivo, *Social Relations,* pp. 211–31.

7. A. Sohn-Rethel, *Intellectual and Manual Labor* (London: Macmillan, 1978); and see my criticisms of his thesis in Restivo, *Social Relations*, pp. 205–7.

8. The material in this section is based on Collins and Restivo, "Sociology of Science," D. Chubin and S. Restivo, "The 'Mooting' of Science Studies: Research Programs and Science Policy," pp. 53–83 in K. Knorr-Cetina and M. Mulkay (eds.), *Science Observed* (Beverly Hills, CA: Sage, 1983); S. Restivo, "Some Perspectives in Contemporary Sociology of Science," in *Science, Technology & Human Values* 6 (1981): 22–30; and "Supporting Laboratory Life: Funds and Funding Sources as Contingencies in the Social Production of Science," paper prepared under a contract with the Division of Policy Research and Analysis of the National Science Foundation and presented in the PRA-NSF Seminar on Funding Sources and the Direction of Science, September 1983, Washington, DC. The contributions of my collaborators Randall Collins and Daryl Chubin are gratefully acknowledged without assigning any responsibility to them for my editing and rending of co-authored materials.

9. H. Small and B. Griffith, "The Structure of Scientific Literatures I: Identifying and Graphing Specialties," *Science Studies* 4 (1974): 17–40; D. Sullivan, D. E. White, and E. J. Barboni, "The State of a Science: Indicators in the Specialty of Weak Interactions," *Social Studies of Science* 7 (1977): 167–200.

10. S. Cozzens, "Taking the Measure of Science: A Review of Citation Theories," *Newsletter of the International Society for the Sociology of Knowledge* (special issue on new directions in the sociology of science, S. Restivo, editor) 7 (1981): 16–21.

11. See the critical discussions of citation analysis in A. Porter, "Citation Analysis: Queries and Caveats," *Social Studies of Science* 7 (1977): 257–67; D. Edge, "Quantitative Measures of Communication in Science: A Critical Review," *History of Science* 17 (1979): 102–34; and E. T. Morman, "Citation Analysis and the Current Debate Over Quantitative Methods in the Social Studies of Science," *4S Newsletter* 5 (1980): 7–13.

12. Diana Crane, *Invisible Colleges* (Chicago: University of Chicago Press, 1972); J. Ben-David and R. Collins, "Social Factors in the Origins of a New Science: The Case of Psychology," *American Sociological Review* 31 (1966): 451–65; N. Mullins, "The Distribution of Social and Cultural Properties in Informal Communication Networks Among Biological Scientists," *American Sociological Review* 33 (1968): 786–97, "The Development of a Scientific Specialty: The Phage Group and the Origins of Molecular Biology," *Minerva* 10 (1972): 51–82, and *Theories and Theory Groups in American Sociology* (New York: Harper and Row, 1973); B. Griffith and N. Mullins, "Coherent Social Groups in Scientific Change," *Science* 177 (1972): 959–64.

13. See J. Ben-David, "Roles and Innovation in Medicine," *American Journal of Sociology* 65 (1960): 557–68, on role hybrids; on the bases of scientific production, see J. Ben-David, "Scientific Productivity and Academic Organization in Nineteenth Century Medicine," *American Sociological Review* 25 (1960): 828–43, and Ben-David and A. Zloczower, "Universities and Academic Systems in Modern Societies," *European Journal of Sociology* 3 (1962): 45–85. See J. Ben-David, *The Scientist's Role in Society* (Englewood Cliffs, NJ: Prentice-Hall, 1971) on the comparative sociology of science. R. Collins, *Conflict Sociology* (New York: Academic Press, 1975), pp. 470–523, puts some of Ben-David's ideas into a propositional format and integrates them into a general sociological theory.

14. L. Hargens, *Patterns of Scientific Research: A Comparative Analysis of Research in Three Fields.* (Washington, DC: American Sociological Association Rose Monograph Series, 1975); J. Gaston, *Originality and Competition in Science* (Chicago: University of Chicago Press, 1973).

15. M. Mauss, *The Gift* (New York: Norton, 1967, originally published in 1925); E.

Durkheim and M. Mauss, *Primitive Classification* (Chicago: University of Chicago Press, 1963, originally published in 1903); C. Levi-Strauss, *Structural Anthropology* (New York: Basic Books, 1962), and *The Savage Mind* (Chicago: University of Chicago Press, 1966); B. Bernstein, *Class, Codes, and Control.* (London: Routledge and Kegan Paul, 1971); M. Douglas, *Natural Symbols.* (Harmondsworth: Penguin, 1973); and G. Gurvitch, *The Social Frameworks of Knowledge* (New York: Harper Torchbooks, 1972).

16. D. Bloor, *Knowledge and Social Imagery* (London: Routledge and Kegan Paul, 1976).

17. Collins, *Conflict Sociology.* Other signs of and influences on the growth of the sociology of science in the 1960s include the publication of readers by B. Barber and W. Hirsch (eds.), *The Sociology of Science* (New York: The Free Press, 1962), and N. Kaplan (ed.), *Science and Society* (Chicago: Rand McNally, 1965).

18. S. Cole and J. Cole, *Social Stratification in Science* (Chicago: University of Chicago Press, 1973).

19. H. Rose and S. Rose, *Science and Society* (Baltimore: Penguin, 1970); L. Sklair, *Organized Knowledge* (St. Albans, Herts: Paladin, 1973); and B. Barnes, *Scientific Knowledge and Sociological Theory* (London: Routledge and Kegan Paul, 1974). And see the readers by B. Barnes (ed.), *Sociology of Science* (Baltimore: Penguin, 1972); and S. Restivo and C. K. Vanderpool (eds.), *Comparative Studies in Science and Society* (Columbus, OH: C. E. Merrill, 1974).

20. M. Mulkay, *Science and the Sociology of Knowledge* (Winchester, MA: Allen and Unwin, 1979); and M. Richter, *The Autonomy of Science* (Cambridge, MA: Schenkman, 1980).

21. For an introduction to citation analysis, see E. Garfield, *Citation Analysis* (Philadelphia: Institute for Scientific Information, 1988).

22. L. Hargens, "Theory and Method in the Sociology of Science," pp. 121–39 in J. Gaston (ed.), *Sociology of Science* (San Francisco: Jossey-Bass, 1978).

23. See the report by the National Science Board, *Science Indicators* (Washington, DC: National Science Foundation, 1979); for commentaries, see Y. Elkana et al. (eds.), *Toward a Metric of Science* (New York: Wiley-Interscience, 1977), and H. Zuckerman and R. B. Miller, "Science Indicators: Implications for Research and Policy," *Scientometrics* 2 (1980): 327–448. And on the "behavior" of science, see F. Narin, *Evaluative Bibliometrics: The Use of Citation Analysis in the Evaluation of Scientific Activity* (New Jersey: Computer Horizons, 1976); N. Mullins et al., "The Group Structure of the Cocitation Clusters: A Comparative Study," *American Sociological Review* 42 (1977): 552–62; D. Lindsey, *The Scientific Publication System in the Social Sciences* (San Francisco: Jossey-Bass, 1978); and the review essay by D. Chubin, "Beyond Invisible Colleges: A Bibliographic Essay," pp. 3–63 in D. Chubin, *Sociology of Science: An Annotated Bibliography on Invisible Colleges, 1972–1981* (New York: Garland, 1982).

24. S. Cole, L. Rubin, and J. Cole, *Peer Review in the National Science Foundation* (Washington, DC: National Academy of Sciences, 1978); H. Zuckerman, "Stratification in American Science," pp. 235–37 in E. O. Laumann (ed.), *Social Stratification: Theory and Research for the 1970s* (Indianapolis, IN: Bobbs-Merrill, 1970); Cole and Cole, *Social Stratification,* and J. Gaston, *The Reward System in British and American Science* (New York: Wiley, 1978).

25. S. Cole, J. Cole, and G. Simon, "Chance and Consensus in Peer Review," *Science* 214 (1981): 881–86.

26. S. P. Turner and D. Chubin, "Chance and Eminence in Science: Ecclesiastes II," *Social Science Information* 18 (1979): 437–49; R. G. A. Dolby, "Reflections on Deviant

Science," pp. 9–47 in R. Wallis (ed.), *On the Margins of Science: The Social Construction of Rejected Knowledge* (Staffordshire: University of Keele, 1979); D. Chubin, "Competence is Not Enough," *Contemporary Sociology* 8 (1980): 204–7, and "Values, Controversy, and the Sociology of Science," *Bulletin of Science, Technology and Society* 1 (1981): 427–36.

27. Collins, *Conflict Sociology,* 470–523.

28. Barnes, *Scientific Knowledge*, and *Interests and the Growth of Knowledge* (London: Routledge and Kegan Paul, 1977); and D. Bloor, *Knowledge and Social Imagery*.

29. See Chapter 2 on numbers and culture in the first volume of Spengler's *Decline*.

30. For exemplary studies, see B. Barnes and S. Shapin (eds.), *Natural Order* (Beverly Hills, CA: Sage, 1979); and D. MacKenzie, "Statistical Theory and Social Interest: A Case Study," *Social Studies of Science* 8 (1978): 35–83; and D. MacKenzie, *Statistics in Great Britain 1865–1930* (Edinburgh: University of Edinburgh Press, 1981).

31. For example, see S. Woolgar, "Interests and Explanation in the Social Study of Science," *Social Studies of Science* 11 (1981): 365–95.

32. H. Collins, "The Seven Sexes: A Study in the Sociology of a Phenomenon, Or the Replication of Experiments in Physics," *Sociology* 9 (1975): 205–24, and "Stages in the Empirical Program of Relativism," *Social Studies of Science* 11 (1981): 3–10; T. Pinch, "What Does a Proof Do if it Does Not Prove?," pp. 171–215 in E. Mendelsohn et al. (eds.), *The Social Production of Scientific Knowledge* (Dordrecht: D. Reidel, 1977); on parapsychology, see H. Collins and T. Pinch, *Frames of Meaning: The Social Construction of Extraordinary Science* (London: Routledge and Kegan Paul, 1982); on solar neutrinos see T. Pinch, "Theoreticians and the Production of Experimental Anomaly: The Case of Solar Neutrinos," pp. 77–106 in K. Knorr et al. (eds.), *The Social Process of Scientific Investigation* (Dordrecht: D. Reidel, 1980); and on planaria, see G. D. L. Travis, "On the Construction of Creativity: The Memory of Transfer Phenomenon and the Importance of Being Earnest," pp. 165–93 in K. Knorr et al. (eds.), *Scientific Investigations*.

33. T. Gieryn, "Relativist/Constructivist Programmes in the Sociology of Science: Redundance and Retreat," *Social Studies of Science* 12 (1982): 279–97; K. Knorr, "Scientific Communities as Transepistemic Arenas of Research? A Critique of Quasi-Economic Models of Science," *Social Studies of Science* 12 (1982): 101–30; and D. Chubin, "Collins' Programme and the 'Hardest Possible Case'," *Social Studies of Science* 12 (1982): 136–39.

34. R. Whitley, "Introduction," pp. 1–10 in R. Whitley (ed.), *Social Processes of Scientific Development* (London: Routledge and Kegan Paul, 1974).

35. D. Campbell, "Evolutionary Epistemology," pp. 413–63 in P. A. Schilpp (ed.), *The Philosophy of Karl Popper* (LaSalle, IL: Open Court, 1974); and "A Tribal Model of the Social System Vehicle Carrying Scientific Knowledge," *Knowledge: Creation, Diffusion, Utilization* 2 (1979): 198; and see S. Restivo, "Notes and Queries on Science, Technology, and Human Values," *Science, Technology, and Human Values* 6 (1981): 20–24, where Campbell's evolutionary epistemology is christened "the mild program."

36. See Campbell (1974), "Evolutionary Epistemology;" "Unjustified Variation and Selective Retention in Scientific Discovery," pp. 139–61 in P. J. Ayala and T. Dobzhansky (eds.), *Studies in the Philosophy of Biology* (London: Macmillan, 1974); and "Descriptive Epistemology: Psychological, Sociological, and Evolutionary," preliminary draft, William James Lectures, Harvard University, 1977. Specific page references are in notes 16 to 22 in Restivo, "Notes and Queries" (1981), 30.

. The question arises whether Campbell's "blind-variation-and-selection" model is a "blind variation." If it is, it must meet the criteria for "blind" in Campbell, "Evolutionary Epistemology" (1974), 422. I do not believe it does. His defense might be that his model is "blind" in the evolutionary long-run. This might also answer Thaggard's criticisms, which I summarize in the next paragraph.

37. Paul Thaggard, "Against Evolutionary Epistemology," pp. 187–96 in Peter D. Asquith and Ronald N. Giere (eds.), *PSA 1980, Proceedings of the Biennial Meeting of the Philosophy of Science Association,* vol. 1 (East Lansing: Michigan State University, 1980).

38. Chubin and Restivo, "The 'Mooting' of Science Studies," divide up the science "circus" into the four rings of the strong program, laboratory studies, scientometrics, and their own "weak program."

39. I have also referred to this as "the mild program."

40. The myth of the Kuhnian revolution in the sociology of science and in science studies generally is affirmed, for example, in L. Sklair, *Organized Knowledge,* 69; S. Blume, *Toward a Political Sociology of Science* (New York: The Free Press, 1974), 7; B. Barnes, "Introduction," in B. Barnes (ed.), *Sociology of Science,* 11; R. G. A. Dolby, "The Sociology of Knowledge in Natural Science," in Barnes (ed.), *Sociology of Science,* 315; P. Weingart, "On a Sociological Theory of Scientific Change," in R. Whitley (ed.), *Social Processes of Scientific Development,* 45; R. D. Whitley, "Introduction," in Whitley (ed.), *Scientific Development,* 2; and P. Suppe, "The Search for Philosophic Understanding of Scientific Theories," in P. Suppe (ed.), *The Structure of Scientific Theories,* 2nd ed. (Urbana: University of Illinois Press, 1977), 127ff. On the alleged convergence of Kuhn and Marx see Sklair, *Organized Knowledge,* 150; and M. Harrington, *The Twilight of Capitalism* (New York: Simon & Schuster, 1976), 18–19. It should be noted that as early as 1971, M. D. King, "Reason, Tradition, and the Progressiveness of Science," *History and Theory* 10 (1971), 30, pointed out convergences between Merton and Kuhn; see also the critical remarks on Kuhn in P. Bourdieu, "The Specificity of the Scientific Field and the Social Conditions of the Progress of Reason," *Social Science Information* 14 (1975), 19–47. For those of my readers who continue to believe my reading of Kuhn is idiosyncratic, I recommend T. S. Kuhn, "Reflections on Receiving the John Desmond Bernal Award," *4S Review* 1 (1983), 26–30. This "lightly polished" version dilutes the original oral presentation somewhat but still makes the points that reinforce my reading.

41. See J. Gaston, "Different Approaches," in J. Gaston (ed.), *The Sociology of Science* (San Francisco: Jossey-Bass, 1979), 118–19; on the critical reaction of historians to Kuhn, see D. Beaver, "Possible Relationships Between the History and Sociology of Science," in Gaston, *Sociology of Science,* 140, and N. Reingold, "Through Paradigm-Land to a Normal History of Science," *Social Studies of Science* 10 (1980), 475–96.

42. See, for example, B. Barnes, *Scientific Knowledge,* 11, "On the Reception of Scientific Beliefs," in Barnes (ed.), *Sociology of Science,* 277, and *Interests and The Growth of Knowledge* (London: Routledge and Kegan Paul, 1977), 23 and *T. S. Kuhn and Social Science* (London: Macmillan, 1982); D. MacKenzie and B. Barnes, "Scientific Judgement: The Biometry-Mendelism Controversy," in B. Barnes and S. Shapin (eds.), *Natural Order,* 207. T. Pinch, "Kuhn—The Conservative and Radical Interpretations: Are Some Mertonians 'Kuhnians' and Some 'Kuhnians' Mertonians?," *4S Review* 7 (1982), 10–25, agrees in part with my interpretation of Kuhn; but I do not agree with him that Kuhn can be given a radical interpretation without destroying what is central to the Kuhnian paradigm.

43. J. Ben-David, "The Emergence of National Traditions in the Sociology of Science: The United States and Great Britain," in Gaston (ed.), *Sociology of Science,* 204–5.

44. On Kuhn's chameleon reception, see R. Merton, *The Sociology of Science*, 554. For an example of how Kuhn is called on to support revisions of the customary view in the sociology of science, see M. Mulkay, *Science and the Sociology of Knowledge*, and "Cultural Growth in Science," in Barnes (ed.), *Sociology of Science*, 134. It should be noted that Kuhn's ideas have not been adopted wholesale and uncritically outside of North America (see Mulkay, *Sociology of Knowledge*, 39, 48, and N. Elias, "The Sciences: Towards a Theory," in Whitley [ed.], *Scientific Development*, 35).

45. R. Merton, "The Sociology of Science: An Episodic Memoir," in R. K. Merton and J. Gaston (eds.), *The Sociology of Science in Europe* (Carbondale: Southern Illinois University Press, 1977), 106–7. The anomaly is self-conscious in Sklair, *Organized Knowledge*, 267, who disembodies the Kuhnian approach from what Kuhn actually writes.

46. T. S. Kuhn, *The Structure of Scientific Revolutions*, 2nd ed. (Chicago: University of Chicago Press, 1970), 166.

47. M. Hesse, *Revolutions and Reconstructions in the Philosophy of Science* (Bloomington: Indiana University Press), 1980, p. 32 is one of the few students of science who recognizes that Kuhn has not explicitly encouraged the sociological study of science; indeed, she argues that if anything Kuhn has discouraged it.

48. Kuhn, *Structure of Scientific Revolutions*, 92–110.

49. See T. S. Kuhn, *Black-Body Theory and the Quantum Discontinuity* (New York: Oxford University Press, 1978).

50. I. Lakatos and A. Musgrave (eds.), *Criticism and the Growth of Knowledge* (Cambridge: Cambridge University Press, 1970).

51. But see R. Collins and S. Restivo, "Robber Barons and Politicians in Mathematics: A Conflict Model of Science," *Canadian Journal of Sociology* 8 (1983), 199–227; this study suggests that the patterns of change in mathematics are substantially different from those identified by Kuhn. Conflicts between rival innovative paradigms rather than struggles between old and new paradigms seem to be the most important form for social change in the cases they examine.

52. R. Collins, "The Social Causes of Philosophies: A Comparative Historical Theory," paper presented in the Lecture Series on Philosophy and Sociology, University of Dayton, Dayton (1979); and "Toward a Theory of Intellectual Change: The Social Causes of Philosophies," *Science, Technology & Human Values* 14 (Spring 1989), 107–40.

53. See the discussion of Bohm's views in Restivo, *Social Relations*, (1983), 121–25.

54. Not all new sociologists are busy developing new accounts of how science works; for an example of the more critical orientation that can be found among some new sociologists of science see D. MacKenzie, "Science and Technology Studies and the Question of the Military," *Social Studies of Science* 16 (1986): 361–71.

55. For example H. Rose and S. Rose (eds.), *The Political Economy of Science* (London: Macmillan, 1976); and R. Arditti, Pat Brennan, and Steve Cavrak (eds.), *Science and Liberation* (Boston: South End Press, 1980).

56. C. W. Mills, *Power, Politics, and People* (New York: Ballantine, 1963), pp. 229–30, 417.

57. See, for example, D. T. Campbell, "Guidelines for Monitoring the Scientific Competence of Preventive Intervention Research Centers: An Exercise in the Sociology of Scientific Validity," *Knowledge* 8 (1987): 390–91.

58. B. Latour and S. Woolgar, *Laboratory Life* (Beverly Hills, CA: Sage, 1979), p. 180; K. Knorr, "Tinkering Toward Success," *Theory and Society* 8 (1979): 369; B. Latour, *Science in Action* (Cambridge: Harvard University Press, 1987), pp. 26–27; and H. Collins, *Changing Order* (Beverly Hills, CA: Sage, 1979), pp. 165–67.

59. Bloor, *Knowledge and Social Imagery,* p. 144.

60. I have stressed paradigms that stand out in my orientation to the *science* studies landscape. For an up-to-date and more comprehensive discussion of the contemporary science and technology studies landscape, see S. Restivo, "The Theory Landscape in Science Studies: Sociological Traditions"; and M. Callon, "Four Models for the Dynamics of Science," both to appear in *Science, Technology, and Society Handbook* in preparation for Sage Publishers and the Society for Social Studies of Science, and edited by G. Markle, J. Petersen, S. Jasanoff, and T. Pinch.

Chapter 2. Ecology, Social Organization, and the Scientific Revolution

1. See Max Weber, *The Protestant Ethic and the Spirit of Capitalism* (New York: Charles Scribner's Sons, 1958), pp. 13–16; D. J. Price, *Science Since Babylon* (New Haven: Yale University Press, 1961), 3; and also H. Butterfield, *The Origins of Modern Science, 1300–1800,* rev. ed. (New York: The Free Press, 1965), 187–202; J. Ben-David, "Scientific Growth: A Sociological View," *Minerva* 2 (1964): 455–76, and "The Scientific Role: The Conditions of its Establishment in Europe," *Minerva* 4 (1965): 15, 54; and J. Needham, "The Poverties and Triumphs of the Chinese Scientific Tradition," pp. 117–53 in A. C. Crombie (ed.), *Scientific Change* (New York: Basic Books, 1963), and "Science and Society in East and West," pp. 127–49 in M. Goldsmith and A. Mackay (eds.), *Society and Science* (New York: Simon and Schuster, 1964); and see also A. R. Hall, *The Scientific Revolution,* 2nd ed. (Boston: Beacon Press, 1962). This chapter is a revised version of H. Karp and S. Restivo, "Ecological Factors in the Emergence of Modern Science," pp. 123–43 in S. Restivo and C. K. Vanderpool (eds.), *Comparative Studies in Science and Society* (Columbus, OH: Charles Merrill, 1974).

2. Weber, *Protestant Ethic,* 24.

3. R. K. Merton, *Science, Technology, and Society in Seventeenth Century England* (New York: Harper and Row, 1970), xxiii, 55. Merton examined numerous factors in the rise of modern science, but commentators and critics have focused on the Puritan ethic thesis. For the most recent round in this battle see George Becker, "Pietism and Science: A Critique of Robert K. Merton's Hypothesis," *The American Journal of Sociology* 89 (1984): 1065–90; and Robert K. Merton, "The Fallacy of the Latest Word: The Case of 'Pietism and Science'," *The American Journal of Sociology* 89 (1984): 1091–1121.

4. Ben-David, "Scientific Role," 15, 48.

5. Ben-David, "Scientific Growth," 457.

6. Needham, "Chinese Scientific Tradition," 127–37; Ben-David, "Scientific Growth," 457.

7. J. Needham, *Science and Civilization in China,* vol. 5, part 2 (Cambridge: Cambridge University Press, 1974), xxvi.

8. O. D. Duncan and L. F. Schnore, "Cultural, Behavioral, and Ecological Perspectives in the Study of Social Organization," *The American Journal of Sociology* 65 (1959): 132–46; O. D. Duncan et. al., *Metropolis and Region* (Baltimore: Johns Hopkins University Press, 1960); O. Duncan, "Social Organization and the Ecosystem," pp. 36–82 in R. E. L. Faris (ed.), *Handbook of Modern Sociology* (Chicago: Rand McNally, 1964).

9. B. Barber, *Science and the Social Order* (New York: The Free Press, 1952), 26, 52.

10. Spengler, *The Decline of the West;* L. Fleck, *Genesis and Development of a Scientific Fact* (Chicago: University of Chicago Press, 1979).

11. Weber, *Protestant Ethic,* 15–16; Ben-David, *Scientific Growth,* 459.

12. Ben-David, "Scientific Growth," 459.

13. Ibid. On "Arab science," see S. Pines, "What Was Original in Arabic Science?," pp. 181–205 in Crombie, *Scientific Change.*

14. Ben-David, "Scientific Role," 19.

15. W. C. Dampier, *A History of Science,* 4th ed. (Cambridge: Cambridge University Press, 1948), 149; Ben-David, "Scientific Role," 49. On the shift of scientific activities to the academies and the impact of this shift on the scientific revolution, see E. Zilsel, "The Sociological Roots of Science," *The American Journal of Sociology* 47 (1942), 544–62; A. Wolf, *A History of Science, Technology and Philosophy in the 16th and 17th Centuries,* vol. 1 (New York: Harper Torchbooks, 1959), 8–9, 54–70; Hall, *Scientific Revolution,* 186–216; and F. R. Johnson, "Gresham College: Precursor of the Royal Society," pp. 328–53 in P. Weiner and A. Noland, *Roots of Scientific Thought* (New York: Basic Books, 1957), 328.

16. Ben-David, "Scientific Growth," 457; J. Needham, *The Grand Titration* (Toronto: University of Toronto Press, 1969), 6–7; and L. Edelstein, "Recent Trends in the Interpretation of Ancient Science," in Weiner and Noland, *Scientific Thought,* p. 121.

17. On the astronomers, see W. Eberhard, "The Political Function of Astronomy and Astronomers in Han China," in J. K. Fairbank (ed.), *Chinese Thought and Institutions* (Chicago: University of Chicago Press, 1957), p. 66; the official nature of Chinese science is discussed in Needham, "Chinese Scientific Tradition," 124; and see K. Yabuuti, "Science in China from the Fourth to the End of the Twelfth Century," in G. S. Métraux and F. Crouzet (eds.), *The Evolution of Science* (New York: New American Library, 1963), p. 188 on the schools of mathematics. On the general "lack of development" of Chinese science, see E. Balazs, *Chinese Civilization and Bureaucracy* (New Haven: Yale University Press, 1964), p. 137. Note that what was "lacking" was a certain kind of organization, not ability, ideas, and inventions. Needham's ("Scientific Tradition," [1963]: 139) term, "spontaneous autochthonous," should not be interpreted literally. The scientific revolution occurred within the boundaries of Western Europe and its culture, but this should not obscure the role of external conditions and infusions. Needham ("Scientific Traditions," 149) is certainly aware of this, and in fact argues that the diffusion of Chinese technology to the West helped set the stage for the scientific revolution beginning in "the favorable social and economic milieu of the Renaissance."

18. Ben-David, "Scientific Growth," 460–64.

19. J. Needham, *Science and Civilization in China,* vol. 1 pp. 146ff; and vol. 2, 1956, pp. 582ff.

20. Ben-David, "Scientific Role," stresses this point.

21. See the discussion in Chapter 6 of B. Moore, Jr., *Social Origins of Dictatorship and Democracy* (Boston: Beacon Press, 1966), especially pages 169ff. For a more detailed look at the emergence of modern science which examines the diffuseness of the process in a way we can ignore here, see M. Crosland (ed.), *The Emergence of Science in Western Europe* (New York: Science History Publications, 1976).

22. See Ben-David, "Scientific Role."

23. Ibid. And see also Crosland, *Science in Western Europe.* On Europe as an "entity" see, for example, Needham, "Chinese Scientific Tradition," (1963): 117, Price, *Science Since Babylon,* 2, Ben-David, "Scientific Role," 17; and T. Parsons, *The Social*

System (New York: The Free Press, 1951), pp. 339ff; on China as an "entity," see, in addition to the works by Needham, Eberhard, Wittfogel, and Balazs cited in this chapter, Chapter 4 in Moore, Jr., *Dictatorship and Democracy*. And see F. Braudel, *Afterthoughts on Material Civilization and Capitalism* (Baltimore: Johns Hopkins University Press, 1977), pp. 31ff.

24. K. Wittfogel, *Oriental Despotism* (New Haven: Yale University Press, 1957), p. 26; J. Steward, *Theory of Culture Change* (Urbana: University of Illinois Press, 1955), p. 54.

25. This tendency has been noted by M. Weber, "Konfuzianismus und Taoismus," in M. Weber, *Gesamelte Aufsatz zur Religionssoziologie* (Tubingen: J. C. B. Mohr, 1920), pp. 298–99, and *General Economic History* (New York: Macmillan, 1927), p. 321; Wittfogel, *Oriental Despotism*, pp. 26ff.

26. Beals (1955: 54) raises this point in his critique of Wittfogel's work.

27. See the evidence for this assembled by W. Eberhard, *Social Mobility in Traditional China* (Leiden: E. J. Brill, 1962), 32–45.

28. Moore, Jr., *Dictatorship and Democracy*, pp. 169–71. Moore follows the argument in O. Lattimore, "The Industrial Impact on China, 1800–1950," pp. 103–12 in *Proceedings of the First International Conference of Economic History* (Paris: Mouton and Company, 1960).

29. G. Lenski, *Power and Privilege* (New York: McGraw-Hill, 1966), pp. 235–38.

30. Wittfogel, *Oriental Despotism*, pp. 31–40; Steward, *Culture Change*, p. 198.

31. H. Pirenne, *Economic and Social History of Medieval Europe* (New York: Harcourt, Brace and World, 1937), pp. 86–88.

32. J. W. Thompson, *The Middle Ages*, 2 vols. (New York: Knopf, 1931), p. 698; Moore, Jr., *Dictatorship and Democracy*, pp. 415–16.

33. Moore, *Dictatorship and Democracy*, p. 416.

34. Ben-David, "Scientific Role," p. 48. This claim reflects a psychologistic view of science (as a "rational" system, for example), and sets the stage for the claim that science is an autonomous social system—not in the sense that it is structurally and functionally differentiated (a social institution) but in the sense that it is independent of wider cultural ("external") influences; in particular, the claim is that "scientific knowledge" is independent of external influences, that it develops in terms of its own "inner logic" and (in the naive realists' account) is a direct reflection of reality.

35. A. Hawley, *Human Ecology* (New York: The Ronald Press, 1950), pp. 201–3.

36. G. Sjoberg, "The Rural-Urban Dimension in Pre-Industrial, Transitional, and Industrial Societies," in Faris, *Handbook*, p. 133.

37. This is a matter of a relative but significant difference. While the comparison has been sometimes overdrawn, the situation has been widely noted and suggests theoretical conclusions which are less ambiguous than the complex historical and cultural realities of the two civilizational areas. See Wittfogel, *Oriental Despotism*, pp. 67ff., Moore, Jr., *Dictatorship and Democracy*, p. 175, and K. Marx, *Pre-Capitalist Economic Formations* (New York: International Publishers, 1965), pp. 70, 83, 91 on the "Asiatic mode of production."

38. J. C. Russell, "The Metropolitan City Region of the Middle Ages," *Journal of Regional Science* 2 (Fall 1960): 55–70; H. Pirenne, *Medieval Cities* (New York: Doubleday Anchor, [c. 1925]), pp. 75–91, and *Medieval Europe*, pp. 54, 80; Moore, Jr., *Dictatorship and Democracy*, p. 174.

39. E. E. Lampard, "Historical Aspects of Urbanization," in P. M. Hauser and L. F. Schnore (eds.), *The Study of Urbanization* (New York: John Wiley, 1965), p. 538; and see W. McNeill, *The Rise of the West* (Chicago: University of Chicago Press, 1963), p.

238, and E. A. Kracke, Jr., *Civil Service in Early Sung China, 960–1067* (Cambridge: Harvard University Press, 1953), pp. 4–5.

40. Moore, *Dictatorship and Democracy,* pp. 178–80.

41. N. Keyfitz, "Political-Economic Aspects of Urbanization in South and South East Asia," pp. 265–309 in Hauser and Schnore, *Study of Urbanization.*

42. Pirenne, *Medieval Cities,* pp. 80–81; and see B. H. Slicher van Bath, *The Agrarian History of Western Europe A.D. 500–1850* (New York: St. Martin's, 1963), pp. 9–14 on the state of pre-modern European agriculture.

43. Thompson, *Middle Ages,* pp. 722–30.

44. On population growth in China and the West, see M. K. Bennett, *The World's Food* (New York: Harper and Brothers, 1954), p. 9; on the land use and food production revolution in China, see Ping-ti Ho, *Studies on the Population of China 1368–1953* (Cambridge: Harvard University Press, 1959), pp. 169–71.

45. R. Murphey, "The Ruins of Ancient Ceylon," *The Journal of Asian Studies* 16 (1957): 191–92.

46. R. Braidwood and G. R. Willey (eds.), *Courses Toward Urban Life: Archeological Considerations of Some Alternatives* (Chicago: University of Chicago Press, 1962), pp. 354–55.

47. See Lampard, "Urbanization," especially pages 529 and 546 for passages relevant to this and the following paragraph.

48. H. Tisdale, "The Process of Urbanization," *Social Forces* 20 (1942): 311–16.

49. For a general overview of scientific development as a function of urban growth, see E. Zilsel, "The Sociological Roots of Science," *The American Journal of Sociology* 47 (1942): 544–62, and L. White, "What Accelerated Technological Progress in the Western Middle Ages?," in Crombie, *Scientific Change,* pp. 272–91.

50. Needham, "Chinese Scientific Tradition," p. 139.

51. Needham, "East and West," pp. 145–46. For theoretical support, see B. Meggers, "Environmental Limitations on the Development of Culture," *American Anthropologist* 56 (1954), p. 822.

52. Weber, *Protestant Ethic,* pp. 127–28; and see Eberhard, *Traditional China,* pp. 5–50, and Balazs, *Chinese Civilization,* pp. 23, 33, 70, 76.

53. R. Merton, *Social Theory and Social Structure*, enlarged ed. (New York: The Free Press, 1968), pp. 628, 633.

54. Ibid., pp. 637, 649.

55. T. Parsons, *The Structure of Social Action* (New York: The Free Press, 1949), p. 549; this is also the source for the discussion of Weber's views below.

56. Balazs, *Chinese Civilization,* p. 22. This is generally consistent with Needham's views, although his argument is a bit more complex. Needham identifies facilitative as well as obstructive consequences of Confucianism for science in China (see the appendices in S. Restivo, "Joseph Needham and the Comparative Study of Chinese and Modern Science," pp. 25–51 in R. A. Jones and H. Kuklick (eds.), *Research in Sociology of Knowledge, Sciences, and Art*, vol. 2 (Greenwich, CT: JAI Press, 1979).

57. Candolle, in his *Histoire des sciences et des savants depuis deux siècles* (Geneva, 1873) remarks that from 1535 to 1735 an authoritarian principle dominated Geneva, preventing any Genevan citizen from gaining real distinction in science. Concerning the Copernican revolution, Protestants as well as Catholics were confronted with the problem of reconciling the new astronomy with Scriptures. Luther and Melanchethon (author of *Physics*, published in 1552) reacted with hostility to the Copernican system. Tycho Brahe, who established the foundation for Kepler's work, rejected Copernicus out of respect for Scriptures. Kepler had to edit out a chapter on the reconciliation of heliocentrism with

Scriptures before he could get his *Mysterium Cosmographicum* into print (1596). He also had difficulties bringing out his account of the comet of 1607 due to the serious theological questions raised by members of the Lutheran University of Leipzig; see F. Russo, "Catholicism, Protestantism, and the Development of Science in the Sixteenth and Seventeenth Centuries," in Métraux and Crouzet, *Evolution of Science,* pp. 300–301.

58. See the discussion in S. Eisenstadt, "The Protestant Ethic Thesis in an Analytical and Comparative Framework," in S. Eisenstadt (ed.), *The Protestant Ethic and Modernization* (New York: Basic Books, 1968), pp. 25–27.

59. See Balazs, *Chinese Civilization,* p. 7, on this point.

60. Needham, *Grand Titration,* pp. 282ff.

61. Merton, *Science, Technology, and Society,* pp. xxviii, 136.

62. J. Ben-David, *The Scientist's Role in Society* (Englewood Cliffs, NJ: Prentice-Hall, 1971), pp. 45ff., 68. It may very well strike the reader as odd that I include "social interests" among the items I claim strain Ben-David's institutional analysis. The reason for this is that he uses "interests" as a companion to values and not primarily as a social structural concept.

Chapter 3. Science, Society, and Progress

1. M. Bakunin, *God and the State* (New York: Dover, 1970; orig. publ. 1916), p. 59.

2. This section is based on the *Oxford English Dictionary* and *Webster's Collegiate Dictionary.*

3. Garfinkel, *Studies in Ethnomethodology* (Englewood Cliffs, NJ: Prentice-Hall, 1967), pp. 272ff., after Karin Knorr-Cetina, *The Manufacture of Knowledge* (Oxford: Pergamon Press, 1981), pp. 21–22. There are obvious limits to this notion set by the boundaries of normal biological functioning. But in the less extreme pathological cases, the problem seems to be one of establishing appropriate referents rather than of being "rational." It may, of course, be true that every living thing is in some sense a practical reasoner. This then leaves open the question of what it is about certain forms of inquiry that recommend themselves to us over others. By grouping paranoids and physicists together I mean to raise and not settle a question.

4. B. Barber, *Science and the Social Order* (New York: The Free Press, 1952), p. 95; Merton, *The Sociology of Science.*

5. L. Laudan, *Progress and its Problems* (Berkeley: University of California Press, 1977), pp. 121–22.

6. Ibid., p. 125.

7. M. Mahoney, *Scientist as Subject: The Psychological Imperative* (Cambridge, MA: Ballinger Publishing Company, 1976), pp. 140–41.

8. W. Bartley, *The Retreat to Commitment* (New York: Knopf, 1962).

9. Laudan, *Progress,* p. 125.

10. B. Barnes and D. Bloor, "Relativism, Rationalism and the Sociology of Knowledge," in M. Hollis and S. Lukes (eds.), *Rationality and Relativism* (Oxford: Basil Blackwell, 1982), pp. 44–45n.

11. Ibid., p. 47n.

12. E. Schwartz, *Overskill* (New York: Ballantine Books, 1972), pp. 27–28.

13. J. A. Camilleri, *Civilization in Crisis* (Cambridge: Cambridge University Press, 1976), p. 42; cf. M. Berman, *The Reenchantment of the World* (New York: Bantam Books, 1984), pp. 7–8.

14. W. E. Moore (ed.), *Technology and Social Change* (Chicago: Quadrangle, 1972), pp. 122–30.

15. G. H. Davis, *Technology—Humanism or Nihilism?* (Washington, DC: University Press of America, 1981), p. 25.

16. T. Veblen, *The Place of Science in Modern Civilization and Other Essays* (New York: Viking, 1919), p. 55.

17. G. Benello, "Wasteland and Culture," in H. P. Dreitzel (ed.), *Recent Sociology* (New York: Macmillan, 1969), pp. 263–64.

18. T. Roszak, *Where the Wasteland Ends* (New York: Anchor Books, 1973), p. 426.

19. G. Woodcock (ed.), *The Anarchist Reader* (Glasgow: Fontana, 1977), pp. 161, 366, is the source of the quotations in this paragraph, in essays by, respectively, Emma Goldman and H. Read.

20. K. Marx, *Economic and Philosophic Manuscripts of 1844*, pp. 110–11, and *Grundrisse*, 699ff.

21. C. A. Hooker, "Philosophy and Meta-Philosophy of Science: Empiricism, Popperianism, and Realism," *Synthese* 32 (1975): 171–231.

22. K. Knorr-Cetina, "The Fabriciation of Facts: Toward a Microsociology of Scientific Knowledge," pp. 223–44 in N. Stehr and V. Meja (eds.), *Society and Knowledge* (New Brunswick, NJ: Transaction, 1984).

23. Hooker, "Philosophy and Metaphilosophy."

24. C. Wright, *Wittgenstein on the Foundations of Mathematics* (Cambridge: Harvard University Press, 1980).

25. Mills, *Power, Politics, and People*, p. 238.

26. C. W. Mills, *The Sociological Imagination* (New York: Grove Press, 1961).

27. See L. Fleck, *Genesis and Development of a Scientific Fact*, pp. 39, 46. Orig. publ. in German in 1935.

28. E. P. Thompson, *The Making of the English Working Class* (New York: Penguin Books, 1980); W. Godwin, *Enquiry Concerning Political Justice* (New York: Oxford University Press, 1971); P. Kropotkin, *Kropotkin's Revolutionary Pamphlets* (New York: Dover, 1970).

29. D. Spender, *Women of Ideas and What Men Have Done to Them* (London: Ark Paperbacks, 1983).

30. Merchant, *The Death of Nature*.

31. Mills, *Power, Politics, and People,* pp. 611, 423–60.

32. Godwin, *Political Justice*, pp. 225–26.

33. Nietzsche, *Twilight of the Idols/The Anti-Christ*, pp. 171–73.

34. W. Morris, *Artist, Writer, Socialist*, 2 vols. (Oxford: Oxford University Press, 1936), vol. 2, p. 393; cf. A. Carter, *The Political Theory of Anarchism* (New York: Harper Torchbooks, 1971), pp. 99–100.

35. G. Woodcock, "The Tyrrany of the Clock," in Woodcock, *Anarchist Reader,* p. 136.

Chapter 4. The Science Machine

1. B. Martin, *The Bias of Science* (Canberra: Australian Society for Social Responsibility in Science, 1979), p. 86.

2. Merchant, *The Death of Nature*, p. 288.

3. Cf. B. Easlea, *Fathering the Unthinkable* (London: Pluto Press, 1983).

4. Merchant, *Death of Nature,* pp. 163, 172.

5. E. Keller, *Reflections on Gender and Science* (New Haven: Yale University Press, 1985), p. 143.

6. S. Harding, *The Science Question in Feminism* (Ithaca: Cornell Univeristy Press, 1986), pp. 82, 246.

7. Harding, *Science Question,* p. 250; and see my remarks on Kuhn in Chapter 1 of this volume.

8. Harding, *Science Question,* pp. 248–50.

9. Keller, *Gender and Science,* pp. 177–78; and E. Keller, "Feminism and Science," *Signs* 7 (1982): 593.

10. E. Fee, "Women's Nature and Scientific Objectivity," in M. Lowe and R. Hubbard (eds.), *Woman's Nature* (New York: Pergamon, 1983), pp. 24–25.

11. Mills, *The Sociological Imagination,* p. 8.

12. Cf. P. Feyerabend, *Science in a Free Society* (London: Verso, 1978).

13. J. B. S. Haldane, *Daedalus, or Science and the Future* (London: Chatto and Windus, 1923); B. Russell, *Icarus, or the Future of Science* (London: Kegan Paul, Trench, Trubner & Company, 1925), p. 5.

14. See, for example, M. Mankoff, *The Poverty of Progress: The Political Economy of American Social Problems* (New York: Holt, Rinehart, and Winston, 1972).

15. Mills, *Power, Politics, and People,* pp. 535–36.

16. Ibid., p. 532n; the quotation is from page 19 of C. M. Rosenquist's 1940 textbook, *Social Problems.*

17. Ibid., pp. 537, 538–40; and see S. Restivo, *The Sociological Worldview* (Oxford: Basil Blackwell, 1991), pp. 79–98.

18. Mills, *Power, Politics,* pp. 530–31n.

19. M. Spector and J. Kitsuse, *Constructing Social Problems* (Menlo Park, CA: Cummings, 1977); J. Gusfield, *The Culture of Public Problems* (Chicago: University of Chicago Press, 1981); J. Schneider, "Social Problems Theory: The Constructionist View," *Annual Review of Sociology* 11 (1985): 209–29; and J. Best, "Rhetoric in Claims Making: Constructing the Missing Children Problem," *Social Problems* 34 (1987): 101–21.

20. S. Woolgar and D. Pawluch, "Ontological Gerrymandering: The Anatomy of Social Problems Explanations," *Social Problems* 32 (1985): 214–37. This is an important "overlap" article since the first author, Woolgar, is a distinguished "new" sociologist of science. The position he adopts on this particular point seems to contradict the statement in the second edition of *Laboratory Life,* co-authored by Woolgar with Bruno Latour, that there is a distinction between relativism and constructivism (*Laboratory Life*); and see p. 277 of the 2nd ed. published at Princeton by Princeton University Press.

21. Mills, *Sociological Imagination,* p. 16.

22. Mills, *Power, Politics,* p. 234; Marx, *Economic and Philosophic Manuscripts of 1844,* pp. 110–11, and *Grundrisse,* pp. 699ff.); and see T. Veblen, *The Place of Science in Modern Civilization and Other Essays* (New York: Viking, 1919), pp. 1–55; W. Broad, "The Men Who Made the Sun Rise," Review of The Making of the Atomic Bomb, by Richard Rhodes, *The New York Times Book Review,* February 8 (1987): 39; Schwartz, *Overskill;* and D. Dickson, *The New Politics of Science* (New York: Pantheon Books, 1984).

23. See, for example, B. J. Bledstein, *The Culture of Professionalism* (New York: W.W. Norton, 1978), pp. 87–88. W. R. Scott, "Professionals in Bureaucracy—Areas of

Conflict," pp. 265–75 in H. M. Vollmer and D. L. Mills (eds.), *Professionalization* (Englewood Cliffs, NJ: Prentice-Hall, 1966) views professions and bureaucracies as institutions; see also E. Friedson, *Profession of Medicine* (New York: Dodd, Mead, 1986), p. 166.

24. But see W. Kornhauser, *Scientists in Industry* (Berkeley: University of California Press, 1962) for a counterexample; he is as much interested in the relations between profession and bureaucracy as institutions as he is in relations between individuals and organizations. On the dysfunctions of the professionalization process, especially in terms of its coincidence with bureaucratization, see S. Restivo, *The Social Relations of Physics, Mysticism, and Mathematics* (Dordrecht: D. Reidel, 1983), pp. 152ff. Bledstein, *Culture of Professionalism,* p. 94; Friedson, *Profession;* and T. H. Brewer, "Disease and Social Class," pp. 143–62 in M. Brown (ed.), *The Social Responsibility of the Scientist* (New York: The Free Press, 1971).

25. See, for example, R. Johnston, "Contextual Knowledge: A Model for the Overthrow of the Internal/External Dichotomy in Science," *Australian and New Zealand Journal of Sociology* 12 (1976): 193–203.

26. H. Collins, *Changing Order* (Beverly Hills, CA: Sage, 1985), p. 165.

27. B. Latour, *Science in Action* (Cambridge: Harvard University Press, 1987), pp. 174–75; cf. Knorr-Cetina, *The Manufacture of Knowledge,* pp. 88ff.

28. T. Pinch and W. Bijker, "The Social Construction of Facts and Artefacts: or, How the Sociology of Science and the Sociology of Technology Might Benefit Each Other," *Social Studies of Science* 14 (1984): 399–441; and see S. Russell, "The Social Construction of Artefacts: A Reply to Pinch and Bijker," *Social Studies of Science* 16 (1986): 333–46, and T. Pinch and W. Bijker, "Science, Relativism, and the New Sociology of Technology: Reply to Russell," *Social Studies of Science* 16 (1986): 347–60.

29. Cf. L. Winner, *Autonomous Technology* (Cambridge: MIT Press, 1977), and "Do Artifacts Have Politics?," pp. 26–38 in D. MacKenzie and J. Wajcman (eds.), *The Social Shaping of Technology* (Philadelphia: Open University Press, 1985); and see W. Bijker, T. Hughes and T. Pinch, *The Social Construction of Technology* (Cambridge: MIT Press, 1986).

30. See, for example, D. MacKenzie and J. Wajcman, "Introductory Essay," pp. 2–25 in MacKenzie and Wajcman, *Social Shaping of Technology* and M. M. Trescott (ed.), *Dynamos and Virgins Revisited: Women and Technological Change in History* (London: The Scarecrow Press, 1979).

31. R. S. Cowan *More Work for Mother* (New York: Basic Books, 1983), pp. 215–16.

32. W. McNeill, *The Rise of the West* (Chicago: University of Chicago Press, 1963), pp. 569–70.

33. Cf. J. Law, "On the Methods of Long-Distance Control: Vessels, Navigation, and the Portuguese Route to India," pp. 234–63 in J. Law (ed.), *Power, Action and Belief: A New Sociology of Knowledge?* (Keele: Sociological Review Monographs, 1986).

34. Cf. D. Noble, *America by Design* (New York: Oxford University Press, 1979), and D. Dickson, "Science and Political Hegemony in the 17th Century," *Radical Science Journal* 8 (1984): 7–37.

35. M. Jacob, *The Cultural Meaning of the Scientific Revolution* (Philadelphia: Temple University Press, 1988), pp. 121–23.

36. M. Berman, *The Reenchantment of the World* (New York: Bantam Books, 1984), p. 37; E. Geller, *Thought and Change* (Chicago: University of Chicago Press, 1964), p. 72.

37. Veblen, *Science in Modern Civilization.*

38. Cf. P. F. Meiksins, "Science in the Labor Process: Engineers as Workers," pp. 121–40 in C. Derber (ed.), *Professionals as Workers* (New York: G. K. Hall, 1982).

39. Noble, *America by Design,* p. 4

40. Jacob, *Scientific Revolution,* p. 259, A. E. Musson and E. Robinson, *Science and Technology in the Industrial Revolution* (Manchester: Manchester University Press, 1969); cf. P. T. Carroll, "American Science Transformed," *American Scientist* 74 (1986): 466–85, and M. M. Poston, D. Hay, and J. D. Scott, *Design and Development of Weapons: Studies in Government and Industrial Organization* (London: H. M. Stationery Office, 1964).

41. Jacob, *Scientific Revolution,* p. 38.

42. Noble, *America by Design.*

43. Cf. W. McNeill, *The Pursuit of Power: Technology, Armed Force, and Society* (Chicago: University of Chicago Press, 1982), and Poston et al., *Weapons.*

44. D. Dickson, *The New Politics of Science* (New York: Pantheon, 1984), p. 107; cf. P. Forman, "Behind Quantum Electronics: National Security as Basis for Physical Research in the United States, 1940–1960, *Historical Studies in the Physical Sciences* 18 (1987): 149–229.

45. Jacob, *Scientific Revolution,* pp. 251–52.

46. R. K. Merton, *Social Theory and Social Structure,* enlarged edition (New York: The Free Press, 1968), pp. 661–63; and see B. Hessen, "The Social and Economic Roots of Newton's 'Principia'," pp. 151–212 in N. Bukharin et al., *Science at the Crossroads* (London: F. Cass, 1931) and G. N. Clark, *Science and Social Welfare in the Age of Newton* (Oxford: Oxford University Press, 1937—a second edition appeared in 1949; and a new impression of the second edition appeared in 1970).

47. T. C. Heath, *The Works of Archimedes* (New York: Dover, n.d. [from the 1897 edition]); Restivo, *Physics, Mysticism, and Mathematics,* pp. 251–52.

48. Quoted in B. Hoffmann, *Creator and Rebel: Albert Einstein* (New York: Viking, 1972), p. 221.

49. G. H. Hardy, *A Mathematician's Apology* (Cambridge: Cambridge University Press, 1967), p. 150; L. Pyenson, *Neohumanism and the Persistence of Pure Mathematics in Wilhelmian Germany* (Philadelphia: American Philosophical Society, 1983).

50. J. R. Newman, "Commentary on G.H. Hardy," pp. 2024–26 in J. R. Newman (ed.), *The World of Mathematics,* vol. 4 (New York: Simon and Schuster, 1956).

51. H. Kennedy, *Peano: Life and Works of Giuseppe Peano* (Dordrecht: D. Reidel, 1980), p. 61.

52. S. Traweek, *Beamtimes and Lifetimes: The World of High Energy Physics* (Cambridge: Harvard University Press, 1988).

53. D. Ozonoff, "The Political Economy of Cancer Research," *Science and Nature* 2 (1979): 14–16.

54. "Secrecy in University-Based Research: Who Controls? Who Tells?" (special issue), *Science, Technology and Human Values* 10 (Spring 1985). ("The Project on Openness and Secrecy in Scientific and Technical Communication was conducted by the American Association for the Advancement of Science under a grant from the Ethics and Values in Science and Technology program [EVIST] of the National Science Foundation. The project, which ran from 1983–1985, was directed by Rosemary Chalk. The special issue contains a number of commissioned essays and excerpts from seminars sponsored by the AAAS Project:" —journal editor's introductory remarks).

55. Dickson, *New Politics,* pp. 9–10. Dickson discusses specific cases that illustrate the general ideas and principles I sketch in this chapter. The control of science and knowledge broadly conceived has always been a central concern of political leaders.

The contemporary problem of secrecy in science has some unique features, but Bernard Barber's discussion of the problem more than forty years ago suggests that the problem is neither new nor more pressing today than it has been throughout the Big Science era (taking into account the fact that mechanisms for the social control of scientific information are more entrenched and more sophisticated today than they were forty years ago). Barber, *Science and the Social Order*, pp. 238–39.

56. E. Holtzman, "Biology Faces Life—Pressures on Communications and Careers," pp. 64–72 in *Science, Technology and Human Values* 10 (Spring 1985): 64–72.

57. R. Chalk, "Overview: AAAS Project on Secrecy and Openness in Science and Technology," *Science, Technology and Human Values* 10 (Spring 1985): 39, and in the same issue C. Grobstein, "Biotechnology and Open University Science," p. 56.

58. D. Chubin, "Open Science and Closed Science: Tradeoffs in a Democracy," *Science, Technology and Human Values* 10 (Spring 1985): 73–81.

59. Collins and Restivo, "Robber Barons," 199–227. This article is about the social structural conditions that affect the forms and intensity of competition in science.

60. Grobstein, "Biotechnology," p. 57.

61. See, for example, the use of the concept of norms in R. M. Rosenzweig, "Research Within the University," *Science, Technology and Human Values* 10 (Spring 1985): 41–42. The rhetoric of "science is . . ." reinforces the myth of an eternal, universal methodology and body of knowledge independent of human beings, and obscures the dynamics of science as a social process and a social activity.

62. For details of these changes see, for example, Dickson, "Science and Political Hegemony." On secrecy and society in general, see S. Bok, *Secrets* (New York: Vintage, 1984).

63. Holtzman, "Biology Faces Life."

64. Chalk, "AAAS Project," p. 33, notes that, with respect to maintaining the diversity of relationships between universities and corporations, and protecting academic standards, "the seminar participants proposed pluralism, laissez-faire, nonregulatory approaches;" and see p. 29 for claims about the "neutral environment" in which the AAAS Project was carried out.

65. Rosenzweig, "Research within the University," p. 40.

66. On eponymy and miseponymy in science, see Robert K. Merton, *The Sociology of Science*, especially Chapter 14 on "priorities in scientific discovery," and my review, S. Restivo, "The Sociology of Science, by Robert K. Merton," Book Review, *Journal of College Science Teaching* 9 (1980): 293–94; and S. Stigler, "Stigler's Law of Eponymy," pp. 147–57 in T. Gieryn (ed.), *Science and Social Structure: A Festschrift for Robert K. Merton* (New York: Transactions of the New York Academy of Sciences, 1980).

67. A. Keatley, "Knowledge as Real Estate," *Science* 222 (18 November 1983): 718.

68. See, for example, D. Hull, "Openness and Secrecy in Science: Their Origins and Limitations," *Science, Technology and Human Values* 10 (Spring 1985): 4–13.

69. M. LaFollette, "Editorial Introduction," *Science, Technology and Human Values* 10 (Spring 1985): p. 3.

Chapter 5. The Anthropology of Science

1. G. H. Hewes, "The Ecumene as a Civilizational Multiplier System," *Kroeber Anthropological Society Papers* 25 (1965), p. 81; and see R. Heilbroner, *The Great Ascent* (New York: Harper Torchbooks, 1963), p. 7. This section is based on S. Restivo,

Visiting Foreign Scientists at American Universities: A Study in the Third-Culture of Science, Ph.D. Dissertation, Michigan State University, 1971. Selected results are reported in my contributions to Restivo and Vanderpool, *Comparative Studies in Science and Society*.

2. See, respectively, B. W. Aginsky, "The Evolution of American Indian Culture: A Method and Theory," *Proceedings of the 32nd International Congress of Americanists* (Copenhagen: Munksgaard, 1958); K. Boulding, "The Emerging Superculture," pp. 336–50 in K. Baier and N. Rescher (eds.), *Values and the Future* (New York: The Free Press, 1969); and J. and R. H. Useem, "Interfaces of a Binational Third-Culture: A Study of the American Community in India," *The Journal of Social Issues* 23 (1967): 130–43, and "American Educated Indians in India: A Comparison of Two Modernizing Roles," *Journal of Social Issues* 24 (1968): 143–58.

3. See, for example, E. Shils, "The Intellectuals and the Powers: Some Perspectives for Comparative Analysis," *Comparative Studies in Society and History* 1 (1958), p. 15.

4. F. Harbison and C. A. Myers, *Education, Manpower, and Economic Growth* (New York: McGraw-Hill, 1964); D. Apter (ed.), *Ideology and Discontent* (New York: The Free Press, 1964), especially p. 436.

5. On the idea of "third culture," see J. Useem, R. H. Useem, and J. D. Donoghue, "Men in the Middle of the Third-Culture: The Role of American and Non-Western People in Cross-Cultural Administration," *Human Organization* 22 (Fall 1963): 169–79; J. Useem, "The Continuity of Man: A Study in Third-Culture," *Centennial Review* 7 (Fall 1963): 481–98; and especially page 131 in Useem and Useem, "American Community in India" (1967). On the third culture of science, see Useem and Useem, "American Educated Indians in India" (1968), p. 143.

6. J. D. Bernal, *The Social Function of Science* (Cambridge: MIT Press, 1967, orig. publ. 1939); H. Brown, *The Challenge of Man's Future* (New York: Viking, 1954); J. D. Brown and F. Harbison, *High-Talent Manpower for Science and Technology* (Princeton: Princeton University Press, 1957), pp. 78ff.; R. Gruber (ed.), *Science and the New Nations* (New York: Basic Books, 1961); W. A. Lewis, "Education for Scientific Professions in the Poor Countries," *Daedalus* 91 (Spring 1962): 310–18; R. Revelle, "International Cooperation and the Two Faces of Science," pp. 122–38 in R. Blum (ed.), *Cultural Affairs and Foreign Relations* (Englewood Cliffs, NJ: Prentice-Hall, 1963), p. 138; UNESCO, *Science and Technology for Development* (New York: UNESCO, 1963), and *Science and Technology in Asian Development* (Paris: UNESCO, 1970); Harbison and Meyers, *Education, Manpower, and Economic Growth*, p. 69; Apter, *Ideology and Discontent*, p. 222; R. L. Meier, *Science and Economic Development*, 2nd ed. (Cambridge: MIT Press, 1966), p. 222; J. A. Perkins, "Foreign Aid and the Brain Drain," *Foreign Affairs* 44 (1966), p. 617; A. B. Shah (ed.), *Education, Scientific Policy and Developing Societies* (Bombay: Massakalas, 1967); M. Halpern, "The Rate and Costs of Political Development," in W. E. Moore and R. M. Cook (eds.), *Readings on Social Change* (Englewood Cliffs, NJ: Prentice-Hall, 1967), p. 183; G. Myrdal, *Asian Drama*, 3 vols. (New York: Pantheon, 1968), pp. 55ff.; B. C. Stone, "Gaps in the Graduate Training of Students from Abroad," (letter to) *Science* 165 (June 6, 1969): 1118; and E. Shils, "Scientific Development in the New States," in R. Gruber (ed.), *Science and the New Nations*, p. 219, "Toward a National Science Policy," in J. W. Hanson and C. S. Brembeck (eds.), *Education and the Development of Nations* (New York: Holt, Rinehart and Winston, 1966), p. 212, and "On the Improvement of Indian Higher Education," in Shah, *Education, Scientific Policy and Developing Societies*, pp. 482f.

7. National Academy of Sciences, *The Invisible University* (Washington, DC: NAS, 1969), p. 209; J. Canter, "American Higher Education for Students of the Developing World," in *Higher Education and the International Flow of Manpower: Implications for the Developing World: Proceedings of the National Conference* (Minneapolis: University of Minnesota, 1967), p. 37.

8. The first quotation is from E. Friedson, *Profession of Medicine* (New York: Dodd, Mead and Company, 1970), pp. 89–90; The second quotation is from H. Wilensky, "Orderly Careers and Social Participation: The Impact of Work History on Social Integration in the Middle Class," *American Sociological Review* 26 (August, 1961), pp. 521f.

9. Vollmer and Mills, *Professionalization*, p. 2; H. Wilensky, "The Professionalization of Everyone?," *American Journal of Sociology* 60 (September, 1964), p. 138; W. Form, "Toward an Occupational Social Psychology," *Journal of Social Psychology* 24 (August, 1946): 85–99; T. Caplow, *The Sociology of Work* (New York: McGraw-Hill, 1954), p. 124; O. Hall, "The Stages of a Medical Career," *American Journal of Sociology* 53 (March 1948): 327–36; E. Greenwood, "Attributes of a Profession," in Vollmer and Mills, *Professionalization,* p. 17.

10. Our definition of "visiting foreign scientists" followed the definition of "visiting foreign scholar" used by the Institute for International Education, in New York City. See their annual report, *Open Doors*, for 1954.

11. *Open Doors*, 1954 through 1968, was our source of data on visiting foreign scholars.

12. See A. M. Carter, *An Assessment of Quality in Graduate Education* (Washington, DC: American Council on Education, 1966).

13. Lists of visitors in residence were obtained from the chairs of an exhaustive list of science departments at four additional midwest universities. Questionnaires were mailed to all the individuals whose names were received. Time and financial limitations prevented following up on the original mailing. The return rate anticipated under these conditions was 50 percent; the actual rate was 53.0 percent, or 140 usable questionnaires. In terms of the limited information available on the lists submitted by the department chairs—fields of study, departmental affiliations, and universities—no systematic bias distinguished respondents and nonrespondents. The total number of respondents for the study was thus 222—82 interviewees and 140 questionnaire respondents. Because of differences in the scope and depth of the interviews and the questionnaires, data are available in some cases only for the interviewees, or only for questionnaire respondents. Interpretations are thus based on a variable data base. Unless otherwise indicated, percentages are based on $n = 82$ (interviewees), $n = 140$ (questionnaire respondents), and $n = 222$ (all respondents). In only three cases are discrepancies the result of missing data; for the most part they are accounted for by the "no answer" category. Not unexpectedly, men outnumber women in the sample by about ten to one. The mean age of all respondents is 32.0 years. More than half of the visitors have advanced degrees (Ph.D. or M.D.) awarded in 1966 or later. Respondents are about equally distributed between "developed" and "developing" home countries; and there are approximately equal numbers in the "physical" and "biological" (including "medical") sciences; twelve respondents are social scientists. The classification of respondents' home countries as "developed" or "developing" follows, with some modifications, the schema of Harbison and Meyers, *Education, Manpower, and Economic Growth,* p. 33. They identify four levels of development based on an index of human resources. I have modified their schema by collapsing the first three levels into a "developing countries" level, and defining countries in level IV as "developed." This modification is justified by: (1) the relatively small size

of my sample and the fact that the distribution of scientists by home country at the universities selected as research sites was not known prior to the collection of data; (2) the range of index numbers between levels I and III is about the same as the range within level IV, suggesting (in a crude way) comparable homogeneity across levels I-II-III, and within level IV; (3) an expectation based on prior studies that there would be few if any scientists in the sample from countries in levels I and II. The classification of scientific fields according to the categories "physical," "biological," and "social" follows the system used by the National Science Foundation at the time of this study.

14. 106 citizens (89.1%) of developed countries are citizens of the developed countries they were born in; 91 citizens (92.8%) of developing countries are citizens of the developing countries they were born in; 13 citizens (10.9%) of developed countries are natives of another developing country.

15. The large discrepancy between N and base n is due primarily to dropping one item which could not be coded "basic" or "applied" unambiguously.

16. Cf. Rose and Rose, *Science and Society*, pp. 180f.

17. Cf. D. Lerner and A. M. Teich, *International Scientists Face World Politics* (Cambridge: Center for International Studies, MIT, 1968).

18. C. Jencks and D. Reisman, *The Academic Revolution* (New York: Doubleday Anchor, 1967), pp. 201f.

19. A. Carr-Saunders, *Professions: Their Organization and Place in Society* (Oxford: The Clarendon Press, 1928), p. 31

20. I. L. Horowitz, "Mainliners and Marginals: The Human Shape of Sociological Theory," in L. T. Reynolds and J. M. Reynolds (eds.), *The Sociology of Sociology* (New York: David McKay, 1970), pp. 345–47; Friedson, *Profession,* p. 371.

21. Jencks and Reisman, *Academic Revolution,* p. 202

22. See, for example, Friedson, *Profession,* and T. H. Brewer, "Disease and Social Class," pp. 149–62 in M. Brown (ed.), *The Social Responsibility of the Scientist* (New York: The Free Press, 1971).

23. C. Schwartz, "Professional Organization," in Brown, *Social Responsibility,* pp. 25–26); B. Commoner, "The Ecological Crisis," in Brown, *Social Responsibility,* p. 174.

24. J. Haberer, *Politics and the Community of Science* (New York: Van Nostrand Reinhold, 1969), p. 321. See also Rose and Rose, *Science and Society,* pp. 159, 179ff., 210ff.; R. Friedrichs, *A Sociology of Sociology* (New York: The Free Press, 1970), p. 114; and A. Gouldner, *The Coming Crisis of Western Sociology* (New York: Basic Books, 1970), pp. 497ff.

25. Gouldner, *Coming Crisis,* p. 55.

26. L. Coser, *Men of Ideas* (New York: The Free Press, 1965), pp. 305ff.; Gouldner, *Coming Crisis,* p. 500.

27. J. C. Martin, *The Tolerant Personality* (Detroit: Wayne State University Press, 1964).

28. Cf. National Academy of Science, *Invisible University,* p. 207, and see also pp. 208, 217, and 219.

29. K. E. Boulding, "The 'National' Importance of Human Capital," in W. Adams (ed.), *The Brain Drain* (New York: Macmillan, 1968), p. 113.

30. G. Lenski, *Human Societies* (New York: McGraw-Hill, 1970), p. 59.

31. J. Useem, "The Study of Cultures," *Studies of Third Cultures,* no. 6 (1971): p. 23.

32. Cf. M. Sahlins and E. Service, *Evolution and Culture* (Ann Arbor: University of Michigan Press, 1960), p. 97; Lenski, *Human Societies,* pp. 55–56; D. Dahlsten, "Pesticides," in Brown, pp. 202f.; E. Durkheim, *The Rules of Sociological Method,* 8th ed. (Chicago: University of Chicago Press, 1938), p. 140.

33. Mary Hesse, *Revolutions and Reconstructions in the Philosophy of Science* (Bloomington: Indiana University Press, 1980), p. vii.

34. G. K. Chesterton, *Heretics* (New York: John Lane Company, 1905), p. 71.

35. The engraving is reproduced on page 110 of Merchant, *The Death of Nature*; see her remarks on pages 9–10, and the Barrias photograph on page 191.

36. J. Clifford, *The Predicament of Culture: Twentieth-Century Ethnography, Literature, and Art* (Cambridge: Harvard University Press, 1988), p. 28.

37. Latour and Woolgar, *Laboratory Life*; D. McKegney, *Local Action and Public Discourse in Animal Ecology: A Communication Analysis of Scientific Inquiry*, unpublished Master's thesis, Department of Communications, Simon Fraser University, 1982; M. Zenzen and S. Restivo, "Mysterious Morphology," 447–73; S. Traweek, *Beamtimes and Lifetimes: The World of High Energy Physics* (Cambridge: Harvard University Press, 1988); K. Knorr-Cetina, *Manufacture of Knowledge*.

38. Latour and Woolgar, *Laboratory Life*, pp. 27–29.

39. This discussion draws on Clifford, *Predicament of Culture*.

40. B. Malinowsky, *The Sexual Life of Savages* (New York: Harcourt, Brace and World, 1929), p. 307, Plate 68; G. Stocking (ed.), *Observers Observed: Essays on Ethnographic Fieldwork* (Madison: University of Wisconsin Press, 1938), p. 101.

41. J. Goodfield, *An Imagined World: A Story of Scientific Discovery* (New York: Harper and Row, 1981).

42. R. Pinxten, "Observation in Anthropology: Positivism and Subjectivism Combined," in R. Pinxten and C. Karnoouh (eds.), *Observation in Anthropology*, special issue of *Communication & Cognition* 14 (1981): 57–83.

43. B. Malinowski, *Magic, Science and Religion* (New York: Doubleday Anchor, 1948), pp. 238f.

44. Ibid., p. 248

45. Ibid., p. 87.

46. See the concluding chapter in Durkheim, *The Elementary Forms of the Religious Life*.

47. Knorr-Cetina, *Manufacture of Knowledge*, p. 5.

48. Latour and Woolgar, *Laboratory Life*.

49. Zenzen and Restivo, "Mysterious Morphology," p. 458; and see K. Knorr-Cetina, "The Ethnographic Study of Scientific Work: Towards a Constructivist Interpretation of Science," in Knorr-Cetina and Mulkay, *Science Observed*, p. 122.

50. Knorr-Cetina, *Manufacture of Knowledge*, p. 5.

51. Ibid., p. 6; cf. Fleck, *Genesis and Development of a Scientific Fact*; D. Campbell, "Evolutionary Epistemology," pp. 413–463 in Schilpp, *Philosophy of Karl Popper*, and L. Apostel et al., "An Empirical Investigation of Scientific Observation," pp. 3–36 in W. Callebaut, M. DeMey, R. Pinxten, and F. Vandamme (eds.), *Theory of Knowledge and Science Policy* (Ghent: University of Ghent Press, 1979).

52. Knorr-Cetina, *Manufacture of Knowledge*, p. 7.

53. K. Knorr-Cetina, "The Ethnography of Laboratory Life: Empirical Results and Theoretical Challenges," *Newsletter of the International Society for the Sociology of Knowledge* 7 (1981): 4–9.

54. Knorr-Cetina follows G. Nicolis and I. Prigogine, *Self-Organization in Non-Equilibrium Systems* (New York: John Wiley, 1977).

55. Knorr-Cetina, *Manufacture of Knowledge*, p. 8.

56. See Knorr-Cetina, *Manufacture of Knowledge* and "Ethnography of Laboratory Life," (1981) for items 1–4.

57. B. Latour, *Science in Action*, p. 162.

58. Ibid., p. 164.

59. S. Leigh Star, "Simplification in Scientific Work: An Example from Neuroscience Research," *Social Studies of Science* 13 (1983): 205–28.

60. Zenzen and Restivo, "Mysterious Morphology."

61. M. Lynch, "Technical Work and Critical Inquiry," *Social Studies of Science* 12 (1982), p. 499; and see M. Lynch, *Art and Artifact in Laboratory Science* (London: Routledge and Kegan Paul, 1983).

62. Lynch, "Technical Work."

63. H. Gil Peach, *Production and Consumption of Applied Social Statistics*, Unpublished Ph.D. Dissertation, Department of Sociology, New York University, 1984.

64. See, for example, C. Bazerman, "Book Review: Laboratory Life, by B. Latour and S. Woolgar," *4S: Newsletter of the Society for Social Studies of Science* 5 (1980): 14–19; S. Cozzens, "Book Review: Laboratory Life, by B. Latour and S. Woolgar," *4S: Newsletter of the Society for Social Studies of Science* 5 (1980): 19–21; T. Nickles, "Book Review: The Manufacture of Knowledge, by K. Knorr-Cetina," *4S: Newsletter of the Society for Social Studies of Science* 7 (1982): 35–39; T. Gieryn, "Relativist/Constructivist Programmes in the Sociology of Science: Redundance and Retreat," *Social Studies of Science* 12 (1982): 293–94.

65. B. Latour, "Book Review: The Manufacture of Knowledge, by K. Knorr-Cetina," *4S: Newsletter of the Society for Social Studies of Science* 7 (1982): 30–34.

66. K. Knorr-Cetina, "Scientific Communities or Transepistemic Arenas of Research? A Critique of Quasi-Economic Models of Science," *Social Studies of Science* 12 (1982), pp. 45–46.

67. Nickles, Book Review, p. 36.

68. Chubin and Restivo, "The 'Mooting' of Science Studies," pp. 53–83 in Knorr-Cetina and Mulkay, *Science Observed*.

69. A. Maslow, *The Psychology of Science* (Chicago: Henry Regnery Company, 1969), p. 49.

70. Sue Curry Jansen, "The Stranger as Seer or Voyeur: A Dilemma of the Peep-Show Theory of Knowledge," *Qualitative Sociology* 2 (1980): 22–55.

71. Nietzsche, *The Gay Science*, p. 36.

Chapter 6. Applied Science Studies

1. J. Law and R. J. Williams, "Putting Facts Together: A Study of Scientific Persuasion," *Social Studies of Science* 12 (1982): 535.

2. Latour and Woolgar, *Laboratory Life*, pp. 192; 200–201.

3. Ibid., p. 200.

4. Ibid., pp. 206–8.

5. Ibid., pp. 212–19.

6. Ibid., pp. 213, 229.

7. Knorr-Cetina, *Manufacture of Knowledge*, p. 83.

8. Ibid., p. 86.

9. Ibid., p. 87.

10. Ibid., p. 91.

11. Star, "Simplification in Scientific Work," 205–28.

12. M. Zenzen and S. Restivo, "Mysterious Morphology," pp. 457, 465.

13. Ibid., p. 457.

14. M. Mulkay, "Sociology of the Scientific Research Community," in D. J. De S. Price and I. Rösing (eds.), *Science, Technology and Society* (London: Sage, 1977), pp. 103, 127; J. J. Salomon, "Science Policy Studies and the Development of Science Policy," in Price and Rösing, *Science, Technology and Society,* p. 62; W. Harvey, "Plausibility and the Evaluation of Knowledge: A Case Study of Experimental Quantum Mechanics," *Social Studies of Science* 11 (1981), p. 104; V. Stolte-Heiskanen, "Externally Determined Resources and the Effectiveness of Research Units," pp. 121–53 in F. Andrews (ed.), *Scientific Productivity* (Cambridge: Cambridge University Press, 1979); Y. de Hemptinne and F. Andrews, "The International Comparative Study on the Organization and Performance of Research Units: An Overview," pp. 3–16 in Andrews, *Scientific Productivity;* I. Mitroff and D. Chubin, "Peer Review at NSF: A Dialectical Policy Analysis," *Social Studies of Science* 9 (1979), pp. 200–201; and see D. Chubin and E. Hackett, *Peerless Science* (Albany: SUNY Press, 1990).

15. See, for example, Andrews, *Scientific Productivity.*

16. Cf. J. Loughlin Makarushka, "The Requirement for Informed Consent on Human Subjects: The Problem of the Uncontrolled Consequences of Health-Related Research," *Clinical Research* 24 (1976): 64–67.

17. M. Mead, "Applied Anthropology: The State-of-the-Art," in A. F. C. Wallace et al. (eds.), *Perspectives in Anthropology 1976* (Washington, DC: American Anthropological Association, 1977), p. 147. The Wallace collection is an important source for much of the material covered in this section.

18. Ibid., p. 146.

19. S. Woolgar, "Laboratory Studies: A Comment on the State of the Art," *Social Studies of Science* 12 (1982): 486–87.

20. W. Schäfer (ed.), *Finalization in Science* (Dordrecht: D. Reidel, 1983).

21. Chubin and Restivo, "The 'Mooting' of Science Studies," pp. 53–83.

22. Whitley, "Black Boxism," pp. 61–92.

23. R. Johnston, "Contextual Knowledge;" R. Whitley, "The Sociology of Scientific Work and the History of Scientific Developments," pp. 21–50 in S. S. Blume (ed.), *Perspectives in the Sociology of Science* (Chichester: J. Wiley, 1977).

24. K. Studer and D. Chubin, *The Cancer Mission: Social Contexts of Biomedical Research* (Beverly Hills, CA: Sage, 1980).

25. See Lakatos and Musgrave, *Criticism and the Growth of Knowledge*, for a progressive view of the content of science. M. Richter, *Science as a Cultural Process* (Cambridge: Schenkman, 1972) summarizes arguments for the inherently adaptive nature of scientific change.

26. On "research trails," see D. Chubin and T. Connolly, "Research Trails and Science Policies: Local and Extra-Local Negotiation of Scientific Work," pp. 293–311 in N. Elias et al. (eds.), *Scientific Establishments and Hierarchies: Sociology of the Sciences Yearbook* vol. 5 (Dordrecht: D. Reidel, 1982).

27. National Science Foundation, *Categories of Scientific Research* (Washington, DC: NSF, 1980).

28. Indeed, two officers of the UK's Social Science Research Council have undertaken a "study of decisions within research funding organizations, in terms of both setting research priorities and of decisions as between individual applications for funds" (Caswill and Healey, 1981, private communication to Chubin). In late 1981, these officers visited their US counterpart, NSF, as well as a smattering of academic researchers, on a fact-finding mission. They report (Chubin, private communication) finding few "facts," but encountering an impenetrable smoke-screen of rhetoric at NSF.

29. For a review, see N. Rescher, "Methodological Issues in Science and Technol-

ogy Forecasting: Users and Limitations in Public Policy Deliberations," *Technological Forecasting and Social Change* 20 (1981): 101–12.

30. With the era of "evaluation research" upon us, surrounding the stereotypes surrounding qualitative versus quantitative analysis is a necessity. For a healthy start toward methodological ecumenism, see C. S. Reichardt and T. D. Cook, "Beyond Qualitative Versus Quantitative Methods," pp. 7–32 in T. D. Cook and C. S. Reichardt (eds.), *Qualitative and Quantitative Methods in Evaluation Research* (Beverly Hills, CA: Sage, 1979).

31. On the "case study" approach, see R. Yin, "The Case Study Crisis: Some Answers," *Administrative Science Quarterly* 26 (1981): 145–52; and see J. J. Salomon, "The Mating of Knowledge and Power," *Impact of Science on Society* 22 (1972): 123–32 on research, power, and policy.

32. G. E. Markle and J. Petersen, "Controversies in Science and Technology: A Protocol for Comparative Research," *Science, Technology and Human Values* 6 (1981): 25–32.

33. M. Wartofsky, "The Critique of Impure Reason II: Sin, Science, and Society," *Science, Technology and Human Values* 33 (1980): 5–23.

34. D. Nelkin, "The Political Impact of Technical Expertise," *Social Studies of Science* 5 (1975): 28.

35. L. Wittgenstein, *On Certainty* (New York: Harper Torchbooks, 1972), p. 61e.

36. Cf. C. Hooker, "Philosophy and Meta-Philosophy of Science: Empiricism, Popperianism, and Realism," *Synthese* 32 (1975): 177–231.

37. See G. Bowden, "The Construction of Validity in Estimates of U.S. Crude Oil Reserves," *Social Studies of Science* 16 (1985): 207–40. The discussion in this section is a response to D. Campbell, "Guidelines for Monitoring the Scientific Competence of Preventive Intervention Research Centers: An Exercise in the Sociology of Scientific Validity," *Knowledge* 8 (1987): 389–430, and originally appeared in S. Restivo and J. Loughlin, "Critical Sociology of Science and Scientific Validity," *Knowledge* 8 (1987): 486–508.

38. L. Johnston, P. O'Malley and L. Eveland, "Drugs and Delinquency: A Search for Causal Connections," in D. Kandel (ed.), *Longitudinal Research on Drug Use* (Washington, DC: J. Wiley, 1978), p. 141. For an argument that validity is distinct from truth, see N. Goodman, *Ways of Worldmaking* (Indianapolis, IN: Hackett, 1978), pp. 125–40.

39. Mills, *The Sociological Imagination.*

40. D. Campbell, *Final Report on Contract Number SSN 442–12–4531* (Rockville, MD: Center for Prevention Research, 1985), pp. 2, 24.

41. E. Goode, *Drugs in American Society* (New York: Knopf, 1984), pp. 20, 23.

42. R. Bonnie and C. Whitebread III, *The Marihuana Conviction: History of Marihuana Prohibition in the United States* (Charlottesville: University of Virginia Press, 1974), p. 225. And see J. Himmelstein, *The Strange Career of Marijuana: The Politics and Ideology of Drug Control in America* (Westport, CT: Greenwood, 1983), Goode, *Drugs;* and J. Helmer, *Drugs and Minority Oppression* (New York: Seabury, 1975).

43. These myths were enumerated and discussed by B. Barber, *Drugs and Society* (New York: Russell Sage, 1967) in the context of a sophisticated but neglected agenda for further research. Goode, *Drugs,* finds it necessary to make the same points that Barber made almost 20 years ago. Extensive discussions of these persistent problems are provided by H. Feldman, M. Agar, and G. Beschner (eds.), *Angel Dust: An Ethnographic Study of PCP Users* (Lexington, MA: Lexington, 1979), A. Trebach, *The Heroin Solution* (New Haven: Yale University Press, 1982), N. Zinberg, *Drug, Set and Setting: The Basis for Controlled Intoxicant Use* (New Haven: Yale University Press, 1984), and B. Glassner and J. Loughlin, *Drugs in the Worlds of Adolescents: Burnouts to Straights* (London: Macmillan, 1986).

44. D. Musto, *The American Disease: Origins of Narcotics Control* (New Haven: Yale University Press, 1973), Bonnie and Whitebread, *Marihuana Conviction,* and Helmer, *Drugs and Minority Oppression.*

45. Goode, *Drugs.*

46. Trebach, *Heroin Solution.*

47. P. Conrad and J. Schneider, *Deviance and Medicalization: From Badness to Sickness* (St. Louis: Mosby, 1983).

48. Bonnie and Whitebread, *Marihuana Conviction,* p. 289.

49. J. Ball and C. Chambers (eds.), *The Epidemiology of Opiate Addiction in the United States* (Illinois: Charles C. Thomas, 1970), p. 20.

50. Glassner and Loughlin, *Drugs in the Worlds of Adolescents;* Goode, *Drugs.*

51. R. Jessor and S. Jessor, "Theory Testing in Longitudinal Research on Marijuana Use," pp. 41–71 in Kandel, *Drug Use.*

52. Trebach, *Heroin Solution,* p. 25.

53. Ibid., p. 77.

54. G. Beschner and H. Feldman, "Introduction," in Feldman et al., *Angel Dust,* p. 2.

55. Campbell, *Final Report,* (1985), p. 5.

56. Glassner and Loughlin, *Drugs in the World of Adolescents;* Zinberg, *Drug, Set and Setting.*

57. P. Cleckner, "Freaks and Cognoscenti: PCP Use in Miami," pp. 183–210 in Feldman, Agar, and Beschner, *Angel Dust.*

58. B. Holzner and J. Marx, *Knowledge Applications* (Boston: Allyn and Bacon, 1979), pp. 102, 112, 129.

59. Ibid., 272.

60. T. Gieryn, "Boundary Work and the Demarcation of Science from Non-Science: Strains and Interests in Professional Ideologies of Scientists," *American Sociological Review* 48 (1983): 781–95.

61. K. Knorr-Cetina, "Fabrication of Facts," pp. 223–44; M. Mulkay, "Knowledge and Utility: Implications for the Sociology of Knowledge," pp. 77–96 in Stehr and Meja, *Society and Knowledge,* M. Bunge, "Technology as Applied Science," *Technology and Culture* 8 (1967): 329–47.

62. N. Cartwright, *How the Laws of Physics Lie* (New York: Clarendon, 1983), M. Gitterman and V. Halpern, *Qualitative Analysis of Physical Problems* (New York: Academic Press, 1981); see also S. Traweek, "Nature in the Age of its Mechanical Reproduction: The Reproduction of Nature and Physicists in the High Energy Physics Community," pp. 94–112 in C. Belisle and B. Schiele (eds.), *Les Savoirs dans les Pratiques Quotidiennes* (Paris: CNRS, 1984), and *Beamtimes and Lifetimes: The World of High Energy Physics* (Cambridge: Harvard University Press, 1988).

63. Holzner and Marx, *Knowledge Application,* p. 167.

64. Restivo, *The Social Relations of Physics, Mysticism, and Mathematics.*

Chapter 7. The Sociology of Objectivity

1. G. Bergmann, "The Logic of Quanta," in *Readings in the Philosophy of Science,* ed. H. Feigl and M. Brodbeck (New York: Appleton-Century Crofts, 1953, p. 477; K. Popper, *The Logic of Scientific Discovery* (New York: Science Editions, Inc., 1961, p. 44; cf. R. Friedrichs, *A Sociology of Sociology* (New York: The Free Press, 1970, p. 207.

2. Gouldner, *Coming Crisis.*

3. H. Feigl, "Naturalism and Humanism," *American Quarterly* 1 (Summer 1949): 135–48; A. Kaplan, *The Conduct of Inquiry* (San Francisco: Chandler, 1964), p. 128.

4. Friedrichs, *Sociology,* p. 209.

5. A. Schutz, "Concept and Theory Formation in the Social Sciences," pp. 231–49 in *Philosophy of the Social Sciences*, ed. M. Natanson (New York: Random House, 1963); K. Pearson, *The Grammar of Science* (New York: Meridian, 1957); orig. publ. 1911, pp. 53–54.

6. On intersubjective testing, see Popper, *Scientific Discovery,* p. 46; on the practical constraints on the range of consensus, see G. Lundberg, "The Postulates of Science and their Implications for Sociology," pp. 33–72 in Natanson, *Social Sciences.*

7. N. Campbell, *Foundations of Science* (New York: Dover, 1957; orig. publ. 1919), p. 21; I. M. Copi, *Introduction to Logic,* 2nd ed. (New York: Macmillan, 1961), p. 449); K. Popper, *The Open Society and its Enemies* (Princeton: Princeton University Press, 1950), pp. 404–7.

8. Campbell, *Foundations of Science.*

9. M. Polanyi, *The Republic of Science: Its Political and Economic Theory* (Chicago: Roosevelt University Press, 1962), pp. 7–8; Goodall, *Science, Logic and Political Action,* p. 78; G. T. Seaborg, "A Scientific Society—The Beginnings," pp. 218–32 in S. Rapport and H. Wright (ed.), *Science: Method and Meaning* (New York: Washington Square Press, 1964).

10. J. Ben-David, "The State of Sociological Theory and the Sociological Community: A Review Article," *Comparative Studies in Society and History* 15 (October 1973): 448–72.

11. Popper, *Open Society,* pp. 404–8, and *Objective Knowledge* (London: Oxford University Press, 1972); L. DeWitt, "On Bloor's Transformation of Popper's Pluralism," *Social Studies of Science* 5 (1975): 208–9.

12. J. Spedding, R. L. Ellis, and D. D. Heath, eds., *The Works of Francis Bacon* (Boston: Houghton, Mifflin and Co., 1863), p. 76.

13. Merton, *Sociology of Science,* p. 24.

14. B. Walter, "The Sociology of Knowledge and the Problem of Objectivity," in L. Gross (ed.), *Sociological Theory: Inquiries and Paradigms* (New York: Harper and Row, 1967), p. 340.

15. Merton, *Sociology of Science,* p. 269.

16. R. La Piere, *Social Change* (New York: McGraw-Hill, 1965), pp. 410–13, 437.

17. C. Jencks and D. Reisman, *The Academic Revolution* (New York: Doubleday-Anchor, 1967), pp. 201–2.

18. Carr-Saunders, *Professions,* pp. 30–31. Carr-Saunders was a eugenicist; the number of eugenicists involved in developing the concept of "profession" suggests to me that as a result of their inability to put eugenic ideas into practice by manipulating biology (because of a lack of technology and knowledge, cultural barriers, and natural limitations), the eugenicists translated their program into social terms. The structural parallels between professionalism and eugenicism as modes of social control are intriguing.

19. Friedson, *Profession of Medicine,* pp. 370–71.

20. I. L. Horowitz, "Mainliners and Marginals: The Human Shape of Sociological Theory," in Reynolds and Reynolds, *Sociology of Sociology,* p. 345.

21. T. Parsons, *Essays in Sociological Theory,* rev. ed. (New York: The Free Press, 1954), pp. 34–49; R. G. Francis and R. C. Stone, *Service and Procedure in Bureaucracy: A Case Study* (Minneapolis: University of Minnesota Press, 1956), pp. 153–57; P. M. Blau and W. R. Scott, *Formal Organizations: A Comparative Approach* (San Francisco: Chandler, 1962), pp. 60–63.

22. W. R. Scott, "Professionals in Bureaucracy-Areas of Conflict," in Vollmer and Mills, *Professionalization*, pp. 266–67.

23. Merton, *Social Theory and Social Structure*, p. 200.

24. Horowitz, "Mainliners and Marginals," p. 347.

25. H. Meynell, "On the Limits of the Sociology of Knowledge," *Social Studies of Science* 7 (1977): 489–500.

26. C. Castaneda, *The Teachings of Don Juan* (New York: Ballantine, 1968).

27. A. Schutz, *The Problem of Social Reality: Collected Papers*, vol. 1 (The Hague: M. Nijhoff, 1971), pp. 10ff., 150ff., 180ff., and 312ff.

28. N. Storer, "The Internationality of Science and the Nationality of Scientists," *International Social Science Journal* 22 (1970): 80–93; and see Meynell, "Sociology of Knowledge," p. 490.

29. L. LeShan, *The Medium, the Mystic, and the Physicist* (New York: Ballantine Books, 1976), pp. 20–24.

30. J. Pearce, "Don Juan and Jesus," pp. 191–219; and C. Oglesby, "Experimental Knowledge," p. 167 in D. Noel (ed.), *Seeing Castaneda* (New York: G. P. Putnam's Sons, 1976).

31. W. James, *Principles of Psychology* (New York: Henry Holt, 1890); Schutz, *Social Reality*, pp. 207, 229–33.

32. Schutz, *Social Reality*, pp. 212–14; C. O. Evans, *The Subject of Consciousness* (New York: Humanities Press, 1970); E. Bourguignon, *Religion, Altered States of Consciousness, and Social Change* (Columbus: Ohio State University Press, 1973).

33. LeShan, *Medium, Mystic, Physicist*, F. Capra, *The Tao of Physics* (Berkeley, CA.: Shambhala Publications, 1975). The historical background of this perspective is discussed at length in Part I of S. Restivo, *The Social Relations of Physics, Mysticism, and Mathematics*.

34. D. Bohm, "Quantum Theory as an Indication of a New Order in Physics. Part B. Implicate and Explicate Order in Physical Law," *Foundations of Physics* 3 (1973), p. 164; on the "boostrap hypothesis" see Restivo, *Physics, Mysticism, and Mathematics*, and see also H. Robinson, *Renascent Rationalism* (Toronto: Macmillan, 1975), pp. 106–7, 274.

35. I discuss this in more detail in Chapters 4 and 6 of S. Restivo, *The Sociological Worldview* (Oxford: Blackwell, 1991). See also S. Restivo and M. Zenzen, "A Humanistic Perspective on Science and Society," pp. 82–116 in W. K. Fishman and G. Benello (eds.), *Readings in Humanistic Sociology* (New York: General Hall, 1986). Struik seems to have this notion in mind when he characterizes the Sophists as "a group of critical men . . . less hampered by tradition than any previous group of learned persons:" D. Struik, *A Concise History of Mathematics* (New York: Dover, 1967), pp. 39–40. See also Dantzig, *Number: The Language of Science*, p. 243 for a view of objective reality as "a living growing organism." Dantzig does not develop this idea, which, in any case, retains too much of the idealistic notion of objectivity and mathematical reality to be considered a significant anticipation of my ideas. His book does, however, contain numerous illustrations which are supportive of the open-ended perspective on inquiry.

36. Campbell, *Foundations of Science*, p. 21.

37. Cf. W. Leiss, "Ideology and Science," *Social Studies of Science* 5 (1975): 196, 200; his critique of "the current hegemony of instrumental rationality" is congruent with my position. See also M. Zenzen, "Sociology of Science as Theory of Rationality," paper presented at the annual meeting of the Society for Social Studies of Science, Bloomington, Indiana, 1978. Zenzen's conception of "critical rationality" leaves open the possibility of a broadening and evolving conception of rationality. I prefer going

further and dropping the term, "rationality" altogether in this context. Regarding the statement by H. Collins and G. Cox, "Recovering Relativity: Did Prophecy Fail?," *Social Studies of Science* 6 (1976), p. 439, "The approach we favour is to push the relativistic heuristic as far as possible: where it can go no further, 'nature intrudes'," nature intrudes everywhere, and therefore the strong sense of the relativistic heuristic must be rejected. To base relativism on research that appeals—implicitly or explicitly—to science, to rationality, or to logic must inevitably lead to knotty paradoxes. This should, at least, be acknowledged.

38. Cf. Bloor, *Knowledge and Social Imagery*, p. ix.

39. Cf. Restivo, "Joseph Needham," pp. 25–51.

40. W. Eckhardt, "Limits to Knowledge," *Limits to Violence Project Paper* #10 (Oakville, Ontario: Canadian Peace Research Institute, 1976), 59.

41. C. Hooker, "Philosophy and Meta-Philosophy of Science: Empiricism, Popperianism, and Realism," *Synthese 32* (1975): 177–231.

42. On (i) see S. Maram, "Pluto's Moon," *Natural History* 88 (1979): 100–101; on (ii) and (iii) see F. Cajori, *A History of Mathematics*, 2nd ed. (New York: Macmillan, 1974; orig. publ. 1919), pp. 191, 465–66; on (iv) see Bloor, *Knowledge and Social Imagery*, p. 113.

43. His argument is sketched in J. Curtis and J. Petras (eds.), *The Sociology of Knowledge: A Reader* (New York: Praeger, 1970), pp. 661–67.

44. More extended discussions can be found in Restivo, *Physics, Mysticism, Mathematics,* Part II; and S. Restivo, J. P. Van Bendegem, and R. Fischer (eds.), *Math Worlds: New Directions in Philosopohy and Social Studies of Mathematics* (Albany: SUNY Press, 1993); and Restivo, *Mathematics in Society and History.*

45. Spengler, *The Decline of the West*; B. Hessen, "The Social and Economic Roots of Newton's 'Principia'," pp. 151–212 in N. Bukharin et al. (eds.), *Science at the Crossroads;* L. Wittgenstein, *Remarks on the Foundations of Mathematics* (Cambridge: MIT Press, 1967), and *On Certainty;* D. Struik, "On the Sociology of Mathematics," *Science and Society* 6 (1942): 58–70, and "Mathematics," pp. 125–52 in R. W. Sellars, V. J. McGill, and M. Farber (eds.), *Philosophy for the Future* (New York: Macmillan, 1949); J. Needham, "Mathematics and Society in China and the West," *Science and Society* 20 (1956): 320–43, and *Science and Civilization in China,* vol. 3: *Mathematics and the Sciences of the Heavens and the Earth* (London: Cambridge University Press, 1959); K. Mannheim, *Idelogy and Utopia* (London: Routledge and Kegan Paul, 1936), p. 79; and see W. Stark, *The Sociology of Knowledge* (London: Routledge and Kegan Paul, 1958), p. 162. On the new sociology of mathematics, see Bloor, *Knowledge and Social Imagery;* MacKenzie, *Statistics in Great Britain;* and Restivo, *Physics, Mysticism, and Mathematics;* see also R. Startup, "The Sociology of Mathematics," *Sociology and Social Research* 64 (1980): 151–67.

46. See, for example, M. Kline, *Mathematics: A Cultural Approach* (Reading, MA: Addison-Wesley, 1962), pp. 582, 661, 665; cf. D. Gasking, "Mathematics and the World," in J. R. Newman (ed.), *The World of Mathematics* (New York: Simon and Schuster, 1956), p. 1710.

47. F. Dostoevsky, "Notes from the Underground," in *The Best Short Stories of Dostoevsky* (New York: Modern Library, n.d.), p. 139 wrote: ". . . twice-two-makes-four is not life, gentlemen. It is the beginning of death. Twice-two-makes-four is, in my humble opinion, nothing but a piece of impudence . . . a farcical, dressed up fellow who stands across your path with arms akimbo and spits at you. Mind you, I quite agree that twice-two-makes-four is a most excellent thing; but if we are to give everything its due, then twice-two-makes-five is sometimes a most charming little thing, too." It is not

clear that this sort of exercise can be "explained" by referring to it as "merely" an expression of literary privilege. The ability to *imagine* "$2 \times 2 = 5$" does not give us a "necessary truth" as would be expected if we adhered to the philosopher and mathematician William Whewell's distinction between necessary and contingent truths, proposed in 1844: J. Richards, "The Art and the Science of British Algebra: A Study in the Perception of Mathematical Truth," *Historia Mathematica* 7 (1980): 362.

48. Bloor, *Knowledge and Social Imagery,* Wittgenstein, *Foundations of Mathematics.*

49. C. Wright, *Wittgenstein on the Foundations of Mathematics* (Cambridge: Harvard University Press, 1980).

50. Spengler, *Decline,* p. 60.

51. Wright, *Wittgenstein,* p. 457, and see also pages 453ff.

52. C. Hooker, "Explanation and Culture: Science and Culture as Adaptation," *Humanities in Society* 2 (1979): 228.

53. Hooker, "Meta-Philosophy of Science."

54. Feyerabend, *Science in a Free Society,* pp. 82 ff.

55. See Restivo, *Physics, Mysticism, and Mathematics;* S. Brush, "The Chimerical Cat: Philosophy of Quantum Mechanics in Historical Perspective," *Social Studies of Science* 10 (1980): 393–447, and Hooker, "Explanation and Culture."

56. G. Bateson, *Steps to an Ecology of Mind* (New York: Ballantine Books, 1972), p. 480.

57. B. Barnes, *Scientific Knowledge and Sociological Theory* (London: Routledge and Kegan Paul, 1974), p. 41.

58. Hooker, "Explanation and Culture," p. 215.

59. M. Kline, *Mathematics: The Loss of Certainty* (New York: Oxford University Press, 1980), pp. 325, 354.

60. Ibid., p. 329; cf. K. Knorr, "Tinkering Toward Success," *Theory and Society* 8 (1979): 347–76.

61. Kline, *Mathematics,* pp. 142, 177, 315.

62. Fleck, *Genesis and Development of a Scientific Fact,* p. 100.

63. R. Rorty, *Philosophy and the Mirror of Nature* (Princeton: Princeton University Press, 1979).

64. Ibid., p. 9.

65. Ibid., pp. 156–57.

66. Ibid., pp. 317–18.

67. Ibid., pp. 225.

68. Ibid., pp. 365–66.

69. Ibid., p. 394.

70. See the articles by McClain, Steiglitz, Pribram and others in volume 5 (1985) of the *Journal of Social and Biological Structures*, pp. 223–88.

71. Hooker, "Meta-Philosophy of Science"; Restivo and Zenzen, "Sociology of Science"; Chubin and Restivo, "The 'Mooting' of Science Studies," pp. 53–83.

72. Bloor, *Knowledge and Social Imagery,* and "Durkheim and Mauss Revisited: Classification and the Sociology of Knowledge," *Studies in History and Philosophy of Science* 13 (1982): 267–97; B. Barnes, *Interests and the Growth of Knowledge* (London: Routledge and Kegan Paul, 1977); Fleck, *Scientific Fact;* Knorr-Cetina, *The Manufacture of Knowledge;* and M. Douglas, *Purity and Danger* (London: Routledge and Kegan Paul, 1966), *Natural Symbols* (Harmondsworth: Penguin, 1973), and *Implicit Meanings* (London: Routledge and Kegan Paul, 1975); M. Douglas, ed., *Rules and Meanings* (Harmondsworth: Penguin, 1973); and see Hooker, "Explanation and Culture."

73. See A. Naess, *The Pluralist and Possibilist Aspect of the Scientific Enterprise* (Oslo: Universitatsforlaget, 1972); and Wright, *Wittgenstein.*

74. Nietzsche, *The Gay Science;* D. T. Campbell, "Evolutionary Epistemology," pp. 413–63 in Schilpp, *The Philosophy of Karl Popper;* Feyerabend, *Science in a Free Society;* and N. Goodman, *Ways of Worldmaking* (Indianapolis, IN: Hackett, 1978).

Bibliography

Aginsky, B. W. "The Evolution of American Indian Culture: A Method and Theory." Proceedings of the 32nd International Congress of Americanists. Copenhagen: Munksgaard, 1958.

Apostel, L., et al. "An Empirical Investigation of Scientific Observation." In *Theory of Knowledge and Science Policy*, edited by W. Callebaut, M. DeMey, R. Pinxten, and F. Vandamme, 3–36. Ghent: University of Ghent Press, 1979.

Apter, D., ed. *Ideology and Discontent*. New York: The Free Press, 1964.

Arditti, R., P. Brennan, and S. Cavrak, eds. *Science and Liberation*. Boston: South End Press, 1980.

Bakunin, M. *God and the State*. 1916; New York: Dover, 1970.

Balazs, E. *Chinese Civilization and Bureaucracy*. New Haven: Yale University Press, 1964.

Ball, J., and C. Chambers, eds. *The Epidemiology of Opiate Addiction in the United States*. Illinois: Charles C. Thomas, 1970.

Barber, B. *Science and the Social Order*. New York: The Free Press, 1952.

———. *Drugs and Society*. New York: Russell Sage, 1967.

Barber, B., and W. Hirsch, eds. *The Sociology of Science*. New York: The Free Press, 1962.

Barnes, B. *Scientific Knowledge and Sociological Theory*. London: Routledge and Kegan Paul, 1974.

———. *Interests and the Growth of Knowledge*. London: Routledge and Kegan Paul, 1977.

———. *T. S. Kuhn and Social Science*. London: Macmillan, 1982.

———., ed. *Sociology of Science*. Baltimore: Penguin, 1972.

Barnes, B., and D. Bloor. "Relativism, Rationalism and the Sociology of Knowledge." In *Rationality and Relativism*, edited by M. Hollis and S. Lukes, 21–47. Oxford: Basil Blackwell, 1982.

Barnes, B., and S. Shapin, eds. *Natural Order*. Beverly Hills, CA: Sage, 1979.

Bartley, W. *The Retreat to Commitment*. New York: Knopf, 1962.

Bateson, G. *Steps to an Ecology of Mind*. New York: Ballantine Books, 1972.

Bazerman, C. "Book Review: Laboratory Life, by B. Latour and S. Woolgar." *4S: Newsletter of the Society for Social Studies of Science* 5 (1980): 14–19.

Beaver, D. "Possible Relationships Between the History and Sociology of Science." In *The Sociology of Science*, edited by J. Gaston, 140–61. San Francisco: Jossey-Bass, 1979.

Becker, G. "Pietism and Science: A Critique of Robert K. Merton's Hypothesis." *The American Journal of Sociology* 89 (1984): 1065–90.

Ben-David, J. "Scientific Productivity and Academic Organization in Nineteenth Century Medicine." *American Sociological Review* 25 (1960): 828–43.

———. "Roles and Innovation in Medicine." *American Journal of Sociology* 65 (1960): 557–68.

———. "Scientific Growth: A Sociological View." *Minerva* 2 (1964): 455–76.

———. "The Scientific Role: The Conditions of its Establishment in Europe." *Minerva* 4 (1965): 15–54.

———. *The Scientist's Role in Society.* Englewood Cliffs, NJ: Prentice-Hall, 1971.

———. "The State of Sociological Theory and the Sociological Community: A Review Article." *Comparative Studies in Society and History* 15 (October 1973): 448–72.

———. "The Emergence of National Traditions in the Sociology of Science: The United States and Great Britain." In *Sociology of Science,* edited by J. Gaston, pp. 197–218. San Francisco: Jossey-Bass, 1979.

Ben-David, J., and R. Collins. "Social Factors in the Origins of a New Science: The Case of Psychology." *American Sociological Review* 31 (1966): 451–65.

Ben-David, J., and A. Zloczower. "Universities and Academic Systems in Modern Societies," *European Journal of Sociology* 3 (1962): 45–85.

Benello, G. "Wasteland and Culture." In *Recent Sociology,* edited by H. P. Dreitzel. New York: Macmillan, 1969.

Bennett, M. K. *The World's Food.* New York: Harper and Brothers, 1954.

Bergmann, G. "The Logic of Quanta." In *Readings in the Philosophy of Science,* edited by H. Feigl and M. Brodbeck. New York: Appleton-Century Crofts, 1953.

Berman, M. *The Reenchantment of the World.* New York: Bantam Books, 1984.

Bernal, J. D. *The Social Function of Science.* 1937; Cambridge: MIT Press, 1967.

Best, J. "Rhetoric in Claims Making: Constructing the Missing Children Problem." *Social Problems* 34 (1987): 101–21.

Bijker, W., T. Hughes, and T. Pinch. *The Social Construction of Technology.* Cambridge: MIT Press, 1986.

Blau, P. M., and W. R. Scott. *Formal Organizations: A Comparative Approach.* San Francisco: Chandler, 1962.

Bledstein, B. J. *The Culture of Professionalism.* New York: W. W. Norton, 1978.

Bloor, D. *Knowledge and Social Imagery.* London: Routledge and Kegan Paul, 1976.

———. "Durkheim and Mauss Revisited: Classification and the Sociology of Knowledge." *Studies in History and Philosophy of Science* 13 (1982): 267–97.

Blume, S. *Toward a Political Sociology of Science.* New York: The Free Press, 1974.

Bohm, D. "Quantum Theory as an Indication of a New Order in Physics. Part B. Implicate and Explicate Order in Physical Law." *Foundations of Physics* 3 (1973): 139–68.

Bok, S. *Secrets.* New York: Vintage, 1984.

Bonnie, R., and C. Whitebread III. *The Marihuana Conviction: History of Marihuana Prohibition in the United States.* Charlottesville: University of Virginia Press, 1974.

Boulding, K. E. "The 'National' Importance of Human Capital." In *The Brain Drain,* edited by W. Adams, 109–19. New York. Macmillan, 1968.

———. "The Emerging Superculture." In *Values and the Future,* edited by K. Baier and N. Rescher, 336–50. New York: The Free Press, 1969.

Bourdieu, P. "The Specificity of the Scientific Field and the Social Conditions of the Progress of Reason." *Social Science Information* 14 (1975), 19–47.

Bourguignon, E. *Religion, Altered States of Consciousness, and Social Change*. Columbus: Ohio State University Press, 1973.

Bowden, G. "The Construction of Validity in Estimates of U.S. Crude Oil Reserves." *Social Studies of Science* 16 (1985): 207–40.

Braidwood, R., and G. R. Willey, eds. *Courses Toward Urban Life: Archeological Considerations of Some Alternatives*. Chicago: University of Chicago Press, 1962.

Braudel, F. *Afterthoughts on Material Civilization and Capitalism*. Baltimore: Johns Hopkins University Press, 1977.

Brewer, T. H. "Disease and Social Class." In *The Social Responsibility of the Scientist*, edited by M. Brown, 143–62. New York: The Free Press, 1971.

Broad, W. "The Men Who Made the Sun Rise." Review of *The Making of the Atomic Bomb* by Richard Rhodes. *The New York Times Book Review*, February 8, 1987: 39.

Brown, H. *The Challenge of Man's Future*. New York: Viking, 1954.

Brown, J. D., and F. Harbison. *High-Talent Manpower for Science and Technology*. Princeton: Princeton University Press, 1957.

Brush, S. "The Chimerical Cat: Philosophy of Quantum Mechanics in Historical Perspective," *Social Studies of Science* 10 (1980): 393–447.

Bunge, M. "Technology as Applied Science." *Technology and Culture* 8 (1967): 329–47.

Butterfield, H. *The Origins of Modern Science, 1300–1800*, Rev. ed. New York: The Free Press, 1965.

Cajori, F. *A History of Mathematics*. 1919; 2nd ed, New York: Macmillan, 1974.

Camilleri, J. A. *Civilization in Crisis*. Cambridge: Cambridge University Press, 1976.

Campbell, D. "Evolutionary Epistemology." In *The Philosophy of Karl Popper*, edited by P. A. Schilpp, 413–63. LaSalle, IL: Open Court, 1974.

———. "Unjustified Variation and Selective Retention in Scientific Discovery." In *Studies in the Philosophy of Biology*, edited by P. J. Ayala and T. Dobzhansky, 139–61. London: Macmillan, 1974.

———. "Descriptive Epistemology: Psychological, Sociological, and Evolutionary." *William James Lectures*, Harvard University, 1977.

———. "A Tribal Model of the Social System Vehicle Carrying Scientific Knowledge." *Knowledge: Creation, Diffusion, Utilization* 2 (1979): 181–201.

———. *Final Report on Contract Number SSN 442–12–4531*. Rockville, MD: Center for Prevention Research, 1985.

———. "Guidelines for Monitoring the Scientific Competence of Preventive Intervention Research Centers: An Exercise in the Sociology of Scientific Validity." *Knowledge* 8 (1987): 389–430.

Campbell, N. *Foundations of Science*. 1919; New York: Dover, 1957.

Canter, J. "American Higher Education for Students of the Developing World." In *Higher Education and the International Flow of Manpower: Implications for the Developing World: Proceedings of the National Conference*, 29–37. Minneapolis: University of Minnesota, 1967.

Caplow, T. *The Sociology of Work*. New York: McGraw-Hill, 1954.

Capra, F. *The Tao of Physics*. Berkeley, CA: Shambhala Publications, 1975.

Carr-Saunders, A. *Professions: Their Organization and Place in Society*. Oxford: The Clarendon Press, 1928.

Carroll, P. T. "American Science Transformed." *American Scientist* 74 (1986): 466–485.

Carter, A. *The Political Theory of Anarchism*. New York: Harper Torchbooks, 1971.

Carter, A. M. *An Assessment of Quality in Graduate Education*. Washington, DC: American Council on Education, 1966.

Cartwright, N. *How the Laws of Physics Lie*. New York: Clarendon, 1983.

Castaneda, C. *The Teachings of Don Juan*. New York: Ballantine, 1968.

Chalk, R. "Overview: AAAS Project on Secrecy and Openness in Science and Technology." *Science, Technology and Human Values* 10 (Spring 1985): 28–35.

Chesterton, G. K. *Heretics*. New York: John Lane, 1905.

Chubin, D. "Competence is Not Enough." *Contemporary Sociology* 8 (1980): 204–7.

———. "Values, Controversy, and the Sociology of Science." *Bulletin of Science, Technology and Society* 1 (1981): 427–36.

———. "Beyond Invisible Colleges: A Bibliographic Essay." In *Sociology of Science: An Annotated Bibliography on Invisible Colleges, 1972–1981*,3–63. New York: Garland, 1982.

———. "Collins' Programme and the 'Hardest Possible Case'." *Social Studies of Science* 12 (1982): 136–39.

———. "Open Science and Closed Science: Tradeoffs in a Democracy." *Science, Technology and Human Values* 10 (Spring 1985): 73–81.

Chubin, D., and E. Hackett. *Peerless Science*. Albany: SUNY Press, 1990.

Chubin, D., and S. Restivo. "The 'Mooting' of Science Studies: Research Programs and Science Policy." in *Science Observed*, edited by K. Knorr-Cetina and M. Mulkay, 53–83. Beverly Hills: Sage, 1983.

Chubin, D., and T. Connolly. "Research Trails and Science Policies: Local and Extra-Local Negotiation of Scientific Work." In *Scientific Establishments and Hierarchies: Sociology of the Sciences Yearbook*, Vol. 5, edited by N. Elias et al., 293–311. Dordrecht: D. Reidel, 1982.

Clark, G. N. *Science and Social Welfare in the Age of Newton*. 1937; Oxford: Oxford University Press, 1970.

Clifford, J. *The Predicament of Culture: Twentieth-Century Ethnography, Literature, and Art*. Cambridge: Harvard University Press, 1988.

Cole, S., and J. Cole. *Social Stratification in Science*. Chicago: University of Chicago Press, 1973.

Cole, S., J. Cole, and G. Simon. "Chance and Consensus in Peer Review." *Science* 214 (1981): 881–86.

Cole, S., L. Rubin, and J. Cole. *Peer Review in the National Science Foundation*. Washington, DC: National Academy of Sciences, 1978.

Collins, H. "The Seven Sexes: A Study in the Sociology of a Phenomenon, Or the Replication of Experiments in Physics." *Sociology* 9 (1975): 205–24.

———. *Changing Order*. Beverly Hills, CA: Sage, 1979.

———. "Stages in the Empirical Program of Relativism." *Social Studies of Science* 11 (1981): 3–10.

Collins, H., and G. Cox. "Recovering Relativity: Did Prophecy Fail?" *Social Studies of Science* 6 (1976): 423–44.

Collins, H., and T. Pinch. *Frames of Meaning: The Social Construction of Extraordinary Science*. London: Routledge & Kegan Paul, 1982.

Collins, R. *Conflict Sociology*. New York: Academic Press, 1975.

———. "The Social Causes of Philosophies: A Comparative Historical Theory." Paper presented in the *Lecture Series on Philosophy and Sociology*, University of Dayton, Dayton, Ohio (1979).

———. "Toward a Theory of Intellectual Change: The Social Causes of Philosophies." *Science, Technology & Human Values* 14 (Spring 1989): 107–40.

Collins, R., and S. Restivo. "Development, Diversity, and Conflict in the Sociology of Science." *Sociological Quarterly* 24 (1983): 185–200.

Collins, R., and S. Restivo. "Robber Barons and Politicians in Mathematics: A Conflict

Model of Science." *Canadian Journal of Sociology* 8 (Spring 1983): 199–227.

Conrad, P., and J. Schneider. *Deviance and Medicalization: From Badness to Sickness.* St. Louis, MO: Mosby, 1983.

Copi, I. M. *Introduction to Logic*, 2nd ed. New York: Macmillan, 1961.

Coser, L. *Men of Ideas.* New York: The Free Press, 1965.

Cowan, R. S. *More Work for Mother.* New York: Basic Books, 1983.

Cozzens, S. "Book Review: Laboratory Life, by B. Latour and S. Woolgar." *4S: Newsletter of the Society for Social Studies of Science* 5 (1980): 19–21.

———. "Taking the Measure of Science: A Review of Citation Theories." In *Newsletter of the International Society for the Sociology of Knowledge* 7 (special issue on new directions in the sociology of science, S. Restivo, editor) (1981): 16–21.

Crane, Diana. *Invisible Colleges.* Chicago: University of Chicago Press, 1972.

Crosland, M., ed. *The Emergence of Science in Western Europe.* New York: Science History Publications, 1976.

Curtis, J., and J. Petras, eds. *The Sociology of Knowledge: A Reader.* New York: Praeger, 1970.

Dampier, W. C. *A History of Science*, 4th ed. Cambridge: Cambridge University Press, 1948.

Dantzig, T. *Number: The Language of Science.* New York: The Free Press, 1954.

Davis, G. H. *Technology—Humanism or Nihilism?* Washington, DC: University Press of America, 1981.

DeWitt, L. "On Bloor's Transformation of Popper's Pluralism." *Social Studies of Science* 5 (1975): 208–9.

Dickson, D. *The New Politics of Science.* New York: Pantheon Books, 1984.

———. "Science and Political Hegemony in the 17th Century," *Radical Science Journal* 8 (1984): 7–37.

Dolby, R. G. A. "The Sociology of Knowledge in Natural Science." In *Sociology of Science*, edited by B. Barnes. Baltimore: Penguin, 1972.

———. "Reflections on Deviant Science." In *On the Margins of Science: The Social Construction of Rejected Knowledge*, edited by R. Wallis, 9–47. Staffordshire: University of Keele, 1979.

Dostoevsky, F. "Notes from the Underground." In *The Best Short Stories of Dostoevsky*, 107–240. New York: Modern Library, n.d.

Douglas, M. *Purity and Danger.* London: Routledge and Kegan Paul, 1966.

———. *Natural Symbols.* Harmondsworth: Penguin, 1973.

———. *Implicit Meanings.* London: Routledge and Kegan Paul, 1975.

Douglas, M., ed. *Rules and Meanings.* Harmondsworth: Penguin, 1973.

Duncan, O. "Social Organization and the Ecosystem," In *Handbook of Modern Sociology*, edited by R. E. L. Faris, 36–82. Chicago: Rand McNally, 1964.

Duncan, O. D., et. al. *Metropolis and Region.* Baltimore: Johns Hopkins University Press, 1960.

Duncan, O. D., and L. F. Schnore. "Cultural, Behavioral, and Ecological Perspectives in the Study of Social Organization." *The American Journal of Sociology* 65 (1959): 132–46.

Durkheim, E. *The Rules of Sociological Method*, 8th ed. Chicago: University of Chicago Press, 1938.

———. *The Elementary Forms of the Religious Life.* 1912; New York: Collier Books, 1961.

Eberhard, W. "The Political Function of Astronomy and Astronomers in Han China," In *Chinese Thought and Institutions*, edited by J. K. Fairbank. Chicago: University of Chicago Press, 1957.

————. *Social Mobility in Traditional China*. Leiden: E. J. Brill, 1962.

Eckhardt, W. "Limits to Knowledge." *Limits to Violence Project Paper* #10. Oakville, Ontario: Canadian Peace Research Institute, 1976.

Edelstein, L. "Recent Trends in the Interpretation of Ancient Science." In *Roots of Scientific Thought*, edited by P. Weiner and A. Noland. New York: Basic Books, 1957.

Edge, D. "Quantitative Measures of Communication in Science: A Critical Review." *History of Science* 17 (1979): 102–34.

Eisenstadt, S. "The Protestant Ethic Thesis in an Analytical and Comparative Framework," In *The Protestant Ethic and Modernization*, edited by S. Eisenstadt, 3–45. New York: Basic Books, 1968.

Elias, N. "The Sciences: Towards a Theory." In *Social Processes of Scientific Development*, edited by R. Whitley, 21–42. London: Routledge and Kegan Paul, 1974.

Elkana, Y. et al., eds. *Toward a Metric of Science*. New York: Wiley-Interscience, 1977.

Evans, C. O. *The Subject of Consciousness*. New York: Humanities Press, 1970.

Fee, E. "Women's Nature and Scientific Objectivity." In *Woman's Nature*, edited by M. Low and R. Hubbard, 9–27. New York: Pergamon Press, 1983.

Feigl, H. "Naturalism and Humanism." *American Quarterly* 1 (Summer 1949): 135–48.

Feldman, H., M. Agar, and G. Beschner, eds. *Angel Dust: An Ethnographic Study of PCP Users*. Lexington, MA: Lexington, 1979.

Feyerabend, P. *Science in a Free Society*. London: Verso, 1978.

Fleck, L. *Genesis and Development of a Scientific Fact*. 1939; Chicago: University of Chicago Press, 1979.

Form, W. "Toward an Occupational Social Psychology." *Journal of Social Psychology* 24 (August 1946): 85–99.

Forman, P. "Behind Quantum Electronics: National Security as Basis for Physical Research in the United States, 1940–1960." *Historical Studies in the Physical Sciences* 18 (1987): 149–229.

Francis, R. G., and R. C. Stone. *Service and Procedure in Bureaucracy: A Case Study*. Minneapolis: University of Minnesota Press, 1956.

Friedrichs, R. *A Sociology of Sociology*. New York: The Free Press, 1970.

Friedson, E. *Profession of Medicine*. New York: Dodd, Mead, 1970.

Garfield, E. *Citation Analysis*. Philadelphia: Institute for Scientific Information, 1988.

Garfinkel, H. *Studies in Ethnomethodology*. Englewood Cliffs, NJ: Prentice-Hall, 1967.

Gasking, D. "Mathematics and the World." In *The World of Mathematics*, vol. 3, edited by J. R. Newman, 1708–22. New York: Simon and Schuster, 1956.

Gaston, J. *The Reward System in British and American Science*. New York: Wiley, 1978.

————. "Different Approaches." In *The Sociology of Science*, edited by J. Gaston, 118–19. San Francisco: Jossey-Bass, 1979.

Geller, E. *Thought and Change*. Chicago: University of Chicago Press, 1964.

Gieryn, T. "Relativist/Constructivist Programmes in the Sociology of Science: Redundance and Retreat." *Social Studies of Science* 12 (1982): 279–97.

Gitterman, M., and V. Halpern. *Qualitative Analysis of Physical Problems*. New York: Academic Press, 1981.

Glassner, B., and J. Loughlin. *Drugs in the Worlds of Adolescents: Burnouts to Straights*. London: Macmillan, 1986.

Godwin, W. *Enquiry Concerning Political Justice*. New York: Oxford University Press, 1971.

Goodall, M. C. *Science, Logic and Political Action*. Cambridge, MA: Schenkman, 1970.

Goode, E. *Drugs in American Society*. New York: Knopf, 1984.

Goodfield, J. *An Imagined World: A Story of Scientific Discovery*. New York: Harper and Row, 1981.

Goodman, N. *Ways of Worldmaking*. Indianapolis, IN: Hackett, 1978.

Gouldner, A. *The Coming Crisis of Western Sociology*. New York: Basic Books, 1970.

Griffith, B., and N. Mullins. "Coherent Social Groups in Scientific Change." *Science* 177 (1972): 959–64.

Grobstein, C. "Biotechnology and Open University Science." *Science, Technology and Human Values* 10 (Spring 1985): 55–63.

Gruber, R., ed. *Science and the New Nations*. New York: Basic Books, 1961.

Gusfield, J. *The Culture of Public Problems*. Chicago: University of Chicago Press, 1981.

Haberer, J. *Politics and the Community of Science*. New York: Van Nostrand Reinhold, 1969.

Haldane, J. B. S. *Daedalus, or Science and the Future*. London: Chatto and Windus, 1923.

Hall, A. R. *The Scientific Revolution*, 2nd ed. Boston: Beacon, 1962.

Hall, O. "The Stages of a Medical Career." *American Journal of Sociology* 53 (March 1948): 327–36.

Halpern, M. "The Rate and Costs of Political Development." In *Readings on Social Change*, edited by W. E. Moore and R. M. Cook, 182–84. Englewood Cliffs, NJ: Prentice-Hall, 1967.

Harbison, F., and C. A. Myers. *Education, Manpower, and Economic Growth*. New York: McGraw-Hill, 1964.

Harding, S. *The Science Question in Feminism*. Ithaca: Cornell Univeristy Press, 1986.

Hardy, G. H. *A Mathematician's Apology*. Cambridge: Cambridge University Press, 1967.

Hargens, L. "Theory and Method in the Sociology of Science." In *Sociology of Science*, edited by J. Gaston, 121–39. San Francisco: Jossey-Bass, 1978.

Harrington, M. *The Twilight of Capitalism*. New York: Simon & Schuster, 1976.

Harvey, W. "Plausibility and the Evaluation of Knowledge: A Case Study of Experimental Quantum Mechanics." *Social Studies of Science* 11 (1981): 95–130.

Hawley, A. *Human Ecology*. New York: The Ronald Press, 1950.

Heath, T. C. *The Works of Archimedes*. 1897; New York: Dover, n.d.

Heilbroner, R. *The Great Ascent*. New York: Harper Torchbooks, 1963.

Helmer, J. *Drugs and Minority Oppression*. New York: Seabury, 1975.

Hemptinne, Y. de, and F. Andrews. "The International Comparative Study on the Organization and Performance of Research Units: An Overview." In *Scientific Productivity*, edited by F. Andrews, 3–16. Cambridge: Cambridge University Press, 1979.

Hesse, Mary. *Revolutions and Reconstructions in the Philosophy of Science*. Bloomington: Indiana University Press, 1980.

Hessen, B. "The Social and Economic Roots of Newton's 'Principia'." In *Science at the Crossroads*, edited by N. Bukharin et al., 151–212. London: F. Cass, 1931.

Hewes, G. H. "The Ecumene as a Civilizational Multiplier System." *Kroeber Anthropological Society Papers* 25 (1965).

Himmelstein, J. *The Strange Career of Marijuana: The Politics and Ideology of Drug Control in America*. Westport, CT: Greenwood, 1983.

Hoffmann, B. *Creator and Rebel: Albert Einstein*. New York: Viking, 1972.

Holtzman, E. "Biology Faces Life—Pressures on Communications and Careers." *Science, Technology and Human Values* 10 (Spring 1985): 64–72.

Hooker, C. "Philosophy and Meta-Philosophy of Science: Empiricism, Popperianism, and Realism." *Synthese* 32 (1975): 177–231.

———. "Explanation and Culture: Science and Culture as Adaptation." *Humanities in Society* 2 (1979): 223–44.

Horowitz, I. L. "Mainliners and Marginals: The Human Shape of Sociological Theory." In *The Sociology of Sociology*, edited by L. T. Reynolds and J. M. Reynolds, 340–70. New York: David McKay, 1970.

Hull, D. "Openness and Secrecy in Science: Their Origins and Limitations." *Science, Technology and Human Values* 10 (Spring 1985): 4–13.

Institute for International Education. *Open Doors*. New York: IIE, 1954–1968.

Jacob, M. *The Cultural Meaning of the Scientific Revolution*. Philadelphia: Temple University Press, 1988.

James, W. *Principles of Psychology*. New York: Henry Holt, 1890.

Jansen, S. Curry. "The Stranger as Seer or Voyeur: A Dilemma of the Peep-Show Theory of Knowledge." *Qualitative Sociology* 2 (1980): 22–55.

Jencks, C., and D. Reisman. *The Academic Revolution*. New York: Doubleday-Anchor, 1967.

Johnson, F. R. "Gresham College: Precursor of the Royal Society." In *Roots of Scientific Thought*, edited by P. Weiner and A. Noland, 328–53. New York: Basic Books, 1957.

Johnston, L., P. O'Malley, and L. Eveland. "Drugs and Delinquency: A Search for Causal Connections." In *Longitudinal Research on Drug Use*, edited by D. Kandel, 137–16. Washington, DC: J. Wiley, 1978.

Johnston, R. "Contextual Knowledge: A Model for the Overthrow of the Internal/External Dichotomy in Science." *Australian and New Zealand Journal of Sociology* 12 (1976): 193–203.

Jones, R. A., and H. Kuklick, eds. *Research in the Sociology of Knowledge, Sciences, and Art*. Greenwich, CT: JAI Press, 1979.

Ho, Ping-ti. *Studies on the Population of China 1368–1953*. Cambridge: Harvard University Press, 1959.

Kaplan, A. *The Conduct of Inquiry*. San Francisco: Chandler, 1964.

Kaplan, N., ed. *Science and Society*. Chicago: Rand McNally, 1965.

Karp, H., and S. Restivo. "Ecological Factors in the Emergence of Modern Science." In *Comparative Studies in Science and Society*, edited by S. Restivo and C. K. Vanderpool, 123–43. Columbus, OH: Charles Merrill, 1974.

Keatley, A. "Knowledge as Real Estate." *Science* 222 (18 November 1983): 718.

Keller, E. "Feminism and Science." *Signs* 7 (1982): 589–602.

———. *Reflections on Gender and Science*. New Haven: Yale University Press, 1985.

Kennedy, H. *Peano: Life and Works of Giuseppe Peano*. Dordrecht: D. Reidel, 1980.

Keyfitz, N. "Political-Economic Aspects of Urbanization in South and South East Asia." In *The Study of Urbanization*, edited by P. M. Hauser and L. F. Schnore, 265–309. New York: John Wiley, 1965.

King, M. D. "Reason, Tradition, and the Progressiveness of Science." *History and Theory* 10 (1971): 3–32.

Kline, M. *Mathematics: A Cultural Approach*. Reading, MA: Addison-Wesley, 1962.

———. *Mathematics: The Loss of Certainty*. New York: Oxford University Press, 1980.

Knorr, K. "Tinkering Toward Success." *Theory and Society* 8 (1979): 347–76.

Knorr-Cetina, K. "The Ethnography of Laboratory Life: Empirical Results and Theoretical Challenges." *Newsletter of the International Society for the Sociology of Knowledge* 7 (special issue on new directions in the sociology of science, S. Restivo, editor) (1981): 4–9.

———. *The Manufacture of Knowledge*. Oxford: Pergamon Press, 1981.

———. "Scientific Communities as Transepistemic Arenas of Research? A Critique of Quasi-Economic Models of Science." *Social Studies of Science* 12 (1982): 101–30.

————. "The Ethnographic Study of Scientific Work: Towards a Constructivist Interpretation of Science." In *Science Observed: Perspectives on the Social Study of Science*, edited by K. Knorr-Cetina and M. Mulkay. Beverly Hills, CA: Sage, 1983.

————. "The Fabriciation of Facts: Toward a Microsociology of Scientific Knowledge." In *Society and Knowledge*, edited by N. Stehr and V. Meja, 223–44. New Brunswick, NJ: Transaction, 1984.

Kornhauser, W. *Scientists in Industry*. Berkeley: University of California Press, 1962.

Kracke, E. A., Jr., *Civil Service in Early Sung China, 960–1067*. Cambridge: Harvard University Press, 1953.

Kropotkin, P. *Kropotkin's Revolutionary Pamphlets*. New York: Dover, 1970.

Kuhn, T. S. *The Structure of Scientific Revolutions*. 2nd ed. Chicago: University of Chicago Press. 1970.

————. *Black-Body Theory and the Quantum Discontinuity*. New York: Oxford University Press, 1978.

————. "Reflections on Receiving the John Desmond Bernal Award." *4S Review* 1 (1983): 26–30.

La Piere, R. *Social Change*. New York: McGraw-Hill, 1965.

LaFollette, M. "Editorial Introduction." *Science, Technology and Human Values* 10 (Spring 1985): 3.

Lakatos, I., and A. Musgrave, eds. *Criticism and the Growth of Knowledge*. Cambridge: Cambridge University Press, 1970.

Lampard, E. E. "Historical Aspects of Urbanization." In *The Study of Urbanization*, edited by P. M. Hauser and L. F. Schnore. New York: John Wiley, 1965.

Lassman, P., and I. Velody, with H. Martins, eds. *Max Weber's "Science as a Vocation."* Boston: Unwin and Hyman, 1989.

Latour, B. "Book Review: The Manufacture of Knowledge, by K. Knorr-Cetina." *4S: Newsletter of the Society for Social Studies of Science* 7 (1982): 30–34.

————. *Science in Action*. Cambridge: Harvard University Press, 1987.

Latour, B., and S. Woolgar. *Laboratory Life*. Beverly Hills, CA: Sage, 1979.

Lattimore, O. "The Industrial Impact on China, 1800–1950." In *Proceedings of the First International Conference of Economic History*, 103–12. Paris: Mouton, 1960.

Laudan, L. *Progress and its Problems*. Berkeley: University of California Press, 1977.

Law, J. "On the Methods of Long-Distance Control: Vessels, Navigation, and the Portuguese Route to India." In *Power, Action and Belief: A New Sociology of Knowledge?*, edited by J. Law, 234–63.

Law, J., and R. J. Williams. "Putting Facts Together: A Study of Scientific Persuasion." *Social Studies of Science* 12 (1982): 535–58.

Le Shan, L. *The Medium, the Mystic, and the Physicist*. New York: Ballantine Books, 1976.

Leiss, W. "Ideology and Science." *Social Studies of Science* 5 (1975): 193–201.

Lenski, G. *Power and Privilege*. New York: McGraw-Hill, 1966.

————. *Human Societies*. New York: McGraw-Hill, 1970.

Lerner, D., and A. M. Teich. *International Scientists Face World Politics*. Cambridge: Center for International Studies, MIT, 1968.

Lewis, W. A. "Education for Scientific Professions in the Poor Countries." *Daedalus* 91 (Spring 1962): 310–18.

Lindsey, D. *The Scientific Publication System in the Social Sciences*. San Francisco: Jossey-Bass, 1978.

Lynch, M. "Technical Work and Critical Inquiry." *Social Studies of Science* 12 (1982): 499–534.

————. *Art and Artifact in Laboratory Science.* London: Routledge and Kegan Paul, 1983.

MacKenzie, D. "Statistical Theory and Social Interest: A Case Study." *Social Studies of Science* 8 (1978): 35–83.

————. *Statistics in Great Britain 1865–1930.* Edinburgh: University of Edinburgh Press, 1981.

————. "Science and Technology Studies and the Question of the Military." *Social Studies of Science* 16 (1986): 361–71.

MacKenzie, D., and B. Barnes. "Scientific Judgement: The Biometry-Mendelism Controversy." In *Natural Order,* edited by B. Barnes and S. Shapin, 191–208. Beverly Hills, CA: Sage, 1979.

Mahoney, M. *Scientist as Subject: The Psychological Imperative.* Cambridge, MA: Ballinger, 1976.

Makarushka, J. Loughlin. "The Requirement for Informed Consent on Human Subjects: The Problem of the Uncontrolled Consequences of Health-Related Research." *Clinical Research* 24 (1976): 64–67.

Malinowsky, B. *The Sexual Life of Savages.* New York: Harcourt, Brace and World, 1929.

————. *Magic, Science and Religion.* New York: Doubleday Anchor, 1948.

Mankoff, M. *The Poverty of Progress: The Political Economy of American Social Problems.* New York: Holt, Rinehart, and Winston, 1972.

Mannheim, K. *Ideology and Utopia.* London: Routledge and Kegan Paul, 1936.

Maram, S. "Pluto's Moon." *Natural History* 88 (1979): 100–101.

Markle, G. E., and J. Petersen. "Controversies in Science and Technology: A Protocol for Comparative Research." *Science, Technology and Human Values* 6 (1981): 25–32.

Martin, B. *The Bias of Science.* Canberra: Australian Society for Social Responsibility in Science, 1979.

Martin, J. C. *The Tolerant Personality.* Detroit: Wayne State University Press, 1964.

Marx, K. *Economic and Philosophic Manuscripts of 1844.* Moscow: Foreign Languages Publishing House, 1956.

————. *Pre-Capitalist Economic Formations.* New York: International Publishers 1965.

————. *Grundrisse.* New York: Vintage Press, 1973.

Marx, K., and F. Engels. *The German Ideology.* New York: International Publishers, 1947.

Maslow, A. *The Psychology of Science.* Chicago: Henry Regnery, 1969.

McKegney, D. *Local Action and Public Discourse in Animal Ecology: A Communication Analysis of Scientific Inquiry.* Unpublished Master's thesis. Department of Communications, Simon Fraser University, 1982.

McNeill, W. *The Pursuit of Power: Technology, Armed Force, and Society.* Chicago: University of Chicago Press, 1982.

————. *The Rise of the West.* Chicago: University of Chicago Press, 1963.

Mead, M. "Applied Anthropology: The State-of-the-Art." In *Perspectives in Anthropology,* edited by A. F. C. Wallace et al., 142–61. Washington, DC: American Anthropological Association, 1976.

Meggers, B. "Environmental Limitations on the Development of Culture." *American Anthropologist* 56 (1954): 801–24.

Meier, R. L. *Science and Economic Development,* 2nd ed. Cambridge: MIT Press, 1966.

Meiksins, P.F. "Science in the Labor Process: Engineers as Workers." In *Professionals as Workers,* edited by C. Derber, 121–40. New York: G. K. Hall, 1982.

Merchant, C. *The Death of Nature*. New York: Harper and Row, 1980.

Merton, R. K. *Social Theory and Social Structure*. Enlarged ed. New York: The Free Press, 1968.

———. *Science, Technology, and Society in Seventeenth Century England*. New York: Harper and Row, 1970.

———. *The Sociology of Science*. Chicago: University of Chicago Press, 1973.

———. "The Sociology of Science: An Episodic Memoir." In *The Sociology of Science in Europe*, edited by R. K. Merton and J. Gaston, 3–41. Carbondale: Southern Illinois University Press, 1977.

———. "The Fallacy of the Latest Word: The Case of 'Pietism and Science'." *The American Journal of Sociology* 89 (1984): 1091–1121.

Meynell, H. "On the Limits of the Sociology of Knowledge." *Social Studies of Science* 7 (1977): 489–500.

Mills, C. W. *The Sociological Imagination*. New York: Grove, 1961.

———. *Power, Politics, and People*. New York: Ballantine, 1963.

Mitroff, I., and D. Chubin. "Peer Review at NSF: A Dialectical Policy Analysis." *Social Studies of Science* 9 (1979): 199–232.

Moore, B., Jr., *Social Origins of Dictatorship and Democracy*. Boston: Beacon, 1966.

Moore, W. E., ed. *Technology and Social Change*. Chicago: Quadrangle, 1972.

Morman, E. T. "Citation Analysis and the Current Debate Over Quantitative Methods in the Social Studies of Science." *4S Newsletter* 5 (1980): 7–13.

Morris, W. *Artist, Writer, Socialist*. 2 vols. Oxford: Oxford University Press, 1936.

Mulkay, M. "Cultural Growth in Science." In *Sociology of Science,* edited by Barnes. Baltimore: Penguin, 1972.

———. "Sociology of the Scientific Research Community." In *Science, Technology and Society*, edited by D. J. De S. Price and I. Rösing. London: Sage, 1977.

———. *Science and the Sociology of Knowledge*. Winchester, MA: Allen and Unwin, 1979.

———. "Knowledge and Utility: Implications for the Sociology of Knowledge." In *Society and Knowledge,* edited by N. Stehr and V. Meja, 77–96. New Brunswick, NJ: Transaction, 1984.

Mullins, N. "The Distribution of Social and Cultural Properties in Informal Communication Networks Among Biological Scientists." *American Sociological Review* 33 (1968): 786–97.

———. "The Development of a Scientific Specialty: The Phage Group and the Origins of Molecular Biology." *Minerva* 10 (1972): 51–82.

———. *Theories and Theory Groups in American Sociology*. New York: Harper and Row, 1973.

———., et al. "The Group Structure of the Cocitation Clusters: A Comparative Study." *American Sociological Review* 42 (1977): 552–62.

Murphey, R. "The Ruins of Ancient Ceylon." *The Journal of Asian Studies* 16 (1957): 191–92.

Musson, A. E., and E. Robinson. *Science and Technology in the Industrial Revolution*. Manchester: Manchester University Press, 1969.

Musto, D. *The American Disease: Origins of Narcotics Control*. New Haven: Yale University Press, 1973.

Myrdal, G. *Asian Drama*. 3 vols. New York: Pantheon, 1968.

Naess, A. *The Pluralist and Possibilist Aspect of the Scientific Enterprise*. Oslo: Universitatsforlaget, 1972.

Narin, F. *Evaluative Bibliometrics: The Use of Citation Analysis in the Evaluation of Scientific Activity*. New Jersey: Computer Horizons, 1976.

National Academy of Sciences. *The Invisible University*. Washington, DC: National Academy of Sciences, 1969.

National Science Board, Science Indicators. Washington, DC: National Science Foundation, 1979.

National Science Foundation, Categories of Scientific Research. Washington, DC: NSF, 1980.

Needham, J. *Science and Civilization in China*. Vol 1. Cambridge: Cambridge University Press, 1954.

————. "Mathematics and Society in China and the West." *Science and Society* 20 (1956): 320–43.

————. *Science and Civilization in China*, Vol. 3: *Mathematics and the Sciences of the Heavens and the Earth*. London: Cambridge University Press, 1959.

————. "The Poverties and Triumphs of the Chinese Scientific Tradition." In *Scientific Change*, edited by A. C. Crombie, 117–53. New York: Basic Books, 1963.

————. "Science and Society in East and West." In *Society and Science*, edited by M. Goldsmith and A. Mackay, 127–49. New York: Simon and Schuster, 1964.

————. *Science and Civilization in China*. Vol. 5, part 2. Cambridge: Cambridge University Press, 1974.

————. *The Grand Titration*. Toronto: University of Toronto Press, 1969.

Nelkin, D. "The Political Impact of Technical Expertise." *Social Studies of Science* 5 (1975): 35–58.

Newman, J. R. "Commentary on G. H. Hardy." In *The World of Mathematics*, vol. 4, edited by J. R. Newman, 2024–26. New York: Simon and Schuster, 1956.

Nickles, T. "Book Review: The Manufacture of Knowledge, by K. Knorr-Cetina." *4S: Newsletter of the Society for Social Studies of Science* 7 (1982): 35–39.

Nicolis, G., and I. Prigogine. *Self-Organization in Non-Equilibrium Systems*. New York: John Wiley, 1977.

Nietzsche, F. *Twilight of the Idols/The Anti-Christ*. New York: Penguin Classics, 1968.

————. *The Gay Science*. New York: Vintage, 1974.

Noble, D. *America By Design*. New York: Oxford University Press, 1979.

Ozonoff, D. "The Political Economy of Cancer Research." *Science and Nature* 2: (1979): 14–16.

Parsons, T. *The Structure of Social Action*. New York: The Free Press, 1949.

————. *The Social System*. New York: The Free Press, 1951.

————. *Essays in Sociological Theory*. Rev. ed. New York: The Free Press, 1954.

Peach, H. Gil. *Production and Consumption of Applied Social Statistics*, Unpublished PhD dissertation. New York: Department of Sociology, New York University, 1984.

Pearce, J. "Don Juan and Jesus." In *Seeing Castenada*, edited by D. Noel, pp.191–219. New York: G. P. Putnam's Sons, 1976.

Oglesby, C. et al. "A Juanist Way of Knowledge," In *Seeing Castenada*, edited by D. Noel, pp.161–85. New York: G. P. Putnam's Sons, 1976.

Pearson, K. *The Grammar of Science*. New York: Meridian, 1957.

Perkins, J. A. "Foreign Aid and the Brain Drain." *Foreign Affairs* 44 (1966): 608–19.

Pinch, T. "What Does a Proof Do if it Does Not Prove?" In *The Social Production of Scientific Knowledge*, edited by E. Mendelsohn, et al., 171–215. Dordrecht: D. Reidel, 1977.

————. "Theoreticians and the Production of Experimental Anomaly: The Case of Solar Neutrinos." In *The Social Process of Scientific Investigation*, edited by K. Knorr, et al., 77–106. Dordrecht: D. Reidel, 1980.

————. "Kuhn—The Conservative and Radical Interpretations: Are Some Mertonians 'Kuhnians' and Some 'Kuhnians' Mertonians?" *4S Review* 7 (1982): 10–25.

Pinch, T., and W. Bijker. "The Social Construction of Facts and Artefacts: or, How the Sociology of Science and the Sociology of Technology Might Benefit Each Other." *Social Studies of Science* 14 (1984): 399–441.

————. "Science, Relativism, and the New Sociology of Technology: Reply to Russell." *Social Studies of Science* 16 (1986): 347–60.

Pines, S. "What Was Original in Arabic Science?" In *Scientific Change,* edited by A. C. Crombie, 181–205. New York: Basic Books, 1963.

Pinxten, R. "Observation in Anthropology: Positivism and Subjectivism Combined." In *Observation in Anthropology*, special issue of *Communication & Cognition* 14, edited by R. Pinxtin and C. Karnoouh (1981): 57–83.

Pirenne, H. *Medieval Cities.* New York: Doubleday Anchor, 1925.

————. *Economic and Social History of Medieval Europe.* New York: Harcourt, Brace and World, 1937.

Polanyi, M. *The Republic of Science: Its Political and Economic Theory.* Chicago: Roosevelt University Press, 1962.

Popper, K. *The Open Society and its Enemies.* Princeton: Princeton University Press, 1950.

————. *The Logic of Scientific Discovery.* New York: Science Editions, 1961.

————. *Objective Knowledge.* London: Oxford University Press, 1972.

Porter, A. "Citation Analysis: Queries and Caveats." *Social Studies of Science* 7 (1977): 257–67.

Poston, M. M., D. Hay, and J. D. Scott. *Design and Development of Weapons: Studies in Government and Industrial Organization.* London: H.M. Stationery Office, 1964.

Price, D. J. *Science Since Babylon.* New Haven: Yale University Press, 1961.

Pyenson, L. *Neohumanism and the Persistence of Pure Mathematics in Wilhelmian Germany.* Philadelphia: American Philosophical Society, 1983.

Reichardt, C. S., and T. D. Cook. "Beyond Qualitative Versus Quantitative Methods." In *Qualitative and Quantitative Methods in Evaluation Research*, edited by T. D. Cook and C. S. Reichardt, 7–32. Beverly Hills, CA: Sage, 1979.

Reingold, N. "Through Paradigm-Land to a Normal History of Science." *Social Studies of Science* 10 (1980): 475–96.

Rescher, N. "Methodological Issues in Science and Technology Forecasting: Users and Limitations in Public Policy Deliberations." *Technological Forecasting and Social Change* 20 (1981): 101–12.

Restivo, S. *Visiting Foreign Scientists at American Universities: A Study in the Third-Culture of Science.* Ph.D. dissertation. Michigan State University, 1971.

————. "Joseph Needham and the Comparative Study of Chinese and Modern Science." In *Research in Sociology of Knowledge, Sciences, and Art*, vol. 2, edited by R. A. Jones and H. Kuklick, 25–51. Greenwich, CT: JAI Press, 1979.

————. "The Sociology of Science, by Robert K. Merton." Book Review. *Journal of College Science Teaching* 9 (1980): 293–94.

————. "Notes and Queries on Science, Technology, and Human Values." *Science, Technology, and Human Values* 6 (Winter 1981): 20–24.

————. "Some Perspectives in Contemporary Sociology of Science." *Science, Technology and Human Values* 6 (Spring 1981): 22–30.

————. "Supporting Laboratory Life: Funds and Funding Sources as Contingencies in the Social Production of Science." Paper prepared under a contract with the Division of Policy Research and Analysis of the National Science Foundation and presented in the PRA-NSF Seminar on Funding Sources and the Direction of Science. September 1983. Washington, DC.

————. *The Social Relations of Physics, Mysticism, and Mathematics*. Dordrecht: D. Reidel, 1983.

————. *The Sociological Worldview*. Oxford: Basil Blackwell, 1991.

————. *Mathematics in Society and History*. Dordrecht: Kluwer Academic Publishers, 1992.

Restivo, S., and C. K. Vanderpool, eds. *Comparative Studies in Science and Society*. Columbus, OH: C. E. Merrill, 1974.

Restivo, S., and J. Loughlin. "Critical Sociology of Science and Scientific Validity." *Knowledge* 8 (1987): 486–508.

Restivo, S., and M. Zenzen. "A Humanistic Perspective on Science and Society." In *Readings in Humanistic Sociology*, edited by W. K. Fishman and G. Benello, 82–116. New York: General Hall, 1986.

Restivo, S., J-P. Van Bendegem, and R. Fischer, eds. *Math Worlds: New Directions in Philosophy and Social Studies of Mathematics*. Albany: SUNY Press, 1993.

Revelle, R. "International Cooperation and the Two Faces of Science." In *Cultural Affairs and Foreign Relations*, edited by R. Blum, 122–38. Englewood Cliffs, NJ: Prentice-Hall, 1963.

Richards, J. "The Art and the Science of British Algebra: A Study in the Perception of Mathematical Truth." *Historia Mathematics* 7 (1980): 343–65.

Richter, M. *Science as a Cultural Process*. Cambridge, MA: Schenkman, 1972.

————. *The Autonomy of Science*. Cambridge, MA: Schenkman, 1980.

Robinson, H. *Renascent Rationalism*. Toronto: Macmillan, 1975.

Rorty, R. *Philosophy and the Mirror of Nature*. Princeton: Princeton University Press, 1979.

Rose, H., and S. Rose, eds. *The Political Economy of Science*. London: Macmillan, 1976.

Rose, H., and S. Rose. *Science and Society*. Baltimore: Penguin, 1970.

Rosenzweig, R. M. "Research as Intellectual Property: Influences Within the University." *Science, Technology and Human Values* 10 (Spring 1985): 41–48.

Roszak, T. *Where the Wasteland Ends*. New York: Anchor, 1973.

Russell, B. *Icarus, or the Future of Science*. London: Kegan Paul, Trench, Trubner & Company, 1925.

Russell, J. C. "The Metropolitan City Region of the Middle Ages." *Journal of Regional Science* 2 (Fall 1960): 55–70.

Russell, S. "The Social Construction of Artefacts: A Reply to Pinch and Bijker." *Social Studies of Science* 16 (1986): 333–46.

Russo, F. "Catholocism, Protestantism, and the Development of Science in the Sixteenth and Seventeenth Centuries." In *The Evolution of Science*, edited by G.S. Métraux and F. Crouzet, 291–320. New York: New American Library, 1963.

Sahlins, M., and E. Service. *Evolution and Culture*. Ann Arbor: University of Michigan Press, 1960.

Salomon, J.-J. "The Mating of Knowledge and Power." *Impact of Science on Society* 22 (1972): 123–32.

Salomon, J.-J. "Science Policy Studies and the Development of Science Policy." In *Scienc, Technology, and Society*, edited by D. J. DeS. Price and I. Rösing, 43–70. London: Sage, 1977.

Schäfer, W., ed. *Finalization in Science*. Dordrecht: D. Reidel, 1983.

Schneider, J. "Social Problems Theory: The Constructionist View." *Annual Review of Sociology* 11 (1985): 209–29.

Schutz, A. "Concept and Theory Formation in the Social Sciences." In *Philosophy of the Social Sciences*, edited by M. Natanson, 231–49. New York: Random House, 1963.
———. *The Problem of Social Reality: Collected Papers*. Vol. 1. The Hague: M. Nijhoff, 1971.
Schwartz, E. *Overskill*. New York: Ballantine, 1972.
Scott, W. R. "Professionals in Bureaucracy—Areas of Conflict." In *Professionalization*, edited by H. M. Vollmer and D. L. Mills, 265–75. Englewood Cliffs, NJ: Prentice-Hall, 1966.
Seaborg, G. T. "A Scientific Society—The Beginnings." In *Science: Method and Meaning*, edited by S. Rapport and H. Wright, 218–32. New York: Washington Square Press, 1964.
Shah, A. B., ed. *Education, Scientific Policy and Developing Societies*. Bombay: Massakalas, 1967.
Shils, E. "The Intellectuals and the Powers: Some Perspectives for Comparative Analysis." *Comparative Studies in Society and History* 1 (1958): 15–22.
———. "Scientific Development in the New States." In *Science and the New Nations*, edited by R. Gruber, 217–26. New York: Basic Books, 1961.
———. "Toward a National Science Policy." In *Education and the Development of Nations*, edited by J. W. Hanson and C. S. Brembeck, 209–17. New York: Holt, Rinehart and Winston, 1966.
———. "On the Improvement of Indian Higher Education." In *Education, Scientific Policy and Developing Societies*, edited by A. B. Shah, 475–99. Bombay: Mankalas, 1967.
Sjoberg, G. "The Rural-Urban Dimension in Pre-Industrial, Transitional, and Industrial Societies." In *Handbook of Modern Sociology*, edited by R. E. L. Faris, 127–59. Chicago: Rand McNally, 1964.
Sklair, L. *Organized Knowledge*. St. Albans, Herts: Paladin, 1973.
Slicher van Bath, B. H. *The Agrarian History of Western Europe A.D. 500–1850*. New York: St. Martin's, 1963.
Small, H., and B. Griffith. "The Structure of Scientific Literatures I: Identifying and Graphing Specialties." *Science Studies* 4 (1974): 17–40.
Sohn-Rethel, A. *Intellectual and Manual Labor*. London: Macmillan, 1978.
Spector, M., and J. Kitsuse. *Constructing Social Problems*. Menlo Park, CA: Cummings, 1977.
Spedding, J., R. L. Ellis, and D. D. Heath, eds. *The Works of Francis Bacon*. Boston: Houghton, Mifflin, 1863.
Spender, D. *Women of Ideas and What Men Have Done to Them*. London: Ark Paperbacks, 1983.
Spengler, O. *The Decline of the West*. 2 vols. New York: Knopf, 1926, 1928.
Star, S. L. "Simplification in Scientific Work: An Example from Neuroscience Research." *Social Studies of Science* 13 (1983): 205–28.
Stark, W. *The Sociology of Knowledge*. London: Routledge and Kegan Paul, 1958.
Startup, R. "The Sociology of Mathematics." *Sociology and Social Research* 64 (1980): 151–67.
Steward, J. *Theory of Culture Change*. Urbana: University of Illinois Press, 1955.
Stigler, S. "Stigler's Law of Eponymy." In *Science and Social Structure: A Festschrift for Robert K. Merton*, edited by T. Gieryn, 147–57. New York: Transactions of the New York Academy of Sciences, 1980.
Stocking, G., ed. *Observers Observed: Essays on Ethnographic Fieldwork*. Madison: University of Wisconsin Press, 1938.

Stolte-Heiskanen, V. "Externally Determined Resources and the Effectiveness of Research Units." In *Scientific Productivity*, edited by F. Andrews, 121–53. Cambridge: Cambridge University Press, 1979.

Stone, B. C. "Gaps in the Graduate Training of Students from Abroad." (Letter to the editor) *Science* 165 (6 June 1969): 1118.

Storer, N. "The Internationality of Science and the Nationality of Scientists." *International Social Science Journal* 22 (1970): 80–93.

Struik D. "On the Sociology of Mathematics." *Science and Society* 6 (1942): 58–70.

———. "Mathematics." In *Philosophy for the Future*, edited by R.W. Sellars, V.J. McGill, and M. Farber, 125–52. New York: Macmillan, 1949.

———. *A Concise History of Mathematics*. New York: Dover, 1967.

Studer, K., and D. Chubin. *The Cancer Mission: Social Contexts of Biomedical Research*. Beverly Hills, CA: Sage, 1980.

Sullivan, D., D. E. White, and E. J. Barboni. "The State of a Science: Indicators in the Specialty of Weak Interactions." *Social Studies of Science* 7 (1977): 167–200.

Suppe, F. "The Search for Philosophic Understanding of Scientific Theories." In *The Structure of Scientific Theories*, 2nd ed., edited by F. Suppe, 1–243. Urbana: University of Illinois Press, 1977.

Thaggard, P. "Against Evolutionary Epistemology." In *PSA 1980, Proceedings of the Biennial Meeting of the Philosophy of Science Association*, vol. 1, edited by Peter D. Asquith and Ronald N. Giere, 187–96. E. Lansing: Michigan State University, 1980.

Thompson, E. P. *The Making of the English Working Class*. New York: Penguin Books, 1980.

Thompson, J. W. *The Middle Ages*, 2 vols. New York: Knopf, 1931.

Tisdale, H. "The Process of Urbanization." *Social Forces* 20 (1942): 311–16.

Travis, G. D. L. "On the Construction of Creativity: The Memory of Transfer Phenomenon and the Importance of Being Earnest." In *The Social Process of Scientific Investigation*, edited by K. Knorr et al., 165–93. Dordrecht: D. Reidel, 1980.

Traweek, S. "Nature in the Age of its Mechanical Reproduction: The Reproduction of Nature and Physicists in the High Energy Physics Community." In *Les Savoirs dans les Pratiques Quotidiennes*, edited by C. Belisle and B. Schiele, 94–112. Paris: CNRS, 1984.

———. *Beamtimes and Lifetimes: The World of High Energy Physics*. Cambridge: Harvard University Press, 1988.

Trebach, A. *The Heroin Solution*. New Haven: Yale University Press, 1982.

Trescott M. M., ed. *Dynamos and Virgins Revisited: Women and Technological Change in History*. London: Scarecrow Press, 1979.

Turner, S. P., and D. Chubin. "Chance and Eminence in Science: Ecclesiastes II." *Social Science Information* 18 (1979): 437–49.

UNESCO. *Science and Technology in Asian Development*. Paris: UNESCO, 1970.

———. *Science and Technology for Development*. New York: UNESCO, 1963.

Useem, J. "The Community of Man: A Study in the Third-Culture." *Centennial Review* 7 (Fall 1963): 481–98.

———. "The Study of Cultures." *Studies of Third Cultures*, no. 6 (1971).

Useem, J., and R. H. Useem. "Interfaces of a Binational Third-Culture: A Study of the American Community in India." *The Journal of Social Issues* 23 (1967): 130–43.

———. "American Educated Indians in India: A Comparison of Two Modernizing Roles." *Journal of Social Issues* 24 (1968): 143–58.

Useem, J., R. H. Useem, and J. D. Donoghue. "Men in the Middle of the Third-Culture:

The Role of American and Non-Western People in Cross-Cultural Administration."
Human Organization 22 (Fall 1963): 169–79.

Veblen, T. *The Place of Science in Modern Civilization and Other Essays*. New York:
Viking, 1919.

Vollmer, H. M., and D. L. Mills, eds. *Professionalization*. Englewood Cliffs, NJ: Prentice-Hall, 1966.

Walter, B. "The Sociology of Knowledge and the Problem of Objectivity." In *Sociological Theory: Inquiries and Paradigms*, edited by L. Gross. New York: Harper and
Row, 1967.

Wartofsky, M. "The Critique of Impure Reason II: Sin, Science, and Society." *Science,
Technology and Human Values* 33 (1980): 5–23.

Weber, M. *The Protestant Ethic and the Spirit of Capitalism*. 1904–5; New York:
Charles Scribner's Sons, 1958.

————. "Konfuzianismus und Taoismus." In *Gesammelte Aufsatze zur Religionsso zi-
ologie*, edited by M. Weber, 298–99. Tubingen: J. C. B. Mohr, 1920.

————. *General Economic History*. New York: Macmillan, 1927.

————. "Science as a Vocation." In *From Max Weber*, edited by H. H. Gerth and C. W.
Mills, 129–56. New York: Oxford University Press, 1946.

Weingart, P. "On a Sociological Theory of Scientific Change," In *Social Processes of
Scientific Development*, edited by R. Whitley, 45–68. London: Routledge and
Kegan Paul, 1974.

White, L. "What Accelerated Technological Progress in the Western Middle Ages?" In
Scientific Change, edited by A. C. Crombie, 272–91. New York: Basic Books, 1963.

Whitley, R. "Black Boxism and the Sociology of Science: A Discussion of the Major
Developments in the Field." In *The Sociology of Science*, edited by P. Halmos,
61–92. Keele: The Sociological Review Monograph, 18, 1972.

————. "Introduction." In *Social Processes of Scientific Development*, edited by R.
Whitley, 1–10. London: Routledge and Kegan Paul, 1974.

————. "The Sociology of Scientific Work and the History of Scientific Developments." In *Perspectives in the Sociology of Science*, edited by S. S. Blume, 21–50.
Chichester: J. Wiley, 1977.

Wilensky, H. "Orderly Careers and Social Participation: The Impact of Work History on
Social Integration in the Middle Class." *American Sociological Review* 26 (August
1961): 521–39.

————. "The Professionalization of Everyone?" *American Journal of Sociology* 60
(September 1964): 138–58.

Winner L. "Do Artifacts Have Politics?" In *The Social Shaping of Technology*, edited by
D. MacKenzie and J. Wajcman, 26–38. Philadelphia: Open University Press, 1985.

————. *Autonomous Technology*. Cambridge: MIT Press, 1977.

Wittfogel, K. *Oriental Despotism*. New Haven: Yale University Press, 1957.

Wittgenstein, L. *Remarks on the Foundations of Mathematics*. Cambridge: MIT Press,
1967.

————. *On Certainty*. New York: Harper Torchbooks, 1972.

Wolf, A. *A History of Science, Technology and Philosophy in the 16th and 17th Centuries*. Vol. 1. New York: Harper Torchbooks, 1959.

Woodcock, G., ed. *The Anarchist Reader*. Glasgow: Fontana, 1977.

Woolgar, S. "Interests and Explanation in the Social Study of Science." *Social Studies of
Science* 11 (1981): 365–95.

Woolgar, S. "Laboratory Studies: A Comment on the State of the Art." *Social Studies of
Science* 12 (1982): 481–98.

Woolgar, S., and D. Pawluch. "Ontological Gerrymandering: The Anatomy of Social Problems Explanations." *Social Problems* 32 (1985): 214–37.

Wright, C. *Wittgenstein on the Foundations of Mathematics.* Cambridge: Harvard University Press, 1980.

Yabuuti, K. "Science in China from the Fourth to the End of the Twelfth Century." In *The Evolution of Science*, edited by G. S. Métraux and F. Crouzet, 108–27. New York: New American Library, 1963.

Yin, R. "The Case Study Crisis: Some Answers." *Administrative Science Quarterly* 26 (1981): 145–52.

Zenzen, M. "Sociology of Science as Theory of Rationality." Paper presented at the annual meeting of the Society for Social Studies of Science, Bloomington, Indiana, 1978.

Zenzen, M., and S. Restivo. "The Mysterious Morphology of Immiscible Liquids: A Study of Scientific Practice." *Social Science Information* 21 (1982): 447–73.

Zilsel, E. "The Sociological Roots of Science." *The American Journal of Sociology* 47 (1942): 544–62.

Zinberg, N. *Drug, Set and Setting: The Basis for Controlled Intoxicant Use.* New Haven: Yale University Press, 1984.

Zuckerman, H. "Stratification in American Science." In *Social Stratification: Theory and Research for the 1970's*, edited by E. O. Laumann, 235–37. Indianapolis, IN: Bobbs-Merrill, 1970.

Zuckerman, H., and R. B. Miller. "Science Indicators: Implications for Research and Policy." *Scientometrics* 2 (1980): 327–448.

Index

263